Xwelíqwiya

Our Lives: Diary, Memoir, and Letters

SERIES EDITOR: JANICE DICKIN

Social history contests the construction of the past as the story of elites—a grand narrative dedicated to the actions of those in power. Our Lives seeks instead to make available voices from the past that might otherwise remain unheard. By foregrounding the experience of ordinary individuals, the series aims to demonstrate that history is ultimately the story of our lives, lives constituted in part by our response to the issues and events of the era into which we are born. Many of the voices in the series thus speak in the context of political and social events of the sort about which historians have traditionally written. What they have to say fills in the details, creating a richly varied portrait that celebrates the concrete, allowing broader historical settings to emerge between the lines. The series invites materials that are engagingly written and that contribute in some way to our understanding of the relationship between the individual and the collective. Manuscripts that include an introduction or epilogue that contextualizes the primary materials and reflects on their significance will be preferred.

SERIES TITLES

A Very Capable Life: The Autobiography of Zarah Petri
John Leigh Walters

Letters from the Lost: A Memoir of Discovery
Helen Waldstein Wilkes

A Woman of Valour: The Biography of Marie-Louise Bouchard Labelle
Claire Trépanier

Man Proposes, God Disposes: Recollections of a French Pioneer
Pierre Maturié, translated by Vivien Bosley

Xwelíqwiya: The Life of a Stó:lō Matriarch
Rena Point Bolton and Richard Daly

Xwelíqwiya

The Life of a Stó:lō Matriarch

Rena Point Bolton and Richard Daly

AU PRESS

Published by AU Press, Athabasca University
1200, 10011 – 109 Street, Edmonton, AB T5J 3S8

ISBN 978-1-927356-56-2 (print) 978-1-927356-57-9 (PDF) 978-1-927356-58-6 (epub)

A volume in the series Our Lives: Diary, Memoir, and Letters
1921-6653 (print) 1921-6661 (electronic)

Printed and bound in Canada by Marquis Book Printers.

Library and Archives Canada Cataloguing in Publication
Point Bolton, Rena, 1927–, author
Xwelíqwiya, The life story of a Stó:lō matriarch /
Rena Point Bolton and Richard Daly.

(Our lives: diary, memoir, and letters series, ISSN 1921-6653 ; 5)
Includes bibliographical references and index.
Issued in print and electronic formats.
ISBN 978-1-927356-56-2 (pbk.). — ISBN 978-1-927356-57-9 (pdf). —
ISBN 978-1-927356-58-6 (epub)

1. Point Bolton, Rena, 1927–. 2. Stó:lō Indians — Biography. 3. Native artists — British
Columbia — Biography. 4. Native women — British Columbia — Biography. I. Daly,
Richard, 1942–, author II. Title. III. Series: Our lives : diary, memoir, and letters ; 5

E99.S72P64 2013   305.897'943   C2013-905399-9
                                              C2013-905400-6

We acknowledge the financial support of the Government of Canada through the
Canada Book Fund (CBF) for our publishing activities.

Canada Council   Conseil des Arts
for the Arts   du Canada

Assistance provided by the Government of Alberta, Alberta Multimedia Development Fund.

Government

Contents

* ❈ *

Illustrations

* ❋ *

Foreword

I have been asked to pen a few words with regard to my mother's book, and I am very pleased to help in this way. Any time that people put their whole life into written form I think they run the risk of misapprehension and even criticism from others. Richard Daly has taken on the monumental task of listening to and recording my mother's thoughts and memories about her life. For this I am very grateful. This book has been an ongoing project for many years, and both Richard and Rena have devoted countless hours to making this book a reality. Richard's training in the field of anthropology, together with his self-critical attitude toward his work, lends itself very well to the task at hand.

For too long, anthropologists and historians have written about Aboriginal people from a purely academic perspective, with their mind on audiences somewhere else, perhaps in Europe. This has produced some marvellous reports, but in some cases it has resulted in a one-dimensional, ethnocentric, and subjective analysis of people about whom the writer in fact knows very little. That is, such accounts simply describe the surface and not the depth of Aboriginal people's reality.

Richard Daly has chosen a much different approach, in that he spends time with the subjects of his study, attending gatherings and feasts and even residing inside their communities so that he can gain a deeper, inside perspective that later informs his written work. He brings a passion for learning and a compassion for the people he studies. His voice is not demanding, nor is it condescending or fraught with the attitude of superiority that too often prevents some writers from getting at the broader and more complex story before them. I am very pleased with the end product of his long and hard work.

So that there could be no mistake, in September of this year, 2012, at Chilliwack, I presented Richard with a talking stick. This stick was presented to him at my home in the presence of my mother and with her approval, so there is no doubt that he speaks on behalf of my mother in this book. Richard and Mother have done a marvellous job and I know that you will enjoy this book, as I have.

Steven Point
20 October 2012

Acknowledgements

* ❋ *

We would like to thank the acquisitions editor at Athabasca University Press, Pamela MacFarland Holway, for her considerable editorial assistance, her literary, historical, and linguistic vigilance, and her good humour. Thanks as well to copy editor and linguist Joyce Hildebrand. We also acknowledge the constructive work of the anonymous peer reviewers who suggested, among other things, that we make more explicit our actions in the crafting of this book. Thank you to Athabasca University Press's book promotion team and to Rena's daughter Wendy Point Ritchie, a teacher of Halq'eméylem, for her work on the glossary and for standardizing the spelling of the Halq'eméylem words in the text. We are grateful for the encouragement we got from Wendy's siblings and their spouses in the Sardis area, among them Gail, Charlotte, Mark, and Steven.

Will Lawson helped to draw up one of the early clean copies of the work from the hitherto scattered transcripts, notes, and fragments, and this enabled me to see some of the story gaps that needed to be filled in by Rena, who then responded by elaborating on her narrative. Will has also provided sensible advice through the years on the anarchic realm known as "English usage."

Liv Mjelde has kept me on my toes by arguing that the problematic of "told-to" autobiographies is coloured more by social stratification than simply by colonial heritage and that the questions being raised about "who contributed what" to the life story are usually fewer when the subject enjoys power and influence in society than when they do not. I hope that this project answers her question about why textual accounts of life stories of people with less power and influence in society are subject to more skepticism regarding authorship. This project has shown me that telling a life story, writing it down, organizing it, and then "writing it up" can be a true and deep cooperation, even though the formal presentation may obscure much of this cooperative and consultative work.

I deeply appreciate the long years of unflagging support, warmth of spirit, and good talks that both I and my wife, Liv, enjoyed with both Rena and the late Cliff Bolton. And finally, Rena and I are grateful for the introductory words provided by Steven Point.

Richard Daly

Maps

* ❋ *

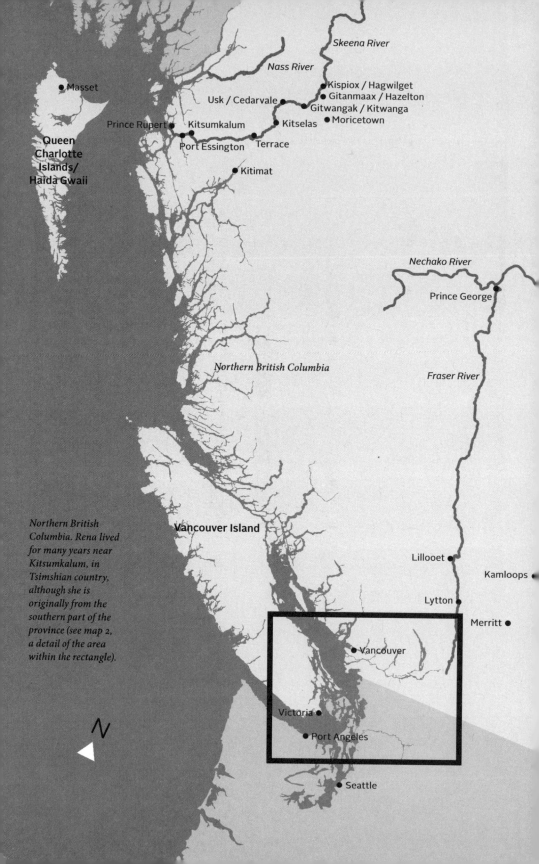

Masset

Queen
Charlotte
Islands/
Haida Gwaii

Skeena River

Nass River

Kispiox / Hagwilget
Gitanmaax / Hazelton
Gitwangak / Kitwanga
Moricetown

Usk / Cedarvale

Prince Rupert
Kitsumkalum
Kitselas
Kitselas

Port Essington
Terrace

Kitimat

Nechako River

Prince George

Northern British Columbia

Fraser River

Vancouver Island

*Northern British
Columbia. Rena lived
for many years near
Kitsumkalum, in
Tsimshian country,
although she is
originally from the
southern part of the
province (see map 2,
a detail of the area
within the rectangle).*

Lillooet

Kamloops

Lytton

Merritt

Vancouver

Victoria

Port Angeles

Seattle

N

Xwélmexw (Stó:lō) territory and nearby Coast Salish areas. Born at Kilgard, Rena was raised at Devil's Run, on the banks of the Fraser River, and spent much of her life in Sardis (Skowkale), just south of Chilliwack.

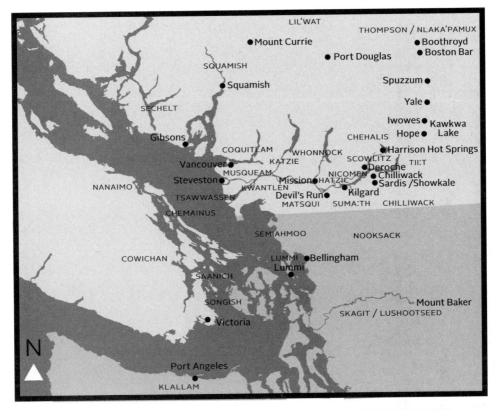

TRIBAL AFFILIATIONS
Places

Introduction

* ❄ *

An indigenous culture with sufficient territory, and bilingual and intercultural education, is in a better position to maintain and cultivate its mythology and shamanism. Conversely, the confiscation of their lands and imposition of foreign education, which turns their young people into amnesiacs, threatens the survival not only of these people but of an entire way of knowing. It is as if one were burning down the oldest universities in the world and their libraries, one after another—thereby sacrificing the knowledge of the world's future generations.

Jeremy Narby, *The Cosmic Serpent: DNA and the Origins of Knowledge* (1999), 155

Back in the days when we both had more bounce to our step, Rena, Mrs. Point Bolton, asked whether I would help to prepare a book about her life. She wanted to leave a document "for those who come after" to show how she was raised and what the culture she grew up in was like. She also wanted to record the teachings she had learned from her grandparents and other elders, as well as the insights about life that she has acquired over the years—not to mention the values she stands for in regard to addressing the ecological and spiritual imbalance between the natural and the human worlds.

We first met in December 1988, while I was working for what was then known as the Alliance of Tribal Councils, gathering data on the past and present use of the Fraser River and its salmon fishery by local First Nations—the Secwepemc, the Nlaka'pamux, and the Stó:lō, who also call themselves the Xwélmexw.[1] In the course of my research, two of Rena's sons, Mark and Steven Point, recommended her to me as someone knowledgeable about the river's importance. Rena was living and working far from the Fraser River at the time, residing with her second husband, Cliff Bolton, outside Kitsumkalum, on the Skeena River west of the town of Terrace. Cliff, a Kitsumkalum Tsimshian *simoogit* (chief), was known for his wood and jade carving, as well as for the canoes that he and Rena's son Mark jointly produced.

1   In the mainland dialect of the Halq'eméylem language spoken by Central Salish peoples (the dialect that, with some variations, extends up the Fraser Valley, as far north as the Fraser Canyon), "Stó:lō" is the word for the Fraser River, but the term is now commonly used to refer to the people who live along the river's lower reaches. Based in the town of Lytton, the Alliance of Tribal Councils (today the Alliance of Tribal Nations, headquartered in New Westminster) represented First Nations living along the watershed of the lower Fraser and Thompson rivers and was engaged in collecting information about the life histories of its members. The histories—which centred on a salmon fishery that extended along much of the river system and had, in some locations, existed for at least six thousand years—were to be used as evidence in a potential legal action, known as the "double-tracking case." The trans-Canada rail system had put forward a plan to double-track the Fraser-Thompson railway corridor, which would involve altering the river flow by dumping tons of riprap (broken stone material) along the river banks to provide a new, improved rail bed. This posed a serious threat to the old salmon-based way of life in the Fraser-Thompson watershed: in many places along the route, disturbing the river's natural flow would eliminate the back eddies (the Aboriginal fishing locations) where the salmon rested on their upstream journey of hundreds of miles to their spawning beds. The alliance and its legal team assembled much potential evidence and prepared for trial, but the railways decided to withdraw their plan and reorganize their transport system, agreeing to use one rail line for westbound traffic and another for eastbound. This has allowed for increased traffic without a great deal of additional environmental and social damage.

Our first meeting occurred neither in Xwélmexw territory nor in Tsimshian country, but rather at a motor inn on Burrard Street in Vancouver—which, of course, sits on traditional lands of the closely related Musqueam and Tsleil-Waututh peoples. We got down to work, and Rena told me how, when she was a girl, she had lived on the banks of the Fraser River, and it was there that her family had survived the Depression years of the 1930s by relying on what the river provided. She explained that they had also suffered from the loss of their main source of food, Sumas Lake, the body of water that once stretched south from Abbotsford to Yarrow and across the border near Lummi, in Washington State. In 1924, just two years before Rena's birth, the lake had been drained to create rich farmland. "Those were hard times," she told me. "The next meal had to be earned. We really had to work for it." She went on to describe how the family members who raised her "caught ducks with nets suspended from poles" and also survived by fishing. "We carried our nets over Sumas Peak to Murphy's Landing," she recalled. "We took coho in the fall in a creek called Kw'ekw'íqw. Grandmother was so happy to see the fish because then we had food for a whole day."

Of course I had more questions. Rena suggested that I come to visit them at their home since I, too, was living along the Skeena River in northern British Columbia at the time. I met Cliff and Rena again six months later, in July of 1989, at their home on the Zymacord River, where it joins the Skeena, some miles west of Terrace. When we finished talking, Rena handed me a sheaf of papers and a couple of brown envelopes containing news clippings and other writings. "I wonder," she said, "if you would be willing to help write my life story. I've already started. Can you take these pages and look them over?"

* ❀ *

On her mother's side, Rena Point Bolton's origins lie at Sumas, or Semá:th, where she was born.[2] Upon her first marriage, to Roy Point, she moved upriver to live in his family's settlement, the Skowkale (Sq'ewq'éyl) reserve, at Sardis, just south of downtown Chilliwack, where her children, the Point family, live today. On the basis of the old teachings, many of them learned from their mother, Rena's children continue to embrace many of the traditional customs and outlooks of their people, but they have managed to do so without turning their backs on modern life.

The name Rena carries is Xwelíqwiya—a name with a history rooted at Semá:th, as she explains in chapter 2.[3] Her mother's grandmother, the last daughter of Chief X̱éyteleq, was matriarch of the Steqó:ye Wolf People. Her matriarchal duties were passed to her daughter and eventually to her daughter's granddaughter, Rena. Through her maternal grandfather, who belonged to the upriver Tii:t people, Rena has also, by birthright, become custodian of the ceremonial Sxwóyxwey masks (about which see chapter 5).[4]

In her turn, as Xwelíqwiya, Rena Point Bolton has become the mother, grandmother, great-grandmother, or foster mother of many. She is also an artist and craftswoman and a hereditary carrier of specific traditions and spiritual practices. She has been an activist, inspiring her family, her people, and First Nations in general both to persist in acquiring formal education and to learn how to build their lives on the basis of locally situated knowledge. For her, this knowledge encompasses the spiritual, meditative, artistic, and scientific traditions lived by her people in their daily life on the land and river.

2   The main settlement at Semá:th is Kilgard (Kw'ekw'íqw), a few kilometres east of Abbotsford. It sits on the edge of Sumas Prairie, or what was originally the north shore of Sumas Lake.

3   Rena's name begins with a blowing sound and is roughly pronounced "Hwe-lee-kwee-yah." For details, see the pronunciation guide at the end of the book.

4   On the Sxwóyxwey, or Sxwaixwe, see the works by Boas (1889), Duff (1952a), Dufresne (1996), Haeberlin (1918), Jenness (1955, 12, 72, 91, 92), Jilek (1974a, 1974b), Shiell (1990), Suttles (1982), Wade (1976), and Wike (1941). The name Tii:t is frequently pronounced and written "Te:it," a form used by some early ethnographers that has gained currency.

Silence

The creation and maintenance of silence in any human relationship is often transactional. It can be a perverse form of dialogue, albeit one in which the participants seldom interact with an equal degree of power, social standing, or influence. Those who have been denied power and influence, who have been silenced by figures of authority, are often silenced internally as well, of their own volition. As a means of self-protection, they choose to maintain silence, to refuse interaction—but their silence can also be a powerful form of communication.

During the late nineteenth and the early twentieth century, like other First Nations across Canada, the people of the lower Fraser River were silenced, and efforts were made to obliterate their culture. Under the banner of social and moral improvement, a process of forced assimilation was undertaken by Canadian institutions that variously administrated, policed, schooled, and proselytized among Aboriginal peoples. These actions were informed by the values and protocols of the "Dominion of Canada," a component of the British Empire, which provided the social infrastructure on which Canada still models itself.

In Xwélmexw culture—before the great silence—the values, stories, histories, and protocols governing interfamily life had been sources of power and legitimacy and were accordingly well-guarded by elders, who passed these traditions carefully down along socially sanctioned lines of kinship and marriage to a new generation of custodians. There was a subtlety to this process of transmission, such that the members of each generation were guided by a flow of silent, family-based knowledge that "felt right," as a result of their upbringing, and yet could be adapted to variations in personal abilities and talents as well as to changing conditions of life. As the colonial administration extended its reach, however, the old procedures for passing on culture and knowledge met with new legal and ideological pressures. The federal government imposed on First Nations communities, previously organized in many and different ways, a standardized administrative model of Indian band membership and elective band councils. For good measure, it carried off most of the children to residential schools and placed decision making in the hands of Indian agents rather than family elders.[5] More recently, provincial and local governance has consistently sought to alienate First Nations from lands, rivers, and coastal regions whenever such peoples are deemed to be getting in the way of development—hindering the activities of those seeking to exploit the raw materials that lie in, and beneath, the home territories of these peoples.[6]

These Canadian initiatives were modelled on the idea of freeing First Nations peoples from their kin-based systems of land holding and land use, by replacing relations based on kinship with those that, while decidedly Christian, would also be market driven.[7] Part of the overall plan was to convert such peoples into modern wage earners equipped with European parliamentary democracy—that is, to impose a system of community political management based not on kinship alliances but rather on the individual's relation to the nation-state. Officials were to be recruited by means of a "one-man, one-vote" electoral process oriented toward individual decision making (a model that imperial Western nations have been trying to spread to the rest of the world for over a century). These government initiatives overrode the kinship-based, hereditary system of governance that existed in most small-scale Aboriginal societies—a system that relied on elders and on interfamily diplomacy couched in the metaphors of competitive and cooperative gift giving, alliance building, and power balancing,

5   Residential schools were, of course, powerful weapons of assimilation. An elderly lady from Spences Bridge once explained to me how she had managed to retain so much knowledge of her traditional Nlaka'pamux ways: "They never took me off to school. That's why I know so much."

6   *In the Way of Development: Indigenous Peoples, Life Projects and Globalization* (Blaser, Feit, and McRae 2004) is one of several books that documents cases, mostly from Aboriginal communities in Canada but also in the United States, Chile, Mexico, India, and Russia, in which indigenous—often tribal—populations have suffered at the hands of resource extractors and the governments that support such economic development.

7   The impact of the globalization of capital on Aboriginal peoples is a theme comprehensively addressed by the late Eric Wolf. See, in particular, *Europe and the People Without History* (1982), especially chapter 6, in which he analyzes the fur trade and its focus on the commercial development of the Northwest Coast of North America.

as well as on kin-based knowledge transmission in the form of family lore, history, stories, and other teachings passed down the generations.[8]

In the area of the lower Fraser River, the hereditary keepers of Xwélmexw culture were silenced by the standard combination of traumas: dispossession from their lands, paternalistic attitudes on the part of both government and church bureaucracies, and massive intimidation born from the stern mother of colonial prejudice, as well as a fundamentally racist contempt for Indigenous knowledge and ways of life. Those administering the infrastructure of government, church, and education were deaf to concerns voiced by local communities. They would not listen to the hereditary carriers of culture, and, for their part, the hereditary carriers responded by refusing to attempt to talk to people who would neither listen nor respect what they had to say about the preferred ways of conducting local society. Here is Rena's description of the onset of the silence:

> When the elders found out that the new society had such contempt for our ways, when the churches called our respected ancestors "naked savages" and "children of Satan," then the old people who were the guardians of the culture, they said to themselves, "Oh goodness, the only dignified thing to do is to say absolutely nothing." They went silent and were ready to take the knowledge to the grave with them. It became *sxaxá*—taboo—to talk about private matters. The old people were afraid. They stopped talking, mainly because there was nobody to listen to them any longer.

8 Throughout Aboriginal Canada, elders have traditionally played the important role of storytellers, passing down knowledge and instructing new generations about how to live life. These narratives have provided a cultural bridge between generations. Anishinabek writer and storyteller Basil Johnston affirms this. He describes how, in the course of conducting training programs for young people, elders would pay special attention to those who were considered gifted and showed concern for the cultural and spiritual heritage. "Young men and women who were chosen to receive special tutelage," he explains, "would be the learned elders when their time came, accredited to interpret and adjudicate" (Johnston 1995, xx).

By the 1950s, this situation had resulted in a deafening two-way silence and considerable social breakdown across First Nations communities, now largely confined to reserves.[9] On the one side, family knowledge, always jealously protected, became even more secretive; on the other side, shared cultures based on hunting, fishing, and gathering were undermined by individual proprietorship and the commercialization of the land. Old ways, tried and true, were of no interest to the dominant commercial and cultural forces in a society that wanted "Indians" to forget the past and become, at first, Christian small farmers and then later job seekers and minor entrepreneurs in the new resource-based industrial economy.[10]

* ❋ *

9 These reserves later became models for the Bantustans, or Bantu "homelands," set up by South Africa's apartheid government. In both countries, such controlled spaces functioned as camps in which to collect non-industrialized people once they had been dispossessed of their lands by newcomer populations.

10 The aggressive assimilation policies of the Canadian government were well summed up by Eddie Gardner, who works for the Stó:lō Nation:

> Now, when you take a look at what happened to Aboriginal people—people were not asked to come and adapt to our culture, system, form of government, or our way of doing things. No, they come in and imposed an awful lot on Aboriginal people and have attempted to completely assimilate Aboriginal people—to squash them right out—they say, "Look, you see us, you become one of us." There was no encouragement you know for this cultural mosaic kind of happiness that everyone would like to have. (Quoted in Thom 1996)

As Gardner points out, immigrants to Canada face similar pressures to conform. The difference, of course, is that Aboriginal peoples were never immigrants—a fact that has often been greeted with a certain amnesia on the part of mainstream Canadian society.

Prior to the inauguration of the government-imposed system of bands and councils, Indigenous governance along the Fraser River consisted of small communities that largely ran their own affairs. As Wayne Suttles (1990, 464) explains, "Most local groups consisted of the household of an established kin group and several dependent households. Men identified as chiefs of local groups were probably heads of leading households or kin groups." For the most part, these local communities would act together as united political bodies, in the modern sense, only in moments of crisis such as raids and attacks from abroad.[11] Politics and administration were conducted in large cedar houses, where extended families lived, worked, and held their ceremonies.[12]

Before the colonial conquest of what is now western Canada, knowledgeable elders played a pivotal role as forces of moral influence, as advisors, and often indirectly, in the course of steering communities of kinfolk and affines (in-laws), as shapers of local political decisions. In many places, the moral and political influence of elders continued long after the advent of the Department of Indian Affairs (DIA), which presumed the right to administer these affairs in the best interests of the Canadian government. The knowledge, experience, and social managerial skills of elders were family-centered and kin-based, and

11 This is not to suggest that each group was otherwise an isolated unit. As Suttles (1990, 464) tells us: "The larger winter villages consisted of several houses representing several kin and local groups. Members of different households within the village cooperated in some subsistence activities, as in a deer drive or building a salmon weir, and the houses within the village, like the families within the house, shared temporary abundances of perishable foods. Houses also cooperated in some ceremonial activities and in mutual defense." He goes on to point out, however, that "such cooperation was not forced upon them by any village organization; houses also acted independently in such matters. Larger winter villages, being composed of kin groups with different inherited rights and different external ties, were not culturally homogeneous. Segments of a village might even differ in speech."

12 Early European visitors claimed, and archaeologists have confirmed, that some of these Salish cedar houses were as much as 640 feet long and 60 feet wide (that is, roughly 210 m × 20 m). See the examples in Carlson (2001, 42).

their skills and wisdom extended to those families into which they and their descendants had married. They also exerted moral influence and enjoyed respect and a reputation for wisdom in the wider society of the day.

But legislation was enacted, and official reports were published. As far as Rena's elders were concerned, the legislation that affected them most was, first, the Indian Act of 1876, which gave government the exclusive right to administer the affairs of First Nations; second, the potlatch ban of 1885, inspired by missionaries, which outlawed ceremonies by which kinship rights and duties were passed from one generation to another; and, third, the recommendations of the McKenna-McBride Royal Commission (1913–16), which established and delimited reserves for First Nations in British Columbia. These legal and administrative activities were, and continue to be, predicated on the assimilation of the First Nations into mainstream Euro-Canadian life. In the eyes of nineteenth-century missionaries and government agents, Aboriginal peoples were, in their "natural" state, childlike and backward, ignorant of the virtues of modernity and the Christian faith. The original inhabitants needed to be raised to social and political adulthood, brought into a civilized state under the stern but dispassionate parental guidance of the government and its supporters. It was therefore assumed that they would benefit from severe tutelage in Euro-Canadian ways.

Over the decades that ensued, the accumulated actions on the part of government intimidated and in fact traumatized the old kinship societies; their members had to become furtive and adept in subterfuge if they were to continue to fulfill their ceremonial responsibilities to each other and to the land. The era of silence was most pronounced during the period marked by the so-called potlatch law, enacted in 1885. This amendment to the Indian Act of 1876 made illegal Aboriginal ceremonial practices, including the hosting of feasts in the course of which families gave away, in what missionaries and others saw as an "improvident" manner, their wealth to their guests. In so doing, of course, the families demonstrated not only their industriousness but also their proprietary rights to land and fishing sites (as was evidenced by the fact that the hosts always announced to their guests the names of the family places from which these gifts originated).[13]

Once ceremonial practices were outlawed and customary family-based forms of leadership usurped by the Canadian government, Aboriginal elders and leaders were encouraged, as well as bribed and pressured, to conform to the ways prescribed by the new society. In the name of equality and democracy, and under the gaze of the European version of the Creator, Aboriginal communities were expected to shun their spiritual beliefs, give up their ceremonial life, and convert to some form of Christianity, to embrace the individualism of the modern ethic, and to try their hand at entrepreneurship and competition in the capitalist market. They were expected to forget their collective heritage and their seasonal round of living from the land, as well as to reject social practices of hospitality and veneration for the natural world. They were further expected to destroy their material culture, to cease to produce their visual arts, their crafts, and their music, to relinquish their storytelling traditions, to abandon the kin-based status system and the taking and keeping of captives from other tribal groups, and to apply themselves to becoming literate and learning a trade. This was the wider world into which Rena Point Bolton's grandparents were born, and, as the twentieth century replaced the nineteenth, they witnessed the fruits of government policy.

13 In the 1927 version of the Indian Act, the "potlatch law" is described in section 140 (1):

> Every Indian or other person who engages in, or insists in celebrating, or encourages, either directly or indirectly, another to celebrate any Indian festival, dance or other ceremony of which the giving away or paying or giving back of money, goods or articles of any sort forms a part, or is a feature, whether such gift of money, goods or articles takes place before, at, or after the celebration of the same, or who engages or assists in any celebration or dance of which the wounding or mutilation of the dead or living body of any human being or animal forms a part or is a feature, is guilty of an offence and is liable on summary conviction to imprisonment for a term not exceeding six months and not less than two months.

The ban on Aboriginal ceremonies remained in force until the 1951 amendments to the Indian Act.

Rena is of the opinion that those who were most willing to adapt to modernity and who therefore responded most readily to the new order often belonged to sections of extended families whose members had not enjoyed much authority in the pre-existing society or had fallen in status owing to some calamity, such as being taken captive by raiding tribes from along the coast. Another category consisted of those family members who had intermarried with the newcomer settlers. Such persons, raised at least partially outside the old culture, possessed little of what was by then esoteric Xwélmexw knowledge and had little to lose socially by cooperating with the new society and new power structure.[14] For their part, those who had been the "old guard," or had, in a sense, occupied the position of cultural elite, often refused to participate in the new ways. Here is how Rena explains the split between new and old. Speaking rather formally and diplomatically but at the same time acknowledging the hierarchy inherent in the old society, she begins by describing those who welcomed the new order:

> These people often were not from the high-born families, or at least not people who were in the traditional line to inherit responsibility for guarding the culture. They did not have the right or responsibility to be, as you say, stewards for the old

14 Both the Xwélmexw old guard and the Indian Act refused to consider persons of mixed heritage as full human beings. From the Xwélmexw perspective, such people were tolerated but not considered good candidates for carrying the culture forward. In the eyes of what was then the Department of Indian Affairs (now Aboriginal Affairs and Northern Development Canada), any First Nations person with a non–First Nations parent was deemed racially impure and hence "non-status." Such persons were ineligible for the benefits pertaining to housing, health, or education guaranteed to "status" Indians under the Indian Act. (Early on in her story, Rena explains how this so-called racial impurity affected her immediate family of origin and its access to DIA support.) Neither "Indians" nor fully enfranchised Canadians "in good standing," they were deprived of rights and were regarded as among the least worthy members of society. On many occasions, First Nations elders related to me the lamentable experiences they endured when, only a few decades earlier, they were categorized as "breeds" or "half-breeds," neither one thing nor the other.

culture. Anyway, some of them wanted to move with the times and abandon all the old ways, leave them behind. Their aim was to be modern. So when the anthropologists came around, the people who would talk to them were usually those who were most familiar with the white ways, and often, these people were the ones least sympathetic with the old ways of our people.

The old society had a pecking order. Those who were high-born, they sort of kept the culture and the procedures among themselves. They looked after it. [. . .] The free people, the ones without such responsibility for the culture, they didn't have such restrictions on them. They seem to have been able to mobilize ties to people through both sides of their family. In the Xwélmexw times, such people were usually treated as "younger brothers and sisters." The oldest were respected. [. . .]

The high-born had responsibilities. They were stewards on behalf of their people and on behalf of their relatives in other species, the ones who lived out on the land. These duties were not imposed on the rest of the people to the same degree. Oh dear, what's the word I want? Yes, "privilege"! The DIA has privileged those who have been educated in the Canadian way. They have never recognized the hereditary leaders. The old hierarchies have been broken up like kindling wood. The large family units that ran the village affairs, they've been broken up.

So the real Xwélmexw were silenced. They became timid. And most of the knowledgeable ones had died in the epidemics. As I said, those with Chinese, Scottish, Japanese, or English blood mixed in their veins, they survived. And the new DIA way of organizing things narrowed our possibilities.

When the old guard witnessed the paternalistic contempt exhibited by teachers, missionaries, police, and government administrators toward Aboriginal ways of living, they tried to withdraw from the new society as far as was possible. Rena's maternal grandparents "voted with their feet" by loading Rena and her brother into their freight canoe and paddling away from the main Semá:th village, Kw'ekw'íqw (Kilgard), to live through the Depression years behind Sumas Mountain, on the banks of the Fraser River. Here, a day's travel from the village, they occupied an old cedar smokehouse and survived by means of fishing, hunting, and casual labour at nearby farms. They preferred to live in self-imposed exile. Their exile may have been marked by poverty, but it allowed them to keep their freedom and continuing reliance on their own productive efforts. They refused to compromise their principles by accepting the subservient "recipient" position in the donor-recipient relationship fundamental to the colonialism of the Indian Act.

Gradually, then, what Rena calls the "real Xwélmexw" were sidelined and silenced, in part by an active assault on their culture and in part of their own volition, in response to that assault. In the 1960s, Rena was asked by Harry Hawthorn, a professor of anthropology at the University of British Columbia, to explain the esoteric or secretive nature of the Stó:lō. Still relatively young, she was not authorized to speak on behalf of her culture, out of respect for her elders. In fact, the heavy silence of the era is reflected in her response to Hawthorn:

> And he said, "Your people were very unique. Why is it that none of the Stó:lō will talk to us?" I told him because Stó:lō people are not allowed to. We're not allowed to talk about things. It's just our way. You don't hear about us because no one will tell you anything. He said, "Well, that's no good. The world should know about you!"

Chief Earl Maquinna George, of the Ahousaht First Nation, has written eloquently on this silencing, underscoring its origins in fears inspired by the Indian Act:

> Part of the reason for the lack of understanding in the writings about us is that for much of the time we have existed under the control of the Indian Act, which we believe prevented us from discussing our culture. We believed that to do so would land us in jail. Whether or not such a law exists is not the issue;

the point is, we believed that was the case. The entire story of our people exists as a large body of information carried in our memories, sometimes with conflicting details between families, but always subject to the same sorts of forces that shape our culture. It is an ongoing conversation among the people. (George 2003, 38)

As Chief George suggests, maintaining silence runs the risk not only of misunderstanding on the part of outsiders but also of the loss of some of the riches of an oral tradition. During a focus group discussion on Native education that took place in 1993, Rena's first husband, the late Roy Point, called attention to the need to redress this loss:

How are we going to learn our history, now that it's getting lost, without telling it? We are taught to not let go of any of our own teachings and our own ways, medicines, our own teachings of each tribe, our own secrets. That's the way it was. Now that [knowledge] is being lost. How to keep it alive is a really big question, because so many of our older people are gone, just a handful of us left . . . I don't know how we can keep it alive. (Quoted in Archibald 2008, 78)

A century after the active years of the generation that raised Rena, the community has indeed moved far from its traditional foundations, from the time when the people lived directly from the land and when the exchanging of salmon and other foods, ceremonial goods, craft products, and services was more extensive than is the case today. Many younger people have little familiarity with the old ways, the old knowledge, philosophy, and ways of being. This knowledge fails to come alive for them in the way it did for earlier generations, who lived their lives on the land and river and carried out, on a daily basis, the rights and duties that had descended to them through birth and marriage.

As I have said, Rena was raised on the land and the river, away from the trappings of modernity. Because her parents were still young at the time, busy working in various jobs and locations, she was raised by her grandparents, in the customary way. Her grandparents' lives remained enmeshed in what urban Euro-Canadians call the "natural world," a world that was as much a part of their lives as were their own body rhythms. These family elders showed Rena the "old way," the way that they had been trained to live. They made sure Rena kept her head clear, her hands busy, and her ears open. She learned to be a good listener and to respect words and use them judiciously.

After these years with her grandparents, Rena was taken to a government-supported church school and subsequently joined modern First Nations life. She worked seasonally—processing fish and farm produce—before marrying Roy and moving to his family's community. She gave birth to and raised a large family and engaged almost daily in her artwork, as well as showing great respect for literacy and formal education. Hers is the story of life within a distinct set of family relationships, but it is also a story of moving beyond a quiet domestic life into a larger world. She was among the first to take action, together with her children, to revive some of the old ways—in crafts and ceremonies—and, relying on her childhood learning, she has shown both Xwélmexw people and the wider society how Aboriginal creativity can enrich modern life. Now, as the years pass, she, like others who have gone before, feels compelled to find ways to pass on what she knows and has experienced, as well as her creativity and her artistic skills, to her descendants and to the broader community.

Readers might wonder how, today, we can speak of silence in relation to the First Nations when so much is currently published by them and about them. Especially during the politically active 1960s and 1970s, the silence began to spring leaks, and, today, the situation appears to be anything but quiet. Aboriginal peoples are often in the media, fighting for their rights, seeking the best media coverage and struggling to mobilize opposition to the latest mega-resource-extraction project to disrupt their lives, whether this be a hydro-electric dam, mammoth cut-block logging, gas fracturing of the earth's crust, petroleum extraction, tar sand pipelines, toxic waste burials, or open-pit mining. As for the Stó:lō (or Xwélmexw), we now have many accounts *by* the people as well as *about* them. These have entered the public arena—memoirs, ethnographies, atlases, archaeological reports, local histories, school texts, poetry, and interactive websites.[15] Why then, despite this abundance of material, have we produced yet another book that purports to break the silence separating Xwélmexw ways of being from those of their mainstream neighbours?

The answer lies mostly in the ever-present need for cultural renewal. Even though, today, Xwélmexw traditional lands have been encroached upon by the urban expansion of Vancouver and its surrounding municipalities, a vibrant Aboriginal culture has somehow continued not only to exist but to flourish. That this culture remains vibrant is due to all those who ceaselessly "break the silence" and now manage to do so much more overtly than was possible in the past, people who are willing to share their knowledge and insights and to hand down their traditions to coming generations in a perpetual, always evolving process.[16]

Still, much work remains to be done to get information, understanding, and respect flowing back and forth between the two sides in the war of

15 Some of this material can be found in books cited in the list of references. See, for instance, Archibald 2008, Carlson 1997, 2001, 2003; Carlson and McHalsie 1998; Kew 1990; Mohs 1987, 2000; Pennier 2006; Simon Fraser University Museum of Archaeology and Ethnology 2008–9; Sleigh 1983; Tataryn 2009; Thom 1994, 1996, 2003; Suttles 1990; and Wells 1987.

16 Those engaged in efforts to keep Xwélmexw cultural practices alive sometimes go about their activities with a heavy heart as they observe the impact of urban encroachment not only on their day-to-day lives but on the balance between human beings and the natural environment. Rena's son Steven Point recently wrote me about this with deep passion. He ended as follows: "Something odd is happening to the deer and the bear. They are coming down from the mountains and seeking food in our towns and cities. In Victoria, hundreds of deer live inside the city limits, living off the gardens and lawns of Europeans. The Bear who once lived off the salmon runs and berry fields, they are coming to the cities to eat the garbage at the dumps. It is sad to see these, our brothers, reduced to living in this manner. Our whole life is one that must be lived in harmony and balance with mother earth. This is a universal law that even the Europeans must adhere to. I fear that something very bad will happen to return us all to this balance. Perhaps we can avoid even our own disappearance if we can find harmony with the land and environment again" (personal communication, July 5, 2013).

silence—a silence that is "both embedded in and also continually reborn from our praxis and from our inability to listen" (Sider and Smith 1997, 17). When cultural continuity is disrupted and traumatized, the silences tend to grow more intense. Moreover, cultural and historical transmission, just like food and shelter, are essential to the success of each new generation. Indigenous activists living within modern nation-states such as Canada thus feel the necessity to recall, to speak out, to elaborate on and pass down their community heritage and distinct ways of being to their descendants. Not to do so is to risk cultural inundation, the total loss of identity. Mrs. Point Bolton's story is part of this concerted effort at cultural continuity and renewal.

The Book Process: From Dialogue to Monologue

Dialogue

"Sit down and listen, that's what our ancestors used to say," Chief Simon Baker, of the Squamish Nation, told Jo-ann Archibald (quoted in Archibald 2008, 47). Learning to be still, to listen quietly and absorb, was an important part of traditional Xwélmexw culture, as well as other Salish cultures. Young people were encouraged not to speak out or talk back to their elders, not to argue and attempt to justify themselves if they were criticized. The young were taught instead to listen, to take criticism and learn from it, to bide their time, to strengthen the mind by practicing patience and learn to use both their hands and their heads to gain skills in life, and to sift out from the old wisdom whatever was relevant to their present lives.

There was a degree of hierarchical discipline built into this training, as there often is in any apprenticeship. Indeed, the need to obey the instructions and wishes of one's elders would silence the learner, possibly causing inner frustrations to build. But the day would come when those learning showed by their actions that they were capable not only of obeying but of taking the words, opinions, and experience of the authorities and using them to build their own lives—not as a carbon copy of those lived by their elders but as an expression of their own generation's energy and outlook. Then, all too quickly, this new generation would become mature and be expected to teach the next generation—those who only yesterday were babies but who now needed to understand who they are and where they came from so that they could, in turn, guide their descendants.

In the 1970s, Archibald, a Stó:lō educational researcher, had begun working with a group of elders from the Central Coast Salish area. The members of the Coqualeetza Elders' Group, as they were called, met regularly at the Coqualeetza Cultural Education Centre, in Sardis, in order to exchange stories and teachings. In *Indigenous Storywork* (2008), Archibald discusses her project, which focused on the erosion of the culture of the old Salish world and on how to transmit the remaining knowledge, values, and stories in ways that would preserve their character and integrity despite radical changes in the society. In addition to the late Roy Point and other elders (many of them Xwélmexw), Archibald worked closely with Aboriginal storytellers, teachers, and writers, all of whom were concerned to find ways to keep the stories flowing down the generations, especially today when Salish people's lives have become highly urbanized and increasingly divorced from daily experiences on the land.

In any "told-to" project, perhaps the principal goal of both teller and listener is to record the past for use and appreciation in the future, in hopes of providing assistance in cultural continuity. As Chief Baker said to his "told-to" collaborator, First Nations educator Verna Kirkness, a couple of decades earlier, "I would like to tell about my life, what I've seen, what I've done, so my grandchildren and their children will learn things that happened in these last hundred years. I believe my story will be interesting for schools" (Baker 1994, 173, cited in Archibald 2008, 23). Our collaborative project in this book is very much in the same vein as the work described by Archibald. The younger generations that Rena hopes to reach have imbibed many cultural prejudices and values from the dominant culture, including the assumption that Xwélmexw ways of the past are quaint and old-fashioned, with little to say to people starting out in modern life. Her aims are thus very similar to those of Chief Baker and all the various Coast Salish elders with whom Archibald worked.

Telling any story is a social act, one that involves a teller, a listener (or listeners), and a cultural context, which is necessary to an understanding of the story and which the listener must be able to supply. Telling a story to someone is thus a dialogue, even if most of the tongue action comes from one side and most of the ear action from the other. When the aim is to publish the results, the "listener" in the dialogue must be prepared to provide whatever assistance potential readers may need in order to understand what is being told. In such cases, the listener is asked to "witness" the story of the speaker, and witnessing is acknowledged as an essential element in legitimating important oral narratives and decisions in Salish and other Northwest Coast cultures, all of which found such alternative ways of recording important social events without the aid of written documents.[17]

Nevertheless, collaborative, "told-to" life stories such as this one are problematic, both for the witness who listens to, records, and edits the narration and for the narrator herself or himself. The two active participants in the interaction seldom share the same influence, reputation, and access to power, the same cultural understanding, or the same personal background. How then do we *cooperate* as equals, rather than creating the sort of "collaboration" in which one side is forced to compromise its principles so as to gain favour with, or even simply recognition from, the more dominant other? Especially in postcolonial countries such as Canada, the act of producing life histories based on the oral narratives of Aboriginal speakers is particularly fraught with historical imbalances of power and with institutionalized prejudice and preconceptions. But it is also weighted down by the degree of ignorance that each side, but particularly the empowered side, tends to possess with regard to the other, in light of the institutional silence that still separates Native and non-Native communities.

In *First Person Plural: Aboriginal Storytelling and the Ethics of Collaborative Authorship* (2011), Sophie McCall explores the cultural hegemony at work in the continuing reluctance to recognize transcribed

---

17 The Xwélmexw speakers whose narratives were presented by Keith Carlson (1997) chose to emphasize this in the title of their book: *You Are Asked to Witness*.

oral accounts as literature, stressing the imbalance of power that exists when oral narratives must try to find a place within the mainstream literary canon by being "told to" someone else, usually someone familiar with the intricacies of today's text-mediated world:

> Told-to narratives do not fit the criteria that govern European concepts of genre; the collaborative process challenges the author-function and notions of the literary by foregrounding process over product, context over text, and audience over author; and literary critics have assigned the study of oral literature to the departments of anthropology and folklore, contributing to the view that transcribed oral narratives are the domain of linguistics or other cultural specialists. Meanwhile, Aboriginal literature in Canada has increasingly come to mean singly authored texts, as if told-to narratives were synonymous with literary colonization. (2011, 4–5)

As McCall points out, dialogic and oral forms of expression—which are simply alternative modalities in which stories can be created and histories recounted—are not accepted as literature in their own right because they are culturally foreign to the dominant culture. Once they have been edited and reshaped, however, they are deemed sufficiently civilized to possess a degree of literary content. Thus "made over," they have, in a sense, been colonized by the mainstream. In McCall's view, then, "told-to" collaborations can be "productive sites for analyzing the shifting dynamics of cross-cultural interaction" (2011, 7).

Apart from this differential of power between the "speaker" culture and the "told-to" culture, there is a striking difference in the way that stories are told, as well as the purpose for which they are told. Situated as we are in a world of written texts, we expect information to be presented in a logical, linear order. Stories (including historical accounts and biographies) are generally told in a straightforward progression, from beginning to end, without what we would regard as needless repetition. In oral cultures, however, stories tend to be recursive. They circle back on themselves and revisit earlier scenes in the plot, such that their repetitions acquire a contrapuntal power—a jazz riff, if you like, or a set of variations on a theme. Moreover, whereas modern Western readers typically view stories as entertainment, in oral cultures stories are more likely to be told for pedagogical purposes, with each telling of the story contributing a new angle or interpretation, a new way of understanding.[18]

Depending on where and when and how it is told, and by whom, the same story can, for example, serve to inform listeners about psychology, social relations, history, politics, the spiritual realm, or the natural environment. As Julie Cruikshank found in her classic study, *Life Lived Like a Story* (Cruikshank et al. 1990; see also Cruikshank 2005), a particular telling of a story tended to reflect issues facing the teller's community at the time, at once illustrating and offering a commentary on the situation in which the telling was embedded. She emphasizes the powerful social and political effects of verbally performed narratives, as well as stressing the constructive power of stories that are told between living interlocutors, as opposed to stories composed for a readership whose lives are largely governed by written texts.

In view of prevailing expectations, however, told-to narratives almost invariably adopt the standard linear chronology familiar from written biographies, even if the teller did not originally tell the story in such a straightforward way. As Kathleen Sands explains in *Telling a Good One,* the life story of Papago elder Theodore Rios (Rios and Sands 2000), while a linear account was the finished product of her collaboration with Rios, it was certainly not how Ted Rios actually told his story. In her introduction, Sands quotes the opening of the biography that she and Rios have created and comments: "This version reads like the beginning of a conventional biography because the dialogic nature of the collaborative

18 It can be argued that, when it comes to entertainment, our attention span is generally shorter today than it was in earlier decades. More and more, it seems, we demand simplicity. As for *learning* things, stories are regarded as inefficient modes of instruction. In the school system, we have a model of learning in which information is presented as a series of facts, with the successful student being the one who can absorb that information quickly and regurgitate it on demand. We don't want to waste time trying to cull lessons and factual information from stories or learning how to assess them and the motives of their tellers as we create a critical sense of the world. We do not have the time.

methodology has been suppressed. But this is, in fact, what Ted expected to go into print—a continuous narrative that I would order and edit from the interviews we did" (Rios and Sands 2000, 3).[19] From the tenor of the book, it seems unlikely that Rios would have been knowledgeable about what publishers would or would not accept; rather, his expectation was presumably grounded in the conviction that, to appeal to mainstream readers, one must create a product that conforms to the prevailing conventions of storytelling.

Another prominent voice in the told-to discourse is Greg Sarris. Sarris (1993) addresses similar issues, but he does so from the standpoint of someone who personally identifies (through blood ties) with a range of American cultures—the mainstream, immigrant minority groups, and the Native American. He argues for an inclusive, "holistic" approach to Native American stories, seeking to find common ground and common cause for encouraging positive and democratic interactions between the storyteller, the listener, and the mass media. As he reminds us, a story is not the product of any one person. It is always enmeshed in a social process of formation and transfer between people.

Sarris also seeks to collapse the personal and the scholarly in research, so that the literary text being examined, or the people under study who tell the stories, are not distanced from the researcher. He rejects the myth of the *cordon sanitaire* that supposedly separates scholars and scientists from what they are studying, counting, recording, and then analyzing—the epistemological demand for objectivity that goes to the extreme of removing from the frame of investigation any sign of the researcher and her or his assumptions and prejudices. Sarris argues that

19 As Sands further explains, she had assumed her collaborative work with Rios was finished in 1975, but instead she had to struggle for twenty-five years to arrive at a version of his story acceptable to academics, to Native Americans, and to the publishing world (and, of course, to Rios). "Lest I seem too sympathetic toward presses," she writes, "be assured I realize how powerful they are in dictating what does and does not get published and how conservative most are in their decisions to invest in Native American literatures and anthropology texts at all" (Rios and Sands 2000, 337n6).

researchers must acknowledge their role in a project—what feminists have called affirming one's "standpoint of knowing."[20] In other words, observers—those listening and recording—must include, as part of the subject matter of the project, the epistemological perspective that they inevitably bring to bear on whatever they study.

When I embarked on this project with Rena, it was certainly not in the spirit of the impersonal observer, someone who strives to be present only as a sort of tabula rasa, with the goal of producing a book that would masquerade as a disembodied, "objective" ethnographic account of Xwél-mexw life. Rather, both Rena and I were materially present as the story was created and the book took form. The result is the product of an ongoing conversation, one that unfolded in episodes that stretched across many months. For the most part, I would ask questions about one or other of the themes we had chosen beforehand to discuss. Rena would then reply, sometimes sitting over tea, with hands idle, and other times while working on a basket. As was the case for Rios, Rena's original narration of her life story was not a continuous monologue. Instead, it took place within the context of what might be characterized as discourse-driven dialogue.

FIGURE 1

Richard Daly, Rena, and Richard's wife, Liv Mjelde, in Rena's workroom at her home on the Zymacord River, not far from Kitsumkalum, 2009. Photo: Richard Daly.

20 For a useful discussion of feminist standpoint theory, see Harding 2004, especially the contributions by Patricia Collins, Donna Haraway, Nancy Hartsock, Dorothy Smith, and Alison Wylie, and by Sandra Harding herself.

By *dialogue,* I am referring to a form of linguistic exchange that has been analyzed by the Russian philosopher and literary theorist Mikhail Bakhtin. Bakhtin was interested in the dialogic nature of speech and writing and, especially, in the question of how, through our social interactions with one another, we arrive at a common, or at least an overlapping, set of understandings that allow for a degree of mutual intelligibility. This is achieved, he argues, through the interactive language of social communication, when people are engaged in the joint activity of speaking and listening to one another (Bakhtin 1986). Mutual understanding depends on two realities—that of the teller and that of the listener—that act in concert. Communication is not based solely on the narrative action of an individual speaker or writer (as linguists sometimes assume) but instead consists of a socially constructed dialectical action involving both parties:

> The fact is that when the listener perceives and understands the meaning (the language meaning) of speech, he simultaneously takes an active, responsive attitude toward it. He either agrees or disagrees with it (completely or partially), augments it, applies it, prepares for its execution, and so on. [. . .] Any understanding of live speech, a live utterance, is inherently responsive, although the degree of this activity varies extremely. Any understanding is imbued with response and necessarily elicits it in one form or another: the listener becomes the speaker. (Bakhtin 1986, 68)

As Bakhtin goes on to point out (1986, 69), in telling a story, or simply making an utterance, the speaker is not "the first speaker, the one who disturbs the eternal silence of the universe," like a god creating the cosmos. Speakers are always, at least to some extent, respondents as well.

Nor does the speaker expect a passive understanding from the listener (or reader), one that merely replicates the speaker's intended meaning. Rather, as Bakhtin puts it (1986, 69), the person speaking "expects response, agreement, sympathy, objection, execution, and so forth." In the case of an oral narrative, the listener reacts to the words of the storyteller with pleasure, interest, distaste, frustration, or some other such response. The listener may also interrupt the speaker to request clarification, elaboration, or illustration and might even seek to deflect the story, so that it heads off in another direction. In other words, the listener—the person on the receiving end of the narration—is often animated by what she or he hears and assists in the communication of what is being told, participating in its overall line of narrative development, its degree of detail, and its future transmission.

Storytelling is thus an ongoing, discursive process that continues across the generations. Stories—including life stories—function as conduits of information, values, and insights, and they are never completely "owned" by the teller. In the words of Annie Ned, one of the Yukon elders with whom Julie Cruikshank worked: "Not *you* are telling it; it's the person who told you that's telling the story" (Cruikshank et al. 1990, 278). Nor is any one narration definitive and final; there are always other things that could be added on, especially by others in the family and community. As Aboriginal legal rights advocate Sharon Venne points out, "One elder may know part of a story and another will know the rest of the story," but "no one Elder knows the complete story" (1997, 174, 176). Rather, "the stories are spread among the people, and only through repeated and continuous contact with Indigenous communities can the complete story be known" (176). Moreover, Elders often deliberately tell stories one piece at a time:

> To a listener, sometimes the stories do not make sense. Often this is a way the Elders communicate the story: they tell a piece and wait to see if there is interest in the whole story. The story is then like a puzzle. . . . The Elder wants the person to want to learn more. There is one piece in this corner, then another piece given at another time. It remains to the listener to put the pieces together and sort out the complete picture. If there are more questions, the listener must make return visits to the Elders. (1997, 176)

In other words, in the social construction of meaning, the audience must take an active interest and assume a participatory role. Jo-ann Archibald affirms this reciprocal process when she writes, "I have heard many Elders say that they wait to be asked to share their knowledge. The term 'share' implies teaching. If a learner is really serious about learning in a traditional manner, then the learner must ask and must make her/himself culturally ready" (2008, 37).

Many of the teachings and anecdotes that are now part of Rena's narrative were told to her by others. Such accounts came to her on the understanding that she would assume responsibility for handing them down to coming generations. Other parts of her story consist of her own life experience, yet these are experiences lived in relation to the teachings she heard as a child. What has prompted her to speak is the need to pass on the teachings of those who were the tellers back in the days when she was the listener, supplemented by what she has learned from life itself. While there is perhaps always a sense of urgency in the task of conveying accumulated knowledge and wisdom to those who will outlive you, Rena has herself already outlived most of her contemporaries, who might otherwise have contributed to her narrative. Indeed, she is probably the last person trained by her elders in the manner she explains, in the course of engaging in daily life along the banks of the river.

* ❧ *

What then happens when a spoken narrative is converted to written form? The elders with whom Cruikshank worked so extensively were from the generation that preceded Rena Point Bolton. Their lives were more directly ruled by the spoken word and face-to-face communication. Rena is informed by a more literate world than were her immediate predecessors, but the living power of oral presentation still remains vital to her life and the lives of those around her. Oral performances of narratives tend to engage the mind and imagination of the listener much more directly than do technologically mediated forms of storytelling, and in turn this engagement feeds back to the storyteller. Rena herself remarks on this change: "Nowadays, the art of storytelling seems to have died. What a tragic loss this has been for my children and grandchildren. The only storyteller today seems to be the television. When you listen to a storyteller, your imagination goes into high gear. That doesn't happen with TV."

Although the situation is changing rapidly, the written text continues to occupy a hegemonic role in modern society. Rena therefore wanted to leave a written account of her life, as a lasting record of a way of living that, for many of her descendants, no longer exists and that may well be completely unfamiliar to broader audiences. But a book is not an artifact in a museum. Even after the story has been placed between the covers of a book, and even though reading is ordinarily a solitary activity, the narrative is passed on from one person to another. It continues to play an active role in society. The act of reading is not carried out passively, in a vacuum. It still entails an interaction—a silent dialogue—between the author (or authors) and the reader. Moreover, as is also the case with oral exchanges, reading involves a relationship between the author, the reader, and the cultural values, ideas, and assumptions that each brings to the dialogue. In written communication, however, this multifaceted interaction is not as direct as it is between speaker and listener, a fact that poses a potentially significant problem when the text's author belongs to a cultural tradition that differs from that of its eventual readers (or at least some of them). Under such circumstances, readers often need to be given a kind of road map, in the form of background information, if they are to arrive at a degree of shared understanding with the author.

Sociologist Dorothy Smith has applied the insights of Bakhtin (among others) in her own thinking about the question of how we socially construct knowledge in a dialogic manner.[21] Keeping dialogic discourse

---

21 See, for example, *Writing the Social: Critique, Theory and Investigation* (1999) and *Institutional Ethnography: A Sociology of People.* In addition to Bakhtin, Smith draws on the classic work of Valentin Vološinov ([1929] 1986), George Herbert Mead (1932, [1934] 1967), and Alfred Schutz (1967). As a feminist scholar, she is a strong proponent of the idea that social research must be conducted from a clearly enunciated standpoint of knowing. In particular, her concern lies with finding ways to do research that capture the world as it is experienced and understood by ordinary people in their everyday lives, including the points at which their lives intersect with the institutions of the state. As one commentator recently explained: "Dorothy Smith wants to equip people to study their own actual situations in society, and to do so to furnish us with a basic understanding of political economy from the point of view of the working people" (Mjelde, forthcoming).

firmly in focus, she explores the way in which people who are interacting seek a common understanding by employing two processes—"mapping" and then "indexing," or "referring," that is, moving back and forth between the map and the local terrain. As Smith explains, in order to make sense of a narrative, "readers/hearers must know how to 'find' objects beyond the text that can be recognized as the object or objects to which the text refers" (2012, 86). In other words, the reader has to bring to the narrative knowledge that he or she has previously accumulated (the map) and use it to "index" items in the text.

In the course of the dialogue between the teller of a story and the listener, the listener uses a similar process of indexing in order to make sense of the narrative, and the teller does the same in response to the listener's reactions. Knowledge is always in circulation among and between people, which opens the possibility of knowing things in common. At the same time, even when those seeking to arrive at a shared meaning share a similar standpoint, no two maps are ever identical. Our individual experiences differ, and thus so do our perceptions. In the case of a "told-to" narrative, it falls to the listener to map and index the significance of the narrator's account, by posing questions in the course of the interaction itself and by subsequent searches for information from other sources that can then be presented to the narrator for comment, rejection, or elaboration. In creating her life story, Rena and I tried to find points of common reference. But we both know that elements in her story will have a significance that extends beyond my own capacity for understanding—my own "mapping" and "indexing" of what I have been told, my own ability to function as an interlocutor. In particular, Rena's family members and others in the Xwélmexw community will understand her words in ways that I cannot fully appreciate. In our joint venture here, Rena speaks to a broad spectrum of reader-listeners, as though they were all sitting with me at the kitchen table of her log house or perched on stools in her workroom, with its coils of cedar bark, its spruce roots soaking in warm water, permeated with the fragrance of Cliff Bolton's fresh-cut yellow cedar and the scent of Rena's herbs and medicines hanging up to dry. But each of these reader-listeners will form their own maps, with which they will proceed to index her story to the world with which they are familiar.

Monologue

As we have seen, oral narratives are fundamentally interactive, implying the presence not only of a narrator and but of a listener who functions as an interlocutor as well. Our interaction generated the story, in the sense that it came out the way it did because she was telling it to me, rather than to somebody else. My contribution was to attend to the meaning of her words and to raise questions when I did not understand.

It was in this dialogic tradition, then, that we worked to assemble the material for this book. Yet, for the purposes of preparing the final text, we have had to relegate our dialogue to the backstage area and produce a soliloquy. We have had to transform what began in first person plural into first person singular. To borrow Sand's image, I, as Rena's text advisor, have chosen to suppress the dialogic nature of our hours of cooperative exchanges, as well as their episodic and recursive quality. I have arranged the content of these hours together into a linear progression in the course of writing up the story as text. However, as readers will discover, some of the ideas that Rena wanted to emphasize still manage to break the linear flow from time to time and repeat themselves as variations on a theme. My other task has been to place within the text some of the poems she handed to me. She usually brought them up herself in the course of the narration.

In addition, I supplied the notes to Rena's narrative, drawing not only on other published sources but on my own personal and professional experience. In contributing this commentary, I have had to keep in mind that, while many of those reading this book will be Xwélmexw, many will not, and the two groups will come to Rena's story with different expectations and assumptions. Of course, neat categorical divisions such as this—"Xwélmexw" versus "non-Xwélmexw"—are inherently somewhat suspect. There are many overlaps between the two, especially today, when Aboriginal outlooks and ways of life and those of the dominant society are increasingly interwoven. Nonetheless, the distinction still holds, and the task is to find ways to redress the imbalances between the two groups, as well as between the prominent and not-so prominent members on either side of the cultural divide. In view of the potential for misunderstanding, readers in both groups need to begin with some road maps with which to orient themselves, so that they will be able to find their way in the monologue,.

On the one hand, then, there are maps for Xwélmexw readers:

- They need to understand that, today, many non-Aboriginal people genuinely wish to know more about the culture of First Nations (who still remain, for far too many, only walking stereotypes of colonial "Indians") and that such people deserve some patience from those who are able to live the culture from the inside.

- They need to be aware that, in the mainstream book publishing world, certain conventions govern the way in which stories are presented, and readers expect these conventions to be observed.

- In addition, they need to allow for the fact that, in mainstream biographies and autobiographies, the narratives always stress the individual point of view. Such life accounts tend to cut out the context of family, as well as setting aside the question of to whom one is related and therefore how one has the right to speak of these things. For the most part, modern society greets preferential treatment based on family connections with embarrassed silence and no longer acknowledges the importance of genealogy and how family influences social legitimacy. For mainstream readers, social legitimacy is based above all on what one makes of oneself, rather than on one's family ties and social connectedness.

- They need to acknowledge that younger generations of Xwélmexw live more fully inside Canadian society than their elders did, as a result of their formal education, their exposure to mainstream media and forms of entertainment, and their absorption of ethics derived from the broader social environment. Consequently, they have begun to lose their own road maps. The process of acculturation has taken hold, to the point that younger Xwélmexw can read the story of Rena Point Bolton's life in order to become acquainted with their history and learn to value their heritage. Together with other young First Nations readers, they can draw on her words in the same way as non-Native readers, acquiring an appreciation of a way of life that came before, yet overlapped with, their own lives.

And, on the other hand, mainstream readers also require maps:

* They need to understand that Rena is primarily addressing her local community—those who can sanction her account, those to whom she is connected by blood or marriage through the generations—for, in the absence of these connections, her story would have much less impact and importance.

* They need to be aware that parts of Rena's story are undoubtedly contested within the local Xwélmexw society. On the basis of what she has learned from the elders, she is seeking to establish who she is in order not only to pass on her rights and obligations to younger persons but also to safeguard these rights and duties, through her elaboration of the family's oral history and its connectedness to earlier generations of people vital to the culture and heritage. In Northwest Coast cultures, the families that do not step forward and present their histories and their rights and duties before their peers will have their claims and their very history eclipsed by families that *do* step forward. In telling what she learned from her elders, Rena puts forward her family background, her cultural heritage, and own experiences for others to confirm, deny, or elaborate upon. There is always some degree of competition among families, some of whom may tell similar stories but with a different emphasis. At the same time, other families often react with pleasure when they see that some people remember their culture and want to pass on that heritage to others, not only within their immediate family but beyond.

* They need to understand why Rena and her brother were removed from the distractions of the village during the

"Hungry Thirties" and raised on the fishing site of Devil's Run. In other words, the reader must understand that, by bloodline, Rena and Peter were destined to be the carriers of the culture since it appeared that most members of their parents' generation were not willing to be apprentices in the old ways. They were busy with jobs in the resource sector and had fallen under the sway of the dominant culture. Rena's grandparents thus concentrated on the next generation as the future carriers of the culture and removed Rena and Peter to the riverside to learn their history and their ways.

* They need to appreciate that Rena's maternal bloodline links her directly to the Steqó:ye Wolf People and their famous warrior of the early European contact period, X̱éyteleq. A luminous figure among the people who lived around the shores of what was once Sumas Lake, X̱éyteleq was said to have cemented ties to various communities dotted along the adjacent coast by taking wives in those places.

* They need to recognize the significance that Rena's family ties—through her maternal grandmother to X̱éyteleq, on the one hand, and through her maternal grandfather to the Sxwóyxwey, on the other—have for the Xwélmexw and the wider Salish community. On the basis of what she learned as a child, Rena traces her family's line of descent from a famous warrior and establishes their claim to the right to conduct and control a prominent healing ceremony. Others can then plot their own genealogical connections, through Rena and her family ties, to these historical persons and to ceremonial rights and duties as well.

* They need to understand the crucial importance of the revival of arts and craft production that took place in the First Nations communities of British Columbia during the 1950s and continued to expand throughout the coming decades. This revival not only enriched the artistic life of the region but also helped

build a new sense of self-identity in cultures that had been so badly battered by generations of colonial administration. As Rena explains in her story, in the days before social welfare, doing craftwork was a way that women could begin to bring their families out of poverty.

When readers draw on these road maps to orient themselves, they will be able, at least to some extent, to override the gap between cultures—to fill in locations that were missing on their respective maps. They will then find that, for the most part, the events in Rena's life, as well as her deep concern for the future of Xwélmexw culture, can be understood as a weft that is woven over and under the warp provided by her heritage and training. Her reflections on her experience elaborate on the way that she has sought to live her life in keeping with the contours of her culture. I hope that, equipped with the necessary maps, readers will be able to relax and enjoy her story, just as if they were sitting around in her workroom listening to her speak as her busy fingers go on plaiting and weaving, trimming and joining.

Time to Speak Out

As a child, sitting at the feet of her mother, grandmother, and aunts, Rena learned the ways of her ancestors and the attitudes and conduct appropriate to a high-born woman in her local cultural community. She experienced an arranged marriage and then lived under the moral authority of her husband's family, away from her home village. While she was still a young woman, the elders of her community recognized in her a worthy successor—someone well trained in Xwélmexw values and seemingly forgotten practices, who had also mastered traditional crafts. They acknowledged that, as she matured, she would have the practical authority to take the culture forward. Later, aided by her relations with her elders and her proficiency in Native arts and crafts, she grew active in the struggles of Canada's First Nations to resist assimilation and to demand that First Nations' ways be respected and that their rights as the country's original inhabitants—including the right to a greater degree of local self-governance and the right to control traditional lands and waterways—be recognized in the Constitution.

With regard to the task of taking her life story to a wider audience, in the form of a book, Rena and her family have appointed me to act has her "speaker," as Steven Point explains in his foreword. The role of speaker in Xwélmexw society, as in other Indigenous societies along the Northwest Coast, is an old one. During pre-colonial, pre-textual times, in local societies all across what would become Canada, words were considered to be very powerful. They had to be thought through, deliberated upon, before being released into the public domain. "Words are medicine that can heal or injure," Basil Johnston told Jo-ann Archibald. "Were a person to restrict his discourse, and measure his speech, and govern his talk by what he knew, he would earn the trust and respect of his listeners." As a result, "people would want to hear the speaker again and by so doing bestow upon the speaker the opportunity to speak, for ultimately it is the people who confer the right of speech by their audience" (quoted in Archibald 2008, 19).

There were, and are, however, differing opinions in the public domain, and thus words must be used carefully when one is meeting others, beyond the boundaries of family. The inappropriate use of words and stories can cause a serious disruption in established social relations, leading to economic disputes, feuding among relatives, retaliatory raids on neighbours, and even war with other peoples. For this reason, leading figures often appointed, and continue to appoint, persons to speak on their behalf. Up to then, the person chosen to speak has been the one listening, as it were, behind closed doors—the person fulfilling the role of witness, learning to understand and appreciate the views and perspective of his or her elder, teacher, or leader.[22]

22 Until fairly recently, women did not normally speak in public. However, they
   often instructed their men beforehand on what to say on public and ceremonial
   occasions, as Rena points out with reference to her grandparents. Women also
   played a leading role in planning and preparing social and ceremonial events
   and took an active part in certain aspects of ceremonial life.

However, once a listener has been appointed speaker, he or she steps into a new role. Whatever the speaker says and writes on behalf of the other person will be closely scrutinized. The speaker's knowledge and understanding are never perfect, of course, and thus the elder or leader can add to or modify the speaker's account as need be. This can become necessary in order to get the point across more indirectly or eloquently or diplomatically, and in a manner that emphasizes reflection and deliberation and the sharing of information, values, and knowledge, all the while maintaining respect for the opinions of others.

As we have seen, in a dialogue, mutual understanding depends on the ability of each side in the equation to "live into" the experience of the other. As Rena Point Bolton's speaker, I have done my best to live into her story as I transferred it to the page, such that it will remain her story, not mine. In First Nations cultures, speakers are, after all, judged on the basis of their fidelity to the message they were engaged to represent. Rena has read the resulting text, marked up certain passages, and suggested a few other changes, which were subsequently made.

In some cases, Rena's accounts overlapped or one narration was supplemented by another. In the "Water and the Cycle of Life" section, for example, near the end of the book, I combined a speech that Rena had delivered at a school graduation with a closely similar account she had given me orally in our very first interview in Vancouver, in December 1988. When I had put all this material together, Rena reviewed the results and made a few corrections. "That's fine," she said, handing back the manuscript, "but for goodness sake, don't make me sound too polished. I'm not educated, you know." I protested: "These are not my words. They're yours." The speech she had given was polished the moment it emerged from her mouth.

In the end, Rena and I hope that, between the two of us, we have provided enough contextual background—enough cultural translation—to establish a common ground, such that our readers can trust us. According to biographer and translator David Bellos (2011, 120), if a narrator and a listener are to understand one another, they must trust one another, and this trust is the key to all social relations—a cornerstone of all culture. The question remains, however, whether the silences of the past can ever be wholly overcome, and trust achieved. As Rena talked, I sometimes had the feeling that the spectres of colonialism were still with us, hovering over my shoulder, reminding me of a legacy that remained unspoken. Over the past decades, I have often had occasion to interview First Nations politicians and elders. Even today, there lingers an almost tangible presence of ghostly dialogue in these interviews, in which the speakers, no matter what topic they happen to be addressing, seem to be responding to colonial injustices that still haunt their minds and chill their hearts.

It may well be that even now, in the twenty-first century, we—both the tellers and the told-tos—continue to produce life stories of Aboriginal elders in an effort to exorcise memories of very real moral, psychological, and material trauma visited upon First Nations in the name of civilization and its trappings: notions of the one true God imported from the burning sands of the Middle East, the diamond-studded British Crown and the arrogance of its Empire. Despite the rapid pace of change, and despite our best intentions, the goals of human respect and cooperation, fully functional democracy, and social justice remain tantalizingly beyond the horizon.

Xwelíqwiya

* ❀ *

Born at a Very Young Age

As Hank Pennier used to say, "I was born at a very young age." [1] I was actually born at Kilgard, but when I was a couple of months old, Mum and Dad moved to Boothroyd [in the Fraser Canyon, upriver from Boston Bar], which was my dad's home area. I was baptized there by Father LePine. He was French and he didn't really understand English too well, so he listened to what they said and for me, he put down Boston Bar as my birthplace. I didn't know that until *years* later when I found my baptismal certificate. So that's what the Department of Indian Affairs goes by, my baptismal certificate, because I wasn't born in hospital. There is no official record of my birth, but actually the place was Kilgard, at Semá:th.

---

[1] The cheerful and highly readable account of the life story of Hank Pennier was republished in 2006 under the title *"Call Me Hank": A Stó:lō Man's Reflections on Logging, Living and Growing Old.* The book was originally published in 1972 with the unfortunate title *Chiefly Indian: The Warm and Witty Story of a British Columbia Half Breed Logger.*

Many years ago, I wrote a poem about how I began my life and how that affected me:

Alone

Alone I entered this world
After eight months in the womb
I was hurled out more dead than alive
Crushed skull and with blood in my eye
Fight on, ere you die.

Sweet victory! I am still alive.
On the breast of my mother did I thrive.
Three years did she nurse me tenderly,
But freedom beckoned, the urge to be free.
I was left at the tender age of three.

I struggled alone through the rest of my life,
As mother and father but never as "wife."
Ten children I bore to add to our home,
Love flourished and grew in my heart of stone.
Give your love to the world and you're never alone.

In a lonely cabin far away
From people milling day to day,
I sit alone and while away the hours
That God has lent me to this day.
Alone again, "Thank God," I pray.[2]

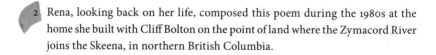

[2] Rena, looking back on her life, composed this poem during the 1980s at the home she built with Cliff Bolton on the point of land where the Zymacord River joins the Skeena, in northern British Columbia.

First Memories

My earliest memories are of life with Mum, Dad, and my brother Peter. We were living in a little cabin just outside the boundaries of the Kilgard Reserve. We were not allowed to live on reserve because my Mum had married my Dad, a non-status Indian, which means he was somebody who had no band membership on any reserve. So Mum lost her own status as an Indian, too. My mother was Annie, daughter of Sarah Vedder Silva and Pete Silva. At that time, my grandmother Sarah was still the one carrying out the duties of the *chu'chelángen*, and my mother was prepared to do só, too. I was born at Kilgard on May 22, 1927, but shortly after that, we lived for a time with my father's people at Boothroyd in the Fraser Canyon.

I guess I was three years old when I had these first memories from when we were back at Semá:th after the time up at Boothroyd. My brother, who was lame and still in a wheelchair, was six years old. He was already learning to sing and play the guitar. His singing hero was already Jimmy Rogers, and would always remain so. He was really something. He played the guitar upside down because he had to use his right hand on the fretboard and pick and strum with the one good finger on his left hand.

FIGURE 2
Rena at five months, with her mother, Annie Silva Bolan, 1927. Photo courtesy of Rena Point Bolton.

I'm not too clear about what happened between my Mum and Dad, but it was around this time that my Mum went away. I don't know how long she was gone. My dad stayed with us as long as he could. He'd been working at the Kilgard brickworks on the night shift. During the day, he'd try to take care of my brother and me.

After my father went back to Lytton, we lived with Grandfather Pete and Grandmother Sarah in a new makeshift DIA house at Kilgard. It was just a plain—like a matchbox house sort of thing. And they had very little furniture. I remember her saying that everything had burned in their big house. And so it was tough times then. The Depression was on. There was no work and they had drained the lake already and so there was very little food. So it was very difficult. I know my uncle used to have to go out and hunt in the mornings, very early in the morning. He'd come back with a sack of ducks, and where he got them, I have no idea. But he'd have a bag of ducks. His wife would pluck them and get them ready for the day's meals. As little as I was, I used to try to help her, although I was probably more in the way than anything. But this was how they lived.

FIGURE 3
Rena around the age of three, in her "Kimiko" period, Vancouver, ca. 1930. Photo courtesy of Rena Point Bolton.

One day when Peter and I were sitting outside our grandparents' house, I suddenly heard my mother's voice. She was calling my name. I jumped up and ran into her arms. She told me not to speak and to be very quiet. I don't recall how this episode ended. There's a memory gap and the next thing I remember is sitting in a doorway to a staircase somewhere in Vancouver. I'm all alone and crying for my grandmother. And I remember sitting under a table drinking pop through a straw. That must have been in the New Pier Café, where my mother was working.

Mum decided to hire a babysitter for when she was working at the café. All I remember is that the lady was a large woman called Mama-san. Mama-san sat in her grocery store all day long and talked to people while her sons waited on the customers. She dressed me up in a small kimono and white socks that looked like gloves. I recall playing, always alone, in the backyard with my little parasol. Mama-san loved me and took very good care of me. She cut my hair, with short bangs in front, and she called me "Kimiko" which means "pretty flower" in Japanese.[3]

One day, I was playing in the backyard when I heard loud voices and my mother sobbing. She was crying because Papa—her father, Pete Silva—had come down to Vancouver from Kilgard. He was very angry with my mother for taking me away to Vancouver without telling anyone. But what really made him boil was my haircut and to see me in those strange clothes. After that, I have a blank spot in my memory. I don't know how we got home or what sort of homecoming there was.

I have another early memory. I'm still three but I remember more. My grandmother has become very strict with me. Every day, I have to sit down and work at something or other. One day, she has me sewing coloured yarn on a piece of cardboard. She's punched a pattern of holes through the cardboard with her bone awl. I am to fill the card with coloured yarns, and I must not miss a single hole. Gradually, I learn to

[3] It seems that Rena's mother was working in the Powell Street area of Vancouver, where many Japanese Canadian families lived until the community was transported away from the coast following Japan's bombing of Pearl Harbor in December 1941.

master the darning needle and the task becomes easy. The next task is teasing wool. Before raw wool can be spun, you have to pull it apart and clean it. This is called "teasing." I used to sit and tease out mountains of wool. Then I would try to card the wool with two hand-carders that Grandmother used.

I guess I must have been around five years old when I mastered the *sélseltel*, the spindle whorl. That whorl was made by Grandfather Pete especially for my small hands. By the age of nine, I had graduated to the old spinning wheel. I don't recall when I learned to weave baskets. It just seems I always knew how. I went to the woods with Grandmother and learned to respect all living things. She taught me how to address the trees and birds and respect them in their own homes. We prayed and we asked the trees for permission before we started to gather what we needed to make our baskets. We took the cedar roots. There were so many old cedar trees. They had long, long roots that made *beautiful* baskets. And the bark! It was top quality. They used that for all kinds of things. They made boxes—storage boxes—and horse baskets and bailers for the canoes. Oh, they used it for everything. They made robes out of the bark, just about everything. That cedar tree, they even used the needles for a medicine. I don't use the needles myself. I don't really know what they were used for but I remember seeing my mother using them to heal people.

They hung the cedar branches up over the door for protection. I know my grandfather was a spiritual healer. He was like a medicine man, and when he worked with sick people, he filled a vessel up with water and he would have a little cedar bough. He would dip it in the water and sprinkle it on the people. And he would work on them. So he always had the water and the cedar bough. The cedar has been very sacred to our people.

I've written a poem about it:

The Cedar Tree

I have a friend so dear to me
A tall and lovely cedar tree
Dressed in splendour of evergreen;
No other tree outranks this queen.

She offers shelter to those in need
Who climb her limbs to hide and feed;
Her trunk will keep a family warm
Through coldest nights of winter storm.

In spring the birds return to build
Their nests she'll hold like those she held
For many years they've come and gone
To fly away at autumn's dawn;
Patiently, really, she stands, always aware
While gentle breezes caress her hair;
The essence of her fragrances fills the air,
Oh lovely, oh beautiful, how came you there!

As I kneel before you loyal friend
A beggar no less for you to tend
With pick and shovel and hiking boots
I've come to seek your tender roots

I'll scrape and split long glowing strands
And weave a basket with loving hands
With red and black and white design
A million stitches to make it fine.

To show the world that you and I
E'en tho' someday we both shall die
We'll leave behind a load of treasure
That time and man shall never measure.

The cedar tree was one of my grandfather's—I don't know what you'd call it—like a spiritual guide. And he also had the brown bear. These were the two spirit guides that helped him with his work, his spirit helpers. He used to tell us, whenever you're not feeling well, you're feeling sad about something, you're in sorrow about something, or you're sick—go sit under a cedar tree and ask for help. And lean on it if you like, and sleep under it, and it will help you heal your body and your mind. The people really believed in this, so I imagine it would work, you know. It would help whatever it was that was bothering them. So the cedar tree was one of our . . . like what we call crests. So we have the cedar tree, the brown bear, the two-headed snake from Dan Milo, and of course, the wolf, which was my Semá:th elders' guide.[4]

If I'm knitting or weaving blankets, or if the boys carve, we use these crests in our designs. We don't really call them crests. We just call them our spirit guides. But we don't wear them like a banner or anything. They are used mostly in the smokehouse or in the privacy of our homes.

My Father and My Brother

What little I know about my father's side is that my father's mother, Grandmother Annie Jamieson, was the daughter of William Jamieson, a Scot who came to Canada and married a lady from Coldwater up near Merritt. Her name was Sally Jim.

Sally Jim used to come over the mountains to do fish at Spuzzum in the Fraser Canyon. They walked through the mountains [Anderson Pass], and afterward, they hiked home [up to the Nicola Plateau], packing their fish with them. One time, she met this Scot, Jamieson, while she was putting up fish at Spuzzum. They married and she stayed on in the Canyon.

---

[4] For a more detailed description of the powers and emanations of the cedar tree, including a listing of three separate avatars, see York, Daly and Arnett (1994, 209–10). This account was gathered around 1990 from a Salish elder living some kilometres further upstream on the same river system.

They ran an inn up at Boothroyd, north of Boston Bar. Their children were Annie, my grandmother and the eldest; Gordon; and a third one. Annie Jamieson worked around the inn as chambermaid and waitress when she was a young girl. The Kanaka workers on the road construction—these Hawaiians—used to come in on the weekends for a break and to clean up and have a good meal.[5] One of the Kanakas, Lena Hope told me, was named John Puliya but was known as Johnny Puleeya.[6] He married Annie and they had children. Gradually, the last name changed to Bolan. The oldest of their children was my father, Francis Bolan. The other children were Janet, John, Martin, and William, or Bill, who died young. John's daughter was my Aunt Janet, who married Jimmy McLinden. McLinden's father was a Scot and his mother was Louie Sqw'átets's sister; he was also Pete Silva's brother in our system—that is, Pete's first cousin. Martin's widow, Louise, lived at Chehalis. Well, those are the only ones I ever heard named.

My father, Francis Bolan, was about two years older than my mother. My mother was born in 1905, so I guess my father was born in 1903, and his parents would have been born between 1870 and 1880. My father's father, John Puliya, came with his family from the United States, and

[5] Kanakas (Hawaiians) were first brought in from the Sandwich Islands to work for the Hudson's Bay Company on the Pacific Coast of North America. They are mentioned regularly in the Fort Langley journal entries of the HBC between 1827 and 1830 (Maclachlan 1998; Tolmie 1963).

[6] Lena Hope, a knowledgeable elder from the Yale Tii:t Xwélmexw people, possessed an intimate knowledge of the Canyon cultures and their interethnic marriages. As a recent student of the ethnohistory of the Fraser Canyon notes:

> In addition, Lena Hope provided evidence that a plethora of Fraser Canyon people were intimately connected as one via travel, marriage, and offspring. She explained to Oliver Wells that, "Some of them I guess go somewhere—get married and go where their husbands are or something." She asserted that these inter-village and geopolitical marriages were of the utmost importance to Fraser Canyon People So much so that grooms would try to cement a marriage and impress the bride's family via a large and handsome dowry. (Opheim 2009, 12–13)

they settled first on Salt Spring Island in British Columbia. I never met anyone from the Salt Spring family, but I did meet my father's mother, Annie Jamieson. She took care of this picture I have on the wall.[7]

Grandmother Annie Jamieson [Bolan Phillips] was living at Lytton with her second husband, George Phillips, who had the Ten-Mile Ranch, not far from St. George's Residential School. We used to go up for visits with our children. When George passed away, she moved onto the reserve right at Lytton.[8]

My father was a tall man with dark curly hair. My brother had the same hair. I asked my mother why, and she said because they were Hawaiian. Those early Kanakas who came here lived in tents and worked on highway construction in the Fraser Canyon. That was during the gold rush when the road was being built into the Cariboo.

[7] Rena is referring here to a photograph of the Silva family (see figure 10) that hung on the wall above the dining room table around which we were sitting during this conversation.

[8] After her mention of Annie Jamieson, Rena added an aside:

> We were in Ottawa one time and I met Andrea Laforet from the Museum of Civilization and we talked about Annie Jamieson and we talked about Andrea's Spuzzum book [Laforet and York 1998]. She invited us for a very good salmon soup that night in her house. I had been longing to have a good fish soup the whole time we were in Ottawa, and there it was! I asked her about the Hawaiians and what she knew about them in the Canyon but she didn't know the details.

> The curator of First Nations collections at the then Museum of Civilization, Andrea Laforet is a leading scholar of Aboriginal cultures and activities in the Fraser Canyon area. She knew the Phillips family, who contributed to our social and historical knowledge of the colonial period and of traditional ways of life in the Fraser and Thompson canyons. George Phillips and his brother, Louie, were successful Nlaka'pamux ranchers on the semi-arid benchland north of Lytton. I knew Louie toward the end of his life and found him to be a most thoughtful and perceptive elder and an invaluable source of information about local Nlaka'pamux history. His knowledge has enriched several books on the region: see, for example, M'Gonicle and Wickwire (1988); York, Daly, and Arnett (1993); and Wickwire (1994).

So my father's parents lived at Boothroyd when he was young, and he worked on the railway in the Canyon. Uncle John Bolan did, too. We were living at Boothroyd, too, until the accident. My brother was agile and quick as a child. One day, he was running along the top of the pig fence and my grandmother [Annie Jamieson] yelled at him to be careful. He turned to look at her and lost his balance. He fell off and landed on his back. That did it; he was paralyzed for life. After that, we moved back to Kilgard. Dad built his cabin right across the creek from Kilgard Reserve, and he got a job at the Clayburn Brickworks, making bricks. He worked the night shift.

After the accident, my brother was so badly paralyzed that he couldn't close his eyes or open his mouth without my mother's help. She spooned food into him, closed his eyes at night and opened them in the morning. They say that one day, when I was about two, I got hold of a box of matches and began to light them and burn my fingers. I got paralyzed by fright and by the pain. I couldn't drop the match. My brother saw me, but he couldn't shout for me to drop it, but he managed to scream anyway, "Sister, throw the match down!" And that's how he began to speak again.

He was paralyzed down the left side but learned to walk stiffly with braces on his legs. He got therapy at the hospital for crippled children. About a year later, like I said, when I was three, my parents separated. My mother found work in Vancouver and my father tried to look after us. Well, it got to be too much for Dad, trying to work and be both parents to us. He decided to take us to his mother, Annie, in Lytton. We called her "Yeyó," which in the Thompson [Nlaka'pamux] language means "grannie." Her first husband, John Bolan [John Puliya], had passed on several years before this. She now lived with her second husband, George Phillips, on that ranch ten miles out of Lytton along the highway to Lillooet.

We were packing up all our belongings, getting ready to move there, when my grandfather Pete Silva appeared. He surveyed the situation

9   This John Bolan was the brother of Rena's father, Francis. They were sons of Annie Jamieson and John Puliya, who was also known as John Bolan.

very quickly and said to my dad, "You can't take Peter and Rena away from the village." The reason was, as Annie Silva's children, we were the children of the "Carrier of the *Chelángans.*" We belonged to the people of Semá:th, and we had to be raised by them. This was an old law of the tribe. We had to stay home and learn from the old people. So Peter and I, we very seldom saw our father after that, because he went back to Lytton, but later on, after I was married, he used to come down and visit my kids sometimes.

Hiding from Destiny

Grandfather Pete and my grandmother could see that my mother was unhappy about taking on the responsibility for *chu'chelángen.* After that time when she worked in Vancouver and she came and took me back with her, my mother went up north to Port Essington, where she worked in the canneries.

And there's another little story. When my mother was still working in Port Essington, she decided to come home for a visit. She made it down the Skeena from the cannery to Prince Rupert all right. She booked passage on this boat, this steamship going to Vancouver. Now I don't remember if that was the *Cardena.* There was a boat named *Cardena.* But then she got together with some of her friends and went to a party and just forgot about the ship, until the next morning. She woke up and then she realized she was supposed to be on that ship, but by the time she got there, it had already steamed away. So she missed the boat. It wasn't until the next week that she was able to book passage again. She had to wait.

When the boat she had missed got partway down the coast toward Vancouver, it sank. Word went out to my grandparents that my mother had gone down with the ship. Her name was on the list of passengers. So they had this big . . . like a memorial. Everybody was crying and they had the wailers out—I remember these elderly women were really howling. What do they call them? They specialize in weeping and wailing. They used to come to the burials. Anyway, after it was all over, the family members were very quiet and my grandparents were sorrowing. They were in mourning. Then the next week, the old Stage [Pacific Stage Lines bus] stopped on the Trans-Canada Highway—it wasn't the Trans-Canada then. It wasn't even a paved road yet. It was just a gravel road—it looked more like a dyke than anything. The Stage stopped and this little woman got off. She had a suitcase. I hadn't seen my mother for three or four years.

My Uncle Ambrose says, "The Stage has stopped. I wonder who's getting off." So we all went out the door. Uncle Ambrose went down the path a way. Then he said, "Oh my goodness, that's my sister Anne!" He went tearing down the trail and down the road. He was so excited. He said, "We heard that you had drowned on the *Cardena*!"

"No," she said, "I came on a different boat."

Well . . . ha ha ha . . . they had a big celebration after that and chased away all the mourning and wailing that had been going on for days. I think my grandfather was ready to give her a good spanking, but he was also just plain glad to see her alive.

My mother left again after a while; she moved over to Deroche. Oh, dear. She did not want to be a carrier! That's why she kept leaving. She did not want to be responsible for . . . she was like my brother. He didn't want to either. He thought that that training was all silly, because, you know, this is the modern day, modern times. Why are we clinging to the old ways? So my mother never wanted any part of it. They each wanted to be a free soul. Like my youngest daughter, the one who left home. She didn't really care for the culture at all. But I think if you keep the good things about your old ways and culture, and if you remember who you are, then you don't get lost in today's society.

And I have another story, too, about the lengths some people go to to hide from their culture and the destiny they have from birth. Have you ever heard of the House of . . . um, it's a Haida House, one of the big Haida Houses, along the coast of the Charlottes. Not the House of Wiah, but it's the House of something else. It's hardly any use telling you if I can't remember the name. Because this fellah, he used to come down, he'd come to Kilgard. He was a little man. He wasn't very big. He was well-spoken. He was educated. He was a cook on one of these ships. His name was Edgar Wilcox. He'd get off the boat and go inland, away from Vancouver and the sea, just to get away. He'd want to rest and go on a holiday. So he'd come out to us at Kilgard.

He was really a good friend of my Aunt Antonia and her husband. He'd come and he'd ask if he could stay for a while. And he'd cook. He'd tell her, "I'll give you a rest. I'll do all your cooking." And he was an excellent cook! Oh my goodness, so many wonderful foods! I would stay there with my aunt and help her out with the children.

Edgar Wilcox would come along and he'd cook, and do a lot of other things. He'd help her repaint or redecorate or whatever. He had a lot of good ideas and he was handy outside. Antonia's husband worked at the factory, making bricks and clay pipes and things. He didn't have too much time to spend around the house, but Edgar was very good. He was a handyman as well as a cook. He'd stay there for about a month. Then he'd say, "Well, I have to go. I have to get back on the ship." He would leave and we wouldn't see him again, maybe not for another year or two years. He came several times. He was a perfect gentleman. He waited on my auntie, hand and foot.

Then, about ten or twelve years ago, I went to the Charlottes [Haida Gwaii] with Cliff. Cliff had a good friend named Tom Green. We went down to Skidegate and I met Tom's mother. She had gone to school at Coqualeetza and she knew the Sepasses. She loved the Sepass family. We would sit and chitchat about the good old days in Sardis. Her name was Essie, Essie Green. One day, I told her about this cook who used to come and cook for my auntie. He was from Skidegate, he used to tell us. He was also a cook on a ship. I told her his name was Edgar Wilcox and did she know him at all? She said, "Edgar Wilcox! He was a cook on a ship and he was my nephew. So that's where he used to disappear to!"

"Do you know," she said, "he was the chief of the House"—what was it called, Cliff? Yes, the House of Ninstints—there was a book written about this deserted House and village.[10] Anyway, she said, "When we were going to make him the head chief of this House, he ran away.

10. The book was George F. MacDonald's *Ninstints: Haida World Heritage Site* (1983). The population moved away from the village in the late nineteenth century.

He got on a ship and he never came back. He said he was going to be *no* chief and he got on that ship and never came back."

She explained that his title was one of the greatest chiefly names in the Haida Nation, and his House was one of the greatest. And here he was cooking for my aunt, you know! Ha ha ha. She didn't ever know who he was. She said, "His name is Chief Ninstints." That's what his name is. But he ran away. He would not face his duties."

Edgar Wilcox, my auntie's cook! Oh my, the things that happen. He used to have so many stories and we never knew if he was telling the truth. If you put this in the book and people from the Haida Nation see it, they are going to say, "Are they talking about our chief? How dare they mention that he was a cook!" We really *didn't* know he was a Haida chief. I told his auntie, Essie, and she was upset: "Oh, that scallywag. If only I could get a hold of him!"

After coming back to Kilgard, my mother moved on to Deroche, where she settled down and lived for twenty-five years. Old Joseph Phillips of Deroche was a second cousin of my grandmother Sarah,[12] X̱éyteleq, our ancestor [see chapter 3], he had his warriors on both sides of the Fraser for defence against raiders, and the Phillips family were descended from those who were across the river at Nicomen and in the Deroche area. The families used to visit back and forth across the river when we were at Devil's Run. I imagine that my mother attended some event over there on the north side and met Alfred Phillips. They were third cousins and my grandmother thought it scandalous when they wanted to marry. She said that third cousins were far too close for a marriage. But my mother and Alfred Phillips had four children together: Merle, Joyce, Selma, and Alfred Jr.

[11] In the early 1800s, the Eagle chief Ninstints took over leadership of the village after a decline in the fortunes of Koyah, the war chief of the Raven Clan who had traded with, and warred against, European and American ships that traded at and raided Haida Gwaii in the late 1700s (Duff 2003).

[12] Joseph Phillips's family is Xwélmexw, whereas the previously mentioned Phillipses were Nlaka'pamux people, living upriver near the town of Lytton. Joseph's family lives in the Fraser Valley, and it also has a Louie Phillips.

All those children are still living today. Alfred and my mother ran a farm—fruit and dairy products. They sold fruit to the canneries. Through the Depression years and during the Second World War, they traded their butter and cheese for staples. I helped her over there sometimes, making butter, lots and lots of butter, thanks to the Jersey cow. There was a butter form carved from wood, with a print that marked the butter.

We used icy cold spring water to keep the dairy products cold, as well as to keep the fish and the meat cold and fresh. We brought that produce to the stores to trade. Alfred used to put a net in the Fraser, so the family ate well—sockeye, springs, coho, pinks, dog salmon, the garden, the dairy, the fruit. There were beans and peas and corn. They got dried corn that they brought down from the Thompson River, too. It would be soaked overnight and then boiled together with beans. My mother grew those green squashes—Mother Hubbards—and two other kinds. She ate lots of greens and had a pretty good life in bad times. They had hundreds of plum trees and hired pickers at harvest time. The plums were sold to the cannery at Mission. They sold milk, too. They worked really hard all the time.

The Cooks were part of that family. Alfred's sister married one and she was the mother of Pat Campo. Alec Joe's mother was a sister to Joseph and Louie Phillips from Deroche, and Alec was the father of the Joe family. And there's Wheeler, too. He was the son of Agnes Phillips. When Alec's mother died, Alec was raised by the Phillips family. They raised him as their own. He married into Tzeachten, and his wife was in Chief Johnny Hall's family.[13] Alec Joe was actually a Phillips, and Nancy Phillips was aware of this. She used to say, "I know Papa came from Deroche." Alec Joe had many daughters, and his grandchildren are everywhere.

---

[13] Marrying into Tzeachten refers to taking up marital residence in the Tzeachten village. In addition to Tzeachten and Skowkale, there are several other First Nations villages around Chilliwack, especially on the southern, or Sardis, side of the town, including Yakweakwioose, the village next door to Skowkale.

Semá:th Lake

I never got to see Semá:th Lake, but I heard about how it looked.[14] And I never got to see the Big House of the Wolves. It burned down before I was born, and we were hard up at that time. My mum talked about Semá:th Lake a lot, and my grandparents, Sarah and Pete Silva. They always talked about the lake because this was where they got their food before times got tough. I always could see it in my mind. It must have been beautiful.

The whole lake was quite shallow. Somebody said it wasn't more than five or six feet deep, but there was a lot of salmon—all kinds of salmon, and sturgeon; trout, too. I think there were eels, different kinds of fish. And there were ducks, all kinds of ducks. And they even gathered duck eggs. And my grandmother said they used to set up little nets—long nets, not very high—among the reeds, the rushes. And when the ducks came in to land, they'd get entangled in these little nets. They'd take them down. They'd use them for food, and for the feathers. They kept the feathers. There was beaver, mink, and marten and—what do you call it? Muskrat. They used them. I heard that they ate the muskrat. I don't remember whether I tasted it or not. I try to think about it, but I can't remember eating muskrat, but I know they did eat them before my time.

They sold the muskrat furs they got. Yes, because I remember seeing my uncle stretching them over boards and hanging them out to dry. But by then, the lake had been drained. He was setting his traps elsewhere. And the reeds, like the cattails and the bulrushes, they were woven into mats. I remember sleeping on those mats. They were called *slewil*. My grandmother wove them. She piled them, stacked them on top of one another, and she would spread a blanket over them and we used this for, like, a mattress when we stayed out at the old smokehouse at Devil's Run.

14 Sumas Lake, or what today is Sumas Prairie, was fed by streams from Washington State. It covered ten thousand acres, which grew to thirty thousand at high water due to snow melt each spring. It was drained in 1924 as part of the Fraser Valley flood control program, and this resulted in much hardship for those who had relied upon it for their living as far back as any of the Xwélmexw could remember (Sleigh 1999).

So I remember her weaving those, but I didn't see . . . the actual lake. I only saw it in my imagination.

The lake had lots of sturgeon and all kinds of salmon. It was Kilgard's larder. It had the finest, straightest cedar trees for splitting planks used in houses. My stepfather, Alfred, used to love sturgeon. My mum did too. We used to make soup out of it. Then if there was any left over, she would fry it. But we ate every part of it. The stuff inside the vertebrae was pulled out. It was like a long snake, a white snake. They cut one end off and they measured it in inches, and each child, depending on how many in the house, each of us would get so many inches from inside the vertebrae. It was squeezed out and was jelly-like when it came out, and we had to open our mouths and swallow it. It was a little bit salty, but it wasn't too bad. Any elders who were really old, they got a share. It must have been some kind of a brain food. I don't know. We asked one of the doctors. He was the pediatrician when we were children, and he said that it was a very precious source of vitamins, because that cord would have gone straight to the sturgeon's brain. He said, "Your people were very clever to do that, to feed this to the children, to give them living vitamins right out of the sturgeon."

Of course, we didn't know. We did what our elders told us. "Open your mouths." And in it went. They would cook sturgeon, too. They would cook the head and make soup out of it. It would have to be boiled for an hour or more—two hours—until it was soft, and we had to eat that, too. We ate the roe thing first. That was cooked and we had to eat that, too. But the fish flesh itself, now that made a beautiful soup! It was like halibut. We put vegetables in with it. We usually had that for breakfast when I was a little girl and my grandmother was cooking.

FIGURE 4

Sumas Lake, looking north. The lake was drained in 1924, and its destruction meant the loss of a crucial food source for local peoples. Photo courtesy of Esther Epps Hardy, second-generation member of a settler family in the area, who reported that "high water, 1910" was pencilled on the back of the original.

I remember my grandmother saying, some babies were being born with blue eyes, and she said, "Oh, that lady must have looked at a sturgeon." They didn't realize there were other sources of blue eyes! I guess that blue-eye thing was just starting to happen. Now when I think about that, I laugh. Why on earth would their eyes get blue or green from looking at a sturgeon? Today, children won't eat it. Neither will a lot of grownups. That is because it was never a part of their diet when they were young. Our people were discouraged from fishing sturgeon because others were overfishing, for the caviar, the roe.

I know the lake was my great-great-grandfather X̱éyteleq's larder. His people lived there at Kilgard, which was called Kw'ekw'íqw. That was what they called that place where Great-great-grandfather X̱éyteleq lived. And the rest of his people—of his tribe—lived on the south side of the lake where the border went through. After they destroyed the lake, those people moved down to Deming and Nooksack territory [Washington State, east of Bellingham]. Most of them lived in Deming, because I had a lot of relatives there. And some of the family moved to Matsqui. But a few stayed at Kw'ekw'íqw, and it was very hard for them because they would have to go over the mountain, over Straiton, the white settlement near Abbotsford, to get to the fishing on the other side, on the Fraser, once Sumas Lake was gone.

Once when I had done a four-day fast, I remember that in my dream, I was sitting on Kilgard Hill and in front of me there was this huge lake, and all along the shoreline there were wolves walking back and forth. They watched me—and they were afraid of me! I descended from the Wolf People and was told by our elders never to forget that we, in our family, came from the wolves. They were grey wolves and Semá:th was their place. These Wolf People owned the place. No other wolves were allowed to be there. We cherish the fact that we are one with the grey wolves, the owners of that land.

When I was dreaming, I looked at that lake and I thought to myself, this land belonged to my ancestors. Everything was here. Our food was here. All the animals, the deer and fishes and birds, came to feed at that lake. Other people were jealous of our good fortune and our prosperity. Those who were not so prosperous raided us. Others grew jealous. This jealousy led to the death of my great-great-grandfather. Then the whites came in. They wanted our land, too. They drained the lake so they could turn it into farmland. Our people had to scatter to other places in order to survive. My grandmother and her mother, Mrs. Vedder, they stayed on at Kilgard after the lake was gone. Getting food was difficult once there was no more lake.

My grandparents and their children lost the lake and they lost their livelihood. Times were tough, but you know, they held their heads high. You might say they suffered in silence. Our old people did not agree when Canada started setting up its band council system. The new ways ignored our laws and our right to choose and train our own leaders from our own families. So they quietly left the village and went to live by the river.

My grandmother Sarah disagreed with the modern reserve ways, and so did Grandfather Pete. Sarah's mother, Th'etsimiya, daughter of Xéyteleq, had been living in a big house and had slaves when the missionaries came in and told her to get rid of her slaves. Then the police came and ordered her to get rid of the slaves because slave-holding was now illegal. Th'etsimiya said, "All right then. I can see times are changing. They can go if they want to. You tell them that."

FIGURE 5

Surveyor's map of Sumas Lake, ca. 1920, prior to land reclamation and flood control work. Photo courtesy of the Vancouver City Museum.

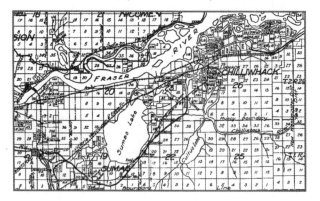

The slaves in her household were very upset. They cried. What would they do? They had spent their lives working for her, picking berries, doing salmon, and she looked after them. "Where are we going to go? Our own people won't take us back on account of the stigma attached to slaves."

The white people said, "No. You have to leave." And they did, and they ended up living in poverty, hand to mouth. So Mama, my grandmother, watched all of this. She could see that the new ways were taking over and the whites were laying down the law about what we could do and could not do. She told me over and over that we had to find ways to keep some of our ways. We must bend with the wind, but we must not give in to everything. We must remember who we have been, who we are, and keep our dignity. This we must do because one day in the future we will have to recall our past and remember who we really are. We have to keep our identity as high *sí:yá:m* people, descendants of the Steqó:ye, who ruled the valley long ago.

Down through the years, I have always remembered that. Although I don't talk about it much, I remember Grandmother Sarah's words. We must never forget who we are. We are the people who ruled in this valley. I have told my children, and this is something they know.

* ❀ *

Xéyteleq

My Xwélmexw name was handed down to me. It was the name held by the mother of X̱éyteleq, the great warrior and defender of the people. He stands at the centre of our family history. We learned all about our names when we lived at Devil's Run.

X̱éyteleq's mother was called Xwelíqwiya. She was the head woman of a prominent family at Semá:th. The family did not tell me anything about the history of her husband. My mother and grandmother did not discuss this with me. They only talked about X̱éyteleq's mother, not about his father.

Anyway, this account begins back in the 1600s, or maybe 1700s. It was a time when our people were being heavily attacked by coastal raiders.

We Stó:lō, or Xwélmexw, people have always felt that we were among the elite in regard to our neighbours. We saw the interior people as quite different and the coastal people as fierce and aggressive. Our own people have been peaceable. They have not initiated wars or raids, but they have certainly defended themselves when attacked.

This history that I am telling, it is about my great-great-great-grand-mother, Xwelíqwiya. *Xwe* means "hungry"; *líqwe,* it just means "flesh," like meat; and *-iya,* it just sort of symbolizes the female gender, just like anything with *-wot* or *-lot* at the end also indicates that it's female. So her name was Xwelíqwiya, the flesh-eating, hungry female. She was our head mother wolf, because we believe that our people were wolves at one time and the Great-Changer-of-All-Things, Laha Xa'als, said that because mother wolves were such good mothers, they would do a good job as human mothers too—so he changed them into people. They became our tribe, the Wolf People, Steqó:ye.

And so Xwelíqwiya was our head woman. They used to tell a strong story about her, and they told me too, when I was small. If a girl comes along and says to Xwelíqwiya, "Look, I'm having your son's or your grandson's child," that is when Xwelíqwiya would do a test to make sure the child belonged to her line. She would take the baby as soon as it was born and pack it up Sumas Mountain. There was a cave up there where the mother wolf took shelter. Xwelíqwiya would place the baby in the cave. If the mother wolf came in and licked the baby clean, that was a sign that it was one of her own kind, but if she ate the baby, of course it wasn't. So this is how we kept our bloodline pure. The name Xwelíqwiya was always given to the hereditary carrier of the Wolf People. Xwelíqwiya is my name. That's the name I carry today.

As for Xéyteleq's father—Xwelíqwiya's husband—I heard recently that there was a family named Th'etsemeltel, or something like that, or Th'itsemeltin. I think it was the male version of the name Th'etsimiya and I kind of have the feeling that this was Xéyteleq's father's name.

Th'etsimiya, my great-grandmother, was Xéyteleq's daughter. From Semá:th territory on the main river [the Stó:lō], all the way down to the Pacific Ocean, we were matrilineal people. The chief belonged to his sister's family. His heir was his sister's son. If he loved his wife's son, he could make something to leave that child, but his family property, songs and names, these belonged to his mother and his sisters. The Lummi, or Dawomish, have the same tradition as us. I'm not sure what the Musqueam and Capilano [Tsleil-Waututh] people do. I think they are the same.

The university people have come to the Xwélmexw—and today we are being called after the river, the Stó:lō—and they studied us. Then they went away and pronounced that our inheritance goes along in all directions and that women have always gone to live at their husband's place after they get married. It's the Christian model, if you like, of the father and the husband ruling wife and children.

This is not how I was raised. The only way I can explain it to myself is that there was an awful lot of smallpox and disease killing off the people. The ones who survived best seem to have been those who intermarried with the whites and whose children had good resistance to the germs— I learned all about germs when I was at Coqualeetza!

These people often were not from the high-born families, or at least not people who were in the traditional line to inherit responsibility for guarding the culture. They did not have the right or responsibility to be, as you say, stewards for the old culture. Anyway, some of them wanted to move with the times and abandon all the old ways, leave them behind. Their aim was to be modern. So when the anthropologists came around, the people who would talk to them were usually those who were most familiar with the white ways, and often, these people were the ones least sympathetic with the old ways of our people.

The old society had a pecking order. Those who were high-born, they sort of kept the culture and the procedures among themselves. They looked after it. When the elders found out that the new society had such contempt for our ways, when the churches called our respected ancestors

1 In 1989, I (Richard Daly) discussed this issue with the late Wayne Suttles, a prominent anthropologist who specialized in Coast Salish studies. He was intrigued. He said that he was not aware of much information about inheritance of rights and knowledge through women on the Central Coast but that he hoped this would lead to more research into Central Coast gender relations and the question of flexibility and variation in studies of systems of descent.

Also, as I mention in the introduction, I have supplied these footnotes to Rena's narrative. So, in the notes that follow, first-person pronouns always refer to me, Richard.

"naked savages" and "children of Satan," then the old people who were the guardians of the culture, they said to themselves, "Oh goodness, the only dignified thing to do is to say absolutely nothing." They went silent and were ready to take the knowledge to the grave with them. It became *sxaxá*—taboo—to talk about private matters. The old people were afraid. They stopped talking, mainly because there was nobody to listen to them any longer.

The free people, the ones without such responsibility for the culture, they didn't have such restrictions on them. They seem to have been able to mobilize ties to people through both sides of their family. In the Xwélmexw times, such people were usually treated as "younger brothers and sisters." The oldest were respected. And part of this was that the eldest daughters always seem to have faced more training and more rules regarding their behaviour. The oldest sister had control over her siblings. She was sort of the authority figure when her parents or grandparents were absent. She could make decisions and she had a lot of say. The younger ones obeyed her.

Chu'chelángen

If the family was high-born, things got passed on at the family's home base—well, you see, the young husbands moved in with their wives' families and learned their ways, at least for a while. I guess it was for lineage reasons. The young husband's mother or sister would make gifts to the bride's family. Both families would have separate meetings, and then joint meetings, to decide what names and rights would be offered to the newlyweds. What I learned in my upbringing was that in high-born families, women controlled names and titles and stories and rights to ceremonies. It's what we called *chelángen* or *chu'chelángen* [plural], the family's own political and spiritual knowledge. These things were always passed down through mothers. They could not be taken by the male line down through brothers and sons. There is one *chelángen* about governing the people and one about the power of the masks, the Sxwóyxwey, and that is a spiritual thing—the responsibility to look after the spiritual powers of the Sxwóyxwey. That's the teachings of the people, the cultural teachings of the people. The governing *chelángen*, well, it was a political thing. So, we carry both of those to this day.

I know most about how the high-born women were trained. Maybe the boys were also trained in the rights, the fishing places, the berry-picking places, the hunting territories. The high-born had responsibilities. They were stewards on behalf of their people and on behalf of their relatives in other species, the ones who lived out on the land. These duties were not imposed on the rest of the people to the same degree. Oh dear, what's the word I want? Yes, "privilege"! The DIA has privileged those who have been educated in the Canadian way. They have never recognized the hereditary leaders. The old hierarchies have been broken up like kindling wood. The large family units that ran the village affairs, they've been broken up.

So the real Xwélmexw were silenced. They became timid. And most of the knowledgeable ones had died in the epidemics. As I said, those with Chinese, Scottish, Japanese, or English blood mixed in their veins, they survived. And the new DIA way of organizing things narrowed our possibilities.

FIGURE 6

Dan Milo and his wife, Agnes Milo (née Edwin), in the 1920s, at Skowkale. Agnes Milo was the mother of Roy Point's mother, Mary Edwin Point. Photo courtesy of Rena Point Bolton.

Here's an example. Dan Milo and his father, Jacob Milo, were from Pópkw'em; they were Tii:t people from the Stó:lō River below Hope—Lhókw'ōlá:leqw's people—and they were more geared to inheriting through the men. The Milos had fishing sites around Pópkw'em, but they also had rights to do some fishing near the mouth of the Chilliwack River. When the Land Commission and DIA came through, they asked Jacob Milo if he wanted an official fishing site at Pópkw'em or at Sardis, and he said, "Right now there's more salmon here in the Chilliwack." So his family were designated residents of Sardis instead of their home Tii:t area. It was on the Milo farm at Sardis that I lived for years and raised my children, and this was because by then, a woman had to move to her husband's village on marriage. My husband, Roy Point, was Mrs. Milo's grandson. In the old hereditary system, my husband would have joined my family, at least for some time, at Semá:th, which was where we were located, but I was not allowed to live at Semá:th as the government said my father, as an Nlaka'pamux, wasn't Indian enough, due to blood he had in his veins from Scotland and Hawaii. We were forced to live off reserve: the Wolf House had to live away from the Wolf Village. So the

2 "The Land Commission and DIA" refers to the McKenna-McBride Royal Commission, 1913–16, which "had a significant impact on Indian peoples' reserve land base by adding to, reducing and eliminating reserves throughout the province" (Union of BC Indian Chiefs, "McKenna-McBride Royal Commission," http://www.ubcic.bc.ca/Resources/final_report.htm#axzz2YVJA9aV3). For more information, see "Background to the McKenna-McBride Commission" (part of the UBCIC's "Our Homes Are Bleeding" digital collection), http://www.ubcic. bc.ca/Resources/ourhomesare/narratives/Background_1.htm. Here one finds the following assessment: "The Report recommended that cut-offs be made from 54 reserves, totalling 47,055.49 acres. At the time, the land cut off had an assessed value of between $1,347,912.72 and $1,533,704.72, with the average acre valued at $26.52 to $32.36. The Report also recommended that 87,291.17 acres be added to reserve land. The added land had an assessed value of only $444,838.80, with the average acre valued at $5.10. Although the acreage of the added reserve land was nearly double that of the cut-off land, the value of the land added was approximately one-third the value of the land cut off. Only 45% of the land applications put forward by Indians were granted, in whole or in part."

arrangement was this. Dan Milo said to my grandfather Pete, "Bring her to Skowkale and she will marry my wife's grandson. The *chelángen* will be moved from Kilgard to Skowkale."

It seems to me that the downriver people were more matrilineal in inheritance than the upriver people, but I'm no expert. I can only relate to what I lived through myself.

In any case, Th'etsimiya, X̱éyteleq's youngest daughter, was my grandmother's mother. After the smallpox swept through, she was the only surviving daughter of X̱éyteleq.[3] She was also known as Mrs. Vedder, and her daughter—Sarah Vedder [Silva], my grandmother—was *her* only daughter. X̱éyteleq's last surviving daughter, Th'etsimiya, was a spirit dancer. She had been initiated into the winter dancing society, the *mí'lha*. She was born into the royal Wolf Clan of Semá:th, the Steqó:ye Xwélmexw. Her family was powerful. They kept slaves. Then, once Sarah grew up and started her own family with Pete Silva, it was Sarah's eldest surviving daughter, Annie Silva, who eventually became my mother.

FIGURE 7

Th'etsimiya, Rena's great-grandmother. The youngest daughter of X̱éyteleq, Th'etsimiya reputedly lived to the age of about 120; she died in 1920, some years before Rena's birth. Photo courtesy of Rena Point Bolton.

3 Robert Boyd (1994, 5–6) dates the first smallpox epidemic to the 1770s; see also Magosci (1999, 89), who maintains that the first "lower Salish epidemic" occurred in 1782.

X̱éyteleq's Story

The original Xwelíqwiya [X̱ételeq's mother] seemed to be barren. She just didn't have children, and the elders were afraid the bloodline was going to peter out. She was starting to get older. I don't know what "older" meant in those days, whether it was thirty or forty or fifty or what. She was getting older and she hadn't had any children yet. Her brother was the family medicine man, Xwelíqweltel—the same name as hers, but the male version. It's the name that my son Steven has now.

Back just before the Europeans came, probably in the late 1700s, the Xwélmexw people were prosperous. That's why they were a prime target for raiding parties from other places. They worked hard and the land was rich. Whatever we needed, and did not have on our land, we traded for. With the [Fraser] Canyon peoples, we bartered our smoked salmon and local foods in exchange for their dried saskatoon berries, their soapberries, and their wind-dried salmon. With people from the west, we bartered smoked clams and other seafood. In addition to our foods, our neighbours loved our cedar-root baskets, as well as our fine Salish rugs and blankets. Because the Xwélmexw had a good life at home, they did not need to spend a lot of time waging war or raiding other nations to get hold of these nations' lands, or their treasures—but anyway, our ancestors did fall prey to many war parties. These foreigners raided and burned the Stó:lō villages. They shed blood and took slaves.

Our Musqueam cousins at the mouth of the river, on Point Grey in Vancouver, were our warriors. They were trained to guard the entrance to the river. They killed invaders and took scalps, which were fashioned into war hats. Copies of these are still worn in today's winter dance ceremonies. In the late 1700s, there were a lot of raids and our family was low in numbers. As I said, the head woman of our Steqó:ye Wolf family was named Xwelíqwiya. She was growing old with no descendants. She sat in her house at Kw'ekw'íqw (Semá:th), bitterly regretting her plight while her brother Xwelíqweltel talked to her. He says to his sister, "We need numbers to defend ourselves. I think we're losing our leaders. Our bloodline is going to come to an end if you don't have children."

Xwelíqweltel was a healer and man of medicine, a *shxwlá:m*. His aging sister was barren and the family had few members. The elders called on Xwelíqweltel to perform a *yeqwá:ls*. As part of the *yeqwá:ls*, food offerings were burned in the fire to feed the spirits and ask them for guidance and protection. The drums beat softly. Xwelíqweltel travelled out of this world, out from his body with his sacred rattles carrying him away. He fell into a trance.

After a long time, he awoke and told his dream prophecy, his *s'elíyá*. He had learned that his sister was to give birth to a son. This son would be the saviour of the Semá:th people. In this dream, he was told by the power of the old people who guided his thinking that he himself would have the task of bringing this about and training this child. As I said, his sister was an older woman at the time of the dream, and her husband was quite old as well. And so Xwelíqweltel, as a doctor and healer, would have to work on them and rejuvenate their bodies.

Xwelíqweltel talked seriously to Xwelíqwiya and her husband about this dream. They agreed to go along with him and his medicine. Xwelíqwiya and her husband were instructed to fast for four days to get rid of impurities and poisons in their bodies. Then they entered the sweat-house and prayed to the Creator for strength and fertility. They were then plunged into the cold snow waters of a creek and kept away from each other for another four days. And so they went to the mountains and they meditated. The uncle, or his mother's brother, who was the *shxwlá:m*, the shaman—he was the one who took them to the mountains to meditate, and to swim in the cold waters, and to fast. And then they would dream. This is how they got their messages about what they were supposed to do.

Xwelíqweltel went up into the mountains and he got some herbal medicines. He spent time up there praying and putting power into those medicines. And he took Xwelíqwiya's husband with him and worked on him and gave him medicine. He also took medicine home to his sister and she used it for many months. I don't know how long. After several months had passed, he allowed the two of them to get together again. It wasn't long before she became pregnant.

During the time she was carrying the child, her brother Xwelíqweltel told her how to take care of herself, how to behave. He explained how the child would be a boy and he himself would have to train the boy how to be a leader. And so it happened; when she had her son, her brother took charge of him because he was the male Wolf leader of our tribe.

When she was expecting, she was told not to lie around and be lazy, but she was not allowed to do any really hard work. And she wasn't to eat anything that was too heavy either. She was to eat lightly, but eat fresh foods and lots of soups. She was not allowed to eat anything very greasy or too rich. And she wasn't allowed to do any climbing. This is what I was told.

And so the child was born and Xwelíqweltel did take charge of training the boy. He trained him right from early childhood. The boy was told the stories of who he was and how he had to learn to take care of his people. He was trained to run, to be what they call a long-distance runner. He was not allowed to sleep on a soft bed of rushes. He had to sleep on a bed of boughs from the red cedar. When he was running long distances, he was not allowed to eat, only to drink water through a bone "straw" he carried, the hollow leg bone of a crane. He learned to jump from high rocks, to jump over creeks—well, he learned to use a pole for pole-vaulting over from one side to another.[4]

When our youths learned to jump and vault over fences and streams, this gave them a feeling that they could overcome challenges, that they were slaves to nothing and to nobody. They felt that they could almost fly. They were not slaves to pain, to emotions, or to other people. When you overcome pain, you learn to be strong in the mind. Otherwise, one tends to fall under the spell and the will of others. We trained our young to be strong-minded. A baby is prey to your thinking. It cannot combat your ideas. In teaching the kids the strength they need to resist the willpower of other people, it is important to stress that they must always deal with what is at hand. Use your mind to solve problems, not to wallow in them.

---

[4] Vaulting over rock crevasses, creeks, and narrow swamps with a long pole was a common feature of travel, especially in the Fraser Canyon area, as explorer Simon Fraser witnessed as he descended the river given his name (Lamb 1960, 96). This use of pole-vaulting was also explained by Nlaka'pamux historian Annie York (Laforet and York 1998, 74).

For example, girls are taught that when they are giving birth, they are not to lose themselves in the pain but to have a single purpose and a strong mind through the whole thing.

X̱éyteleq was very well trained. He was not allowed to eat fat or to lounge around. When at home, he was taught always to squat, not sit or lie down—he always had to be vigilant and ready to spring into action. At puberty, he started his sweathouse sessions, plunging into the cold creeks afterward, sweating and facing the sunrise, scrubbing his body with cedar boughs. Then he would run for miles before returning to Semá:th for his breakfast. After breakfast, he learned to hunt and fish and trap and become one with a canoe—to wear it like clothes—on the lakes and rivers.

Later, as he became a young man, he was taught everything a warrior must learn so that he could protect his people at Semá:th. And so they made him armour. A stone slab was fitted onto his chest and onto his back. Holes were drilled in these slabs and they were tied together with rawhide; the sides were drilled too, and laced up with rawhide. The rocks were dug out or were formed the best way they could to fit his shape. And he had a club made. My mother said the club weighed fifty pounds. That was put onto a strong handle and he was trained to swing it. He grew to be a very tall man. He grew to be over seven feet tall.

He was recognized up and down the coast by the neighbouring tribes. He had seven wives. These women were offered to him by other tribes. They stayed in their own villages and were kept there by their own people, but when X̱éyteleq visited them, they would have a wife waiting for him. He had children with these women, but his one wife—he lived with her at Kw'ekw'íqw, at Sumas Lake. I don't know what her name was. If someone mentioned it, I don't remember.

But X̱éyteleq guarded the river. War canoes that got past Musqueam would make their way up the Fraser, come into Kw'ekw'íqw Creek and into Sumas Lake. That little creek ran by the village. He would hide himself and wait for them. He always got to know when these ocean-going canoes were coming. You see, whoever was the first to see them on the river, that person would pull the plug out of the hollowed log full of water that families kept on the roof of the big house. As the water ran out of the log in a certain way it would start whistling, and this would set the dogs barking furiously—just screaming. Even if the people didn't hear the whistling of the water, the dogs did, and the people sure heard the dogs.

So he would get ready. He knew they were coming. There was this rock at Kilgard Village—they blasted it out recently—and he would sit behind there, near Kw'ekw'íqw Creek, and wait for the canoes to come up. The creek was narrow there and only one war canoe could go through at a time. He would capsize the canoes, swing his club, and kill them all: one canoe at a time. But he usually didn't destroy the last canoe. He would leave one man alive, put him back in the canoe and send him away, saying, "Tell your people not to send any more canoes because they will end up the way these others ended up!"

When he had defended the village, he would bash the canoes into small pieces and burn them. They found lots of human bones near that place—at Albert Kelly's. Some were smashed and some skulls were separated from their bodies. This is how he became known up and down the coast. They would tell you, "Oh, yes, we know the story of this X̱éyteleq because he had a wife from our tribe."

There are many stories about him, and of course, some people didn't like him. The villages on the coast where he had wives became his allies against the invaders. This is the way he built up a defence and there was peace.

After X̱éyteleq was born, Xwelíqwiya conceived again and had a daughter, but the daughter, she was later taken captive during her puberty time in the woods. When a girl is approaching her puberty ceremonies, she has to keep her hands busy. She might be told to make baskets or weave swéqeth, the Salish robes worn by high-born people. While she was out there in the woods, weaving, she would think over what she had learned. She would have been well trained, as one day it would be her task to pass on the women's knowledge and skills to her own daughters, especially since she was from the Wolf People. She had to behave well and never engage in idle chatter. She must speak little and speak softly, and never look into the eyes of the person she is talking to. She had to cover her mouth when she laughed because showing one's teeth was unladylike.

On this occasion, they say she was out picking berries when the raiding party came. The water whistle alarm went off while she was way down the creek. X̱éyteleq, they say, destroyed the war party and sent the last man back downstream in the last canoe, as a warning to his people. This last man came across X̱éyteleq's sister as she was picking berries. She was tattooed with the wolf crest and she wore fine earrings. He could tell she was high-born, and he kidnapped her. The old law said you could not rape or kill a high-born woman because this could cause a huge war when her people found out. Also, if the captor had been violent, his own relatives would not help him when the lady's family came to take revenge. The captor's own family would find it necessary to hold a potlatch to wash away the shame that had fallen on them all. If this was not done, they would lose respect and be in the debt of the girl's family forever. This was the code of all the peoples up and down the coast.

On his way home, this man stopped at Squamish and exchanged X̱éyteleq's sister for food and water. The Squamish sold her to the St'latl'imx Mount Currie people, where she became the wife of a chief's son. She had a daughter whom she tattooed with the wolf like her own. She told her daughter she came from Semá:th. She said, "If you can ever get away, go to Semá:th and look for my brother, X̱éyteleq."

The daughter was sold to Port Douglas at the head of Harrison Lake, where she was taken as the chief's slave wife. She in turn marked her daughter with the wolf. This girl married a white man from Clinton on the Cariboo Highway. His name was Kelly, and with her, he had four sons, Harry, James, Peter, and one other. When she was in her fifties, her husband took her and the boys to Kilgard. This was when Sarah Vedder, my grandmother, was still in charge of our people. She had married Pete Silva by this time.

This is the way my grandfather Pete told the story that this lady told in the words of her grandmother:

"When I was a young girl, I lived in a beautiful valley at a place called Semá:th. My mother's name was Xwelíqwiya and my brother was a very tall man called X̱éyteleq. He was a warrior and many people feared him. One day when I was picking berries a great distance from my village—where the berries grew thick by the little river, I was suddenly dragged into a strange canoe. I fought to get away from this stranger but he was too strong. He hit me on the head and I knew nothing until we were on our way down to the big river. I wept and begged him to release me but he continued to paddle down the river.

"I slept off and on in the bottom of that huge canoe. I don't know how long we travelled. When I woke up, we were out in the saltwater, far away from home. We came to a village called Squamish. My captor traded me for food and water. My new owners laughed at me but did not mistreat me. On their next trip inland, they sold me to a chief at Mount Currie. He became my husband and fathered my children. Following my Semá:th tradition, I trained my eldest daughter to carry my family lineage and duties. I tattooed her wrist the same as mine and told her of her people in the south. I told her never to forget who she is and to train her eldest daughter likewise."

Grandfather Pete continued the story as the lady visitor had told it: "Her daughter married a man from Port Douglas. She trained her eldest daughter—and it was me—and tattooed my wrist. The white settlers had arrived, including an Irish man called Kelly, who fell in love with me, the girl with this strange tattoo. He promised to take me to my grandmother's home some day. He knew the place, and now, here we are."

Grandfather Pete asked to see her wrist. She showed her tattoo. It was the same as the one on my grandmother Sarah's wrist. Kelly and his wife settled down at Kilgard. This lady's son Harry Kelly and his wife, Marianne, lived just outside Kilgard. Their children were Fraser, Fred, Francis, Henry, Arthur, Marie, and Stella. Marie married Frank Clark. She and Frank had a large family: Henry, Dorothy, Irene, Mabel, Nellie, Eva, Doreen, Judy, Eleanor, Fraser (Spud), and maybe there were more. Eva, daughter of Marie and Frank Clark, married Robert Sepass, of Skowkale. He was the son of Chief Billy Sepass (Chief William K'HHalserten Sepass)[5]

5   Chief William K'HHalserten published a book of poems in 1963, which was republished in 2009; see K'HHalserten ([1963] 2009). From the Longhouse Publishing press release, 2009: "As described by His Honour, Grand Chief Steven Point, Lieutenant Governor of BC, in his foreword to the book, '... like the Homeric legends of Western thought, the Sepass Poems are a profound legacy to future Xwélmexw generations as they continue to seek meaning and stability in an ever-changing modern world.'"

Francis married Josie Cooper from Cultus Lake. Josie's father was the chief of the Soowahlie Band, and he adopted Francis, who became a full member of the band. He has many descendants still at Cultus Lake.

James married Charlotte Uslick from Sardis. She was the daughter of Elizabeth and Jack Uslick. They were given some acreage on the Sumas Reserve at Kilgard and were adopted into that band. Their children were Edward, Albert, James, Hugh, Martha, Louise, May, Myrtle, and Norma. They also have numerous descendants in various places across BC and Washington.

So this is why the family could not pass its names and property through X̱éyteleq's sister as was the rule—because she had lost status by being taken into slavery. There was also a lot of disease and death at that time. So the old people made an exception and passed things down from X̱éyteleq to his daughter Th'etsimiya.

I used to be very bitter about the way X̱éyteleq's life came to an end, but nowadays, I believe it is best not to talk much about it at all. I remember Bert Louie talking about the death of X̱éyteleq. Bert was married to Amelia Hilaire, my aunt, a lady from Lummi. She was the daughter of Frank Hilaire. Bert maintained that his grandfather's sister's husband had been an eyewitness to what happened. I don't know why he told us this—maybe because he was married to my aunt, Frank Hilaire's daughter. Frank and his cousin-brother Charlie Point were close to us because they were raised together with Sarah and George Vedder by X̱éyteleq's daughter herself—old Mrs. Vedder.

The location of X̱éyteleq's remains is not something we talk about. He was a huge man and Grandmother was worried that museum people would get their hands on his bones and seize him, so they never put up a headstone for him. Much later, gravediggers found some remains . . . well, at least his arm bones. They recognized them from the size. He

6 Rena decided not to include the details of X̱éyteleq's death in her account of his life, except to say that his remains were hidden for a long time on Sumas Mountain before being buried, together with his remaining war regalia, without a headstone at an undisclosed location. One of Rena's mother's last requests was that the remains of X̱éyteleq be left unmarked and undisturbed.

was really tall and that bone from his arm—what is it called? Yes, the humerus—it reached from a normal man's wrist almost to his shoulder. So there are members of our family who have actually seen X̱éyteleq's bones, his tangible remains. It was Herman and Uncle Ambrose who saw those warrior artifacts.

X̱éyteleq, he was the most important warrior chief of his day, and he was a defender of the people from attack downriver and upriver. X̱éyteleq set up posts at places among the Tii:t and the Chilliwacks [Ts'elxwéyeqw], as well as at Semá:th. His relatives, what you might call subchiefs or wing chiefs, were in charge at these places, and when there were troublemakers, they sent them to him. He sent his young men on to Musqueam for real warrior training. I don't know if he was trained there or not. But anyway, my first husband's uncle, James Point, confirmed the story that troublemakers were sent downriver to Musqueam for warrior training.

Apart from X̱éyteleq, we were peaceful people. In our culture, the major colour of paint of the upriver [spirit] dancers is red, and for the downriver ones, black. Black stands for the guardians and warriors, and red for the holy ones. Our singers mostly use red paint, and thanks to pretty good defence, it was a peaceful place. Upriver Stó:lō country was so rich, and especially Sumas, that war canoes came from other places to attack us. This continued right up to the time they built Fort Langley.[7]

We might have been too prosperous for our own good. Raiders came from near and far, looking for riches. You know, we went on a delegation to New Zealand, and I met a Maori canoe maker down there. Bruce was his name. He said his people used to come to our coast all the time. With their big canoes, they knew our coast. He said, "Some of us stayed there, on your coast."

Those who stayed were possibly from an expedition that paddled from New Zealand to Easter Island, then to South America and up all along the shore to our coast. I told Bruce that the Haida have stories of tall warrior people who landed on the southern tip of Haida Gwaii, and

7 Fort Langley, a garrison and trading post on the lower Fraser River, was built in 1827 by the Hudson's Bay Company.

they were known as headhunters. He laughed and said, "They must have been the guys from the three canoes that never came back. We lost three canoes on that trip and their crews were never seen again."

You know, there are a lot of similarities between them and us. They carve totem poles too, and a lot of them have been coming here for visits in recent years.

Yes, X̱éyteleq was a famous long-distance runner. Our runners were messengers, and messengers were important to our people's defence against raids by other nations. Running is also good for physical training. All my sons were runners. It is just part of the way we bring up children. You just learn to run because you are Semá:th people. My grandsons and great-grandsons all run. Back in the old days of raiding and wars, the runners played a very important role as messengers in defending the home villages.

When X̱éyteleq needed a drink of water, he was restricted. You should drink very little water when on a run, or you'll get cramps in the stomach, so X̱éyteleq was given the hollow leg bone of a crane filled with water. That was all he was allowed to drink when he was on a long run. He would fill it up like a mini-canteen. One leg bone full of water was all he was allowed in the course of a day. If he was on a run of more than a day, he could take along one piece of dried salmon to eat. As far as the powers of water are concerned, I don't know. I am not trained in the arts of the *shxwlá:m* [shamanic healers].

After X̱éyteleq: Family Ties

X̱éyteleq's first wife was from Semá:th. She was not from the Wolves. X̱éyteleq had many children and descendants, but most of them died from smallpox epidemics and things like that Spanish flu that came later. Due to smallpox and other deadly sicknesses, Th'etsimiya, his youngest daughter, was the only living descendant he had in Semá:th. Two of his other daughters died of smallpox, and each one left a little boy behind. The oldest one was Frank Hilaire and the younger one was Charlie Point. Frank Hilaire married into Lummi, and Charlie Point, into Musqueam.

Frank Hilaire grew to be a tall man like his grandfather X̱éyteleq. Frank married a girl from Lummi, across the border in Washington State. In fact, he raised his family there. I don't know who he married, but I heard she was Hawaiian or part Hawaiian. When it came time for Frank to join the spirit dancers, he knew that all spirit dancers must have an Indian name that has been witnessed in the longhouse. Frank went back to Sumas to ask for his grandfather's name. His aunt, old Mrs. Vedder, Th'etsimiya, she refused because he had moved away. He no longer lived at Semá:th. He wept and pleaded with her. She gave in at last and put the name X̱éyteleq on Frank Hilaire, right there in her longhouse by the Sumas River. She told him that because he made his home so far away, the name would end with him. He was not to pass it on to his descendants. She said this since it was such an impor-tant Semá:th name. To make sure that the name stayed on in Kilgard, Th'etsimiya also put it on her little grandson, my mother's only brother, David Ambrose Silva.

Over a thousand people attended Ambrose's naming at the long-house beside the Sumas River. They came from British Columbia and Washington State. Important witnesses were paid with gold nuggets. My great-grandmother Th'etsimiya was a powerful wealthy woman, but nobody knows where she got her gold from. I can still see in my mind the large portrait of her, sitting bolt upright in a straight-backed chair [see figure 7]. She wore a high-necked blouse and a long black skirt. She had small bags of gold sitting in her lap. She lived to the ripe old age of 125.

As I said, Frank Hilaire married a lady from Lummi. His children were Joe, Veronica, and Amelia, and there may have been others, but memory fails me. Many descendants live across Washington State. Some live in La Conner, Washington. Mrs. Gus Stone was a granddaughter of Frank Hilaire, and she lived there. His daughter Amelia married Albert Louie, of Yakweakwioose. Joe Hilaire's son was Ben Hilaire. Veronica had two families. Her first family was two sons, Joe and Louie Washington. With her second husband, Sam Cagey, she had a daughter, Margaret, who became Mrs. Eddie Greene. The Hilaires, Cageys, and Washingtons are eager to learn their family history. Someone should ask who Frank Hilaire married. She must have been an important person or he would not have moved. He carried X̱éyteleq's name, but the name belongs in Semá:th. Ray Silver carries it now.[8]

The other orphaned nephew raised by Th'etsimiya was Charlie Point. The younger of the two boys, he was stubborn and was known to have fits of temper. During one of these tantrums, he left home and never returned. Th'etsimiya was sad about this and made sure she always knew where he was. He went to Bellingham, Washington, and met a half-Native, half-English woman. Her name was Emily Coutts. They married and had five children, as far as I recall. The oldest were John and James, and the younger were twins: Cecilia and Robert. The youngest was Abram. Charlie moved his family to the Musqueam Reserve on Point Grey in Vancouver, where they became duly registered. In his later years, Charlie's eldest son, Johnny, joined the spirit dancers and made his way back to "the Old Lady," as Th'etsimiya was now called with affection by her relatives. Johnny's children were Basil, Ambrose, Dominic, Cyrus, Bertha, and Mabel. There may have been others whose names could have slipped my mind.

---

8 Ray Silver was the eldest son of David Ambrose Silva. The name "Silva" was at some point modified to "Silver," but at this point no one can remember who first made the change.

Th'etsimiya now put a name on Johnny. That name was Yeqwyéqweléqw. His sister Cecilia once told me that before the ceremony, the Old Lady had directed two other ladies to cut off all of Cecilia's long red curls while she was sitting in the audience at her brother's naming. This was to be used to make a "hair hat" for her brother to wear during the ceremony. Cecilia said, "I cried the rest of the night every time anybody so much as glanced at me." Should any reader attend a *mí'lha* dance ceremony and notice a Musqueam dancer wearing a hat with long curly red hair, it just may be Aunt Cecilia's tresses from long ago. May you rest in peace, Auntie!

FIGURE 9

A portrait of Rena's mother and her parents and siblings, at Kilgard, ca. 1910. Clockwise, from the top left: Pete Silva, Sarah Vedder Silva, Antonia, Annie (Rena's mother), David Ambrose, and Margaret. Photo courtesy of Rena Point Bolton.

John's son Dominic lives at Musqueam. Ambrose, another of his sons, married into Chehalis, and the Chehalis Points stem from Ambrose. Cecilia married Francis Thomas from Fort Langley. Their children were Elmer, Roderick, and Robert. Robert lives at Albion. James has lots of grandchildren today in Musqueam.

Charlie Point and Emily were married a long time. After Charlie died, Emily married Qwi'qwitlam, chief of Coquitlam. Tommy Williams was their son.

Most of the Points stayed on in Musqueam but some live in Chehalis and Sardis. Roy Edgar Point, who was chosen for me as my husband and who was the father of my ten children, he was the only son of Abram Point. The Points at Musqueam descended from one of X̱éyteleq's daughters. The Cageys, Washingtons, Hilaires, and Stones are descended from another of his daughters.

As I said, Frank Hilaire and Charlie Point were the grandsons of X̱éyteleq. They were raised by his youngest daughter, Th'etsimiya, together with her own daughter and son, Sarah and George Vedder. Th'etsimiya married Henry Vedder, and when he died, she married his brother George, after whom her second child was named. Vedder is a Dutch name that was given to an Indian family at Kilgard. I don't know much about the Vedders.

After the boys, Frank and Charlie, grew up and moved away, Sarah and George [Vedder] were left alone with the old people at Semá:th. Sarah married Pete Silva from the Tii:t Xwélmexw people from upriver above Chilliwack and below Hope. I think he was from what used to be called Skw'átets but now is the Peters Reserve. I know Pete Silva's sister, Margaret, Mrs. August Jim, lived at Ohamil until she passed away—in that area, anyway. Her name was Margaret Silva before she married. So Sarah Vedder married Pete Silva, and her oldest surviving daughter, Annie Silva, was my mother. My mother's brothers and sisters were Ambrose Silva, Antonia Silva, and Lottie—Charlotte—Silva. Those were the ones who survived. The others all passed away.

More Family Ties

Stó:lō people have lots of family and complicated ties. Outsiders who read this might get lost, but I think it is important to record it for our own people and their connections to the past.[9]

My mother, Annie Silva, came from the *sí:yá:m* family of Steqó:ye, as I said. She was one of seven children. Margaret, the eldest, was trained to be the carrier of family knowledge, but then she drowned. The next children, Elizabeth and Cecilia, died young. Then there was my mother, Annie, followed by David, who was known as Ambrose, then Antonia —the mother of Sweetie Malloway—and Charlotte, the youngest.

My mother's mother, Sarah Vedder Silva, had one brother, George, who died during an epidemic. He was named for the brother of Henry Vedder. When Henry Vedder, the husband of Th'etsimiya, died, his brother George Vedder married Great-grandmother. This was the custom. A brother was responsible for his brother's widow and children. If he did not marry her himself, he looked after her until she married again. So her second child was named after her second husband, George, but he died young. My grandmother Sarah Vedder died at the age of sixty-five in 1936. Her mother, Th'etsimiya, lived to be well over a hundred and she died in about 1924, when Sumas Lake was drained away. From this reckoning, X̲éyteleq was probably born sometime in the 1700s.

My mother Annie's father was Pete Silva from Skw'átets village. The Xwélmexw name "Silver" has been derived from "Silva," and earlier, from "da Silva," from Spanish speakers who came in from the south, maybe in the gold-rush days, and maybe from Chile.[10] Pete Silva was a member

---

[9] Many of the people named in this section have been important resources for historians, linguists, and anthropologists over the past century.

[10] It may be that the original da Silva family was not Spanish. During the nineteenth century, Portuguese pioneers, many of them from the Azores and Madeira islands, settled in British Columbia. Gradually the "da Silva" descendants changed their name to Silvey or Silver and also intermarried with Salish people in the region. See, for example, Jean Barman's *The Remarkable Adventures of Portuguese Joe Silvey* (2004).

of the Upper Stó:lō, the Tii:t tribe. Pete Silva's father was Rafaelito da Silva. He had a dry-goods store at Yale during the gold rush of 1858. Pete's mother was sister to Louis Sqw'átets. Louie and his sister were the two carriers of the Sxwóyxwey. Louie Sqw'átets's son Patrick was the father of Agnes Kelly.

Well, I guess Rafaelito decided to leave the country, or just leave and go elsewhere. He was a person who didn't like to stay too long in one place. So when he was ready to leave—my grandfather (Papa) was telling me this—Rafaelito said to Papa, "Would you like to come with me? I'm going to my home and you will meet your other family down there." Papa was just a young boy, he must have been about six or seven, and he remembered this very clearly. And he said, "Sure, I'd love to go. I'd really like to go."

Papa was the youngest in the family, so he had no qualms about anything. His dad got up early in the morning, and he had a horse and buggy. He woke up my grandfather and carried him out and put him down in the trunk on the wagon, behind him on the seat, and he drove away. He was on what became the Trans-Canada Highway, going toward Vancouver. I guess Louie Sqw'átets woke up and realized—well, his sister had probably told him that her husband, Rafaelito, had stolen her son, the youngest one. This was Louie Sqw'átets's nephew, Pete, his favourite one. He became very angry. He was the *shxwlá:m*, a very strong *shxwlá:m*. He was like the medicine man that everyone was afraid of. He became angry and he got a group of men to go with him—they got the posse together—and they went after them. They paddled like crazy downriver and stopped at Pattullo Bridge in New Westminster. That was the only crossing point at that time. They parked there and waited. By the time Rafaelito da Silva got that far, he had taken my grandfather Pete out of the back of the wagon. He was sitting up with his dad on the wagon when they got to Pattullo Bridge.

That's where the war party stopped them. They were going to kill Rafaelito da Silva. They told him he had no right to the boy. They said the boy belonged to the mother. He handed the boy over and they told him he was never ever to come back to the Fraser Valley and Xwélmexw country again. Then they let him go over the bridge and on his way. They took Papa—that is, Pete—and put him into their canoe. Papa later said he didn't understand why his "Uncle Hees" was so angry and upset, and why he had paint on his face—because it wasn't *mí'lha* time, you know. But anyway, they took him home and he never saw his dad again. He remembered a few Spanish words, and every now and then, he would speak the words to my brother. That's how my brother started learning Spanish, from my grandfather.

So that was one of the exciting stories that I heard from my grandfather.

Pete Silva had an older brother, David, who died young, and a sister, Margaret Silva. She was later known as Mrs. August Jim. Her first husband was an Italian man, Andrew Lorenzetto. They had two children, Edmond Lorenzetto and Kathryn, who was known as Kate. Kate married an Englishman called Eccles. Her son, Andrew Eccles, had a sister, Margaret, who was known as Chickee and would have been the legitimate carrier of the Sxwóyxwey masks and knowledge, except she married an American and moved to the United States. She never came back. Edmond and his wife, Adeline, were parents to Joe Lorenzetto.

Lottie Tom's brother was Johnny Roberts. Johnny had lots of descendants: Bill Roberts was his son. Bill married one of the Joe girls from Tzeachten, Rose Joe, who became Rosie Roberts. Rosie's brothers were Henry Joe and Stan Joe. Rose had several sisters: Minnie, Nancy (Phillips), Helen, Flora, and Adeline. One of them had a daughter, Lorena, and one of Lorena's sisters was Edna Ned of Kilgard. Two other sisters lived at Matsqui. Mary Malloway's mother was one of them. I think her name was Helen. She married a Julian. I think the other one was called Flora and she married a McKay. One of the Joe sisters moved to Nooksack and married Bill Roberts. Another Joe sister married Vincent Malloway. Vincent's son Ivan was the father of Ken Malloway. Ivan married my cousin Georgina. We called her Sweetie.

The father of the Joe girls was Alec Joe. Alec Joe was a younger half-brother to Joe Phillips, or Old Joe Punch, as everybody called him. Old Joe's full brother was Louie Phillips, and they were known as Joe and Louie Punch. They all lived at Deroche. When I was a girl, we used to see them all when we were fishing at Devil's Run. Alec Joe moved to Tzeachten when he married.

Joe Punch and his wife, Josephine, lived at Deroche. Their children were Rose Phillips, Lena Phillips, Agnes Phillips, and Alfred Phillips. Rose, their eldest, married a Lewis and they had two daughters, Winnie and Eva. Then Rose married Steven Charlie of Chilliwack Landing and had Steven Jr. and Verna. Lena, the second daughter, had Sarah and Leonard (Phillips), then she married Clarence Cook and they had Patricia, Verna, Annie Laura, John, Norma, and Eleanor. Rose and Lena's brother, Alfred Phillips, married my mother and they had my half-brothers and half-sisters Merle, Joyce, Selma, and Alfred Jr. Agnes Phillips married one of the Andrews from Seabird Reserve. They had two daughters, Mary and Virginia. She then married James Elkins and had Ralph and Reynold. Reynold is known as Wheeler, and he was cared for by Agnes Kelly at Ohamil. That family has ties with the Louies.

Josephine, Mrs. Joe Punch, had three brothers. The oldest was Edwin. They had no English surname as far as I know. The other brothers were Louie and Antoine. They were from Matsqui.

Edwin married a woman by the name of Agnes. After Edwin's death, Agnes Edwin married Dan Milo. Agnes and Edwin had two daughters, Susan and Mary. Susan Edwin married Ed Coombs of Chilliwack Landing. Their daughter, Clara Coombs, married Alphonse George of Sardis. Clara and Alphonse's daughter, Susan, married Robert Sam of Lytton. Mary Edwin married Abram Point. As I said, their son Roy Point was my first husband.

One of Mrs. Joe Punch's brothers was called Antoine. Antoine's sons were Harry Antoine of Everson, Washington—right across the border—and Joe Antoine of Fort Langley. Harry Antoine married Louise Kelly of Kilgard. Louise was the sister of James Kelly, Charlotte (Uslick), and Hugh and Ed Kelly. Harry and Louise's children live at Nooksack. Their daughter Rowena married a Klein. Their other children were Shirley, Milton, and Melvin.

Louie, the brother of Antoine and Edwin, was the father of Joe and Ed Louie. Ed Louie's son Albert Louie was known as Happy. Albert had a brother and two half-brothers, James and Ernest Louie of Deroche.

Joe and Louie Punch had a sister called Gulastelot. She married Joe Johnson, of Katzie. Down at Katzie, they speak and write with *ns*, like Musqueam and Cowichan, instead of *ls* like we use. Some of the first people to get European names at Matsqui had only one name, like Edwin, Louie, Antoine, or Joseph. Their descendants took some of these as surnames. Today, the Antoines and Louies from Matsqui live over the border on the American side.

I have limited myself in what I have said about my relatives—whether you believe it or not. My grandmother was related to a lot of those who have been chiefs in this area. These hereditary chiefs in all the villages were her cousins. When I was young, and before that too, these hereditary chiefs would come together at places like Chilliwack in the middle of the Fraser Valley and discuss problems. Maybe some villages had bad fortune, or surplus foods, or were fighting or disagreeing. The chiefs decided how to sort things out. Chilliwack, some say, comes from Ts'elxwéyeqw, "a place of meetings." Others say it means "where the river bends." Dan Milo's grandfather, Sí:yá:m Lhókw'ōlá:leqw (the-man-who-flew-like-an-eagle-as-he-danced) was one of those who met with the big *sí:yá:m* of the area in these councils. Dan often talked about these things to us. He was one of my great-uncles and we had lot in common.

* ❀ *

Devil's Run

One thing that always sticks out from my early memories is growing up with our grandparents, away from the village, at Líyómxetel, Devil's Run.[1] Yes, Líyómxetel is a very ancient fishing site on the Fraser River, on the north side of Sumas Mountain but still in Semá:th territory.

Our grandparents had decided to move out from the village. We spent days packing up and getting ready for the canoe trip. It was a long day's pull from Semá:th to Devil's Run. On moving day, all the bundles

---

1 Rena's daughter Wendy Point Ritchie, who teaches Halq'eméylem and very kindly helped to standardize the spelling of Halq'eméylem words in this book, explained the name Líyómxetel as composed of the following elements: *Líyóm* is taken from the Chinook trade language (*liyam* means "devil"), while, in Halq'eméylem, *xe* means "foot" and *tel* means "place": Devil's Foot Place. A powerful shaman was said to have lived here. People were afraid of his diabolical powers, and they reported that he abducted women and brought them to live with him here at this place as his wives (personal communication, September 4, 2012).

and boxes were packed aboard Grandfather's large dugout canoe. People from the village came to say goodbye. They came down to the creek where the canoe was being loaded. It was sad to leave, but my brother and I were young and excited by the adventure. We were off to see the world. It was our first trip. Grandfather Pete, "Papa," sat at the stern and Grandmother Sarah, "Mama," sat in the bow. We sat in the middle, a bit closer to Papa than to Mama.

Some of the men gave us a push and away we went, down Kw'ekw'íqw Creek, heading east. Papa used a pole to shift us down the creek to where it joined Sumas River. And there he began to paddle. Oh! Absolutely nothing could be more exciting! There we were, two small children off to see the world!

After an hour or so, we reached Pump Town, which wasn't really a town at all, just a store and a gas pump. And the dam, or dyke, was there to keep the Sumas from flooding the new farmland that had been exposed by draining Sumas Lake. At Pump Town, we had to portage everything around the dam. While Papa looked for someone to give us a hand, Mama and I went shopping at the store. We bought cheese, crackers, and fresh milk. Once everything had been carried over the dam, we sat on the riverbank and had our lunch. It was a splendid outing for us youngsters. After lunch, we paddled out the mouth of the Sumas and into the milky, murky waters of the Fraser River, the Stó:lō. Now we were heading west, moving with the current down the Stó:lō, along the north side of Sumas Mountain. (Kilgard [Kw'ekw'íqw], our starting point, is on the south side of the mountain.) We passed many creeks and even some waterfalls. At one waterfall, Papa stopped the canoe and filled all our canteens with fresh drinking water. We all had a long cold drink before climbing back into the canoe for the next leg of the journey.

We saw deer running along the bank and disappearing into the underbrush. There were grouse and ducks and helldivers.[2] These ducks

---

2 Helldivers are pied-billed grebes. They probably take this, their current popular name, from an American World War II dive-bomber, the Curtiss sb2c Helldiver, and when Rena was a child, these birds were probably called simply by their Halq'eméylem name.

got that name because of the way they dive really deep and you never seem to see them come back up again. They pop up far away from where they started. But I got tired and began to fall asleep in the canoe. Mama turned around and laid me down on an old Salish blanket that she had folded on the bottom of the canoe. When I woke up, we were landing. We had reached Devil's Run, Líyómxetel, where I would spend the best part of the next four years.

The old smokehouse was on a levelled-off patch on top of a hill. It was surrounded by trees. It had been patched and repaired so many times that I thought it might collapse at any moment. Papa and Mama didn't seem in the least concerned about its condition. We were all busy unloading the canoe and piling everything up on the bank. When everything was out of the canoe, we packed it all up to the smokehouse. It sat about forty feet above the high-water mark. The house was made of cedar planks and shakes, and it had no windows at all. When we entered, a really strange feeling hit me. My jaw dropped. There in the middle of the room was a fire pit. It was built on top of large flat boulders that were buried in the floor with just their tops sticking up and forming a circle. There was a hole in the roof, way up above us. This was to let the smoke out. There were cracks between the planking of the walls, and these let in rays of sunshine. The sun lit up the dust in the air and a mass of cobwebs so that they looked like wispy ghosts hovering in mid-air. The only furniture was some wooden benches around the fire pit.

The next scene that comes to my mind is Mama leaning over the fire in the middle of the room, cooking. I can still picture her bent over the fire and the black cast-iron pot hanging over the flames from an iron tripod, and the wood is crackling. Mama cooks all her soups and stews in this pot. Then, as soon as the soup was done she prepared bannock in an iron fry pan that she placed right on top of the coals with the handle raised from the heat with a piece of firewood. It sat there until the baking was done. Getting the distance exactly right between the hot coals and the bread in the fry pan was something you learned by trial and error.

Sometimes, we put the bannock dough right into the coals to cook and left it for an hour or so. When it was done, you lifted it up and shook off all the ashes on both sides. This was the same way we prepared potatoes, carrots, and other roots. When we had ducks, they were roasted whole on skewers over the coals. When you cut your skewer, you left a couple of branch prongs at the bottom so the duck would not slide down into the fire or onto the rocks. The bottom of this skewer would be sharpened so it could be jammed into the ground between the rocks. Mama placed tin cans and old stone bowls under the roasting duck to collect the drippings. She would turn the bird a quarter every so often and baste with the drippings. We barbecued salmon the same way as the ducks. With salmon, you take a young green tree, a sapling a couple of inches in diameter. You remove the branches and split part way down the trunk. You place the fish inside the partly split sapling. The fish consists of the fillets joined at the belly, but the head, tail, guts, and backbone are removed. The fillets are held out flat with thin cedar cross-slats. Then you tie the split top of the tree stem tightly together with string or wire. The slatted salmon is lifted carefully and its sapling stick is jammed into the ground and leaned over the coals. The stick can be adjusted by piling small rocks against it. Salmon grilled this way is delicious, and the flavour, well, it is really hard to beat.

We had some carved wooden spoons and stone bowls in the smokehouse, too. Our stone bowls were without carvings. The ones with carvings on them belonged to spirit doctors, the *shxwlá:m*. We used the plain ones as bowls and for grinding paint and grinding medicines. Blood from a girl's first menstruation was collected in the special ones. I don't know what they did with it. If you had one with a man carved on the side, it was used for making war and for mixing poisons. The healers used them a lot for mixing medicines to help people. And apart from that, we had wooden bowls for eating from. They were like boats. We had wooden spoons and ladles for eating out of these big bowls. The stone bowls were used for healing and were very sacred.

Once we've moved in, the house no longer looks bare. Now there are huge woven cattail mats attached to the beams overhead. In daytime, they're rolled up, but at night, they are lowered to form walls around our beds, like long straw curtains. The beds are on platforms a couple of feet high, covered with stacks of cattail matting and Salish blankets. On top of us, we have either more Salish blankets or store-bought ones.

My great-grandmother slept on such bedding all her life, until she died at about the age of 120. However, her daughter, Grandmother Sarah, "Mama," she slept on a feather mattress that rested on top of several mats. We never had a table or chairs. We sat on the floor on mats made from cedar bark or cattail rushes. Our dishes were either carved from wood or made of tin. We loved our wooden spoons, but we had metal cutlery as well.

Grandfather fished and Grandmother put up hundreds and hundreds of salmon for the winter. She smoked and dried them, and she salted them, too. We took enough so that nobody among the poor and the elderly at Kilgard would starve. That was the way that *sí:yá:m* families were in those days. The *sí:yá:m* [hereditary chiefs] had a duty to look after their people. Grandmother was highly aware of the responsibility; my mother was, too. The same was passed on to me. I learned to butcher fish, to hang them and smoke them so that there would be enough fish for all those who needed them over the winter.

During the summer months, we always had salmon hanging to dry at the back part of the house, and at the same time, the fire coals were always smouldering; this kept the flies away. All the fish-cutting and butchering was done down at wooden stands by the riverside. Mama used to cut fish with a cutter in the shape of a half-moon. It was made from an old handsaw. Two holes through the straight side of the iron were used to attach two pieces of wood for a handle that was kept in place with bolts or rivets. I guess it was like an Inuit *ulu* and the curved side was sharp. In our language, it was a *lhá:ts'tel*. Using her *lhá:ts'tel*, Mama could clean and fillet a salmon much quicker than somebody using a straight-blade knife.

During the spring, we used to pack up a few things and go camping across the Stó:lō on the north side—at a place called Dewdney. While we were there, Papa would work for local farmers, hoeing strawberries and raspberries and picking rhubarb in the fields. This was the 1930s, during the Great Depression, and money was very scarce. Every cent that Papa earned, he saved for the winter, for the staples like sugar, salt, flour, baking powder, pilot bread, matches, and tea. Mama used to sun-dry the rhubarb, cutting them in long strips but leaving them joined at one end. She hung these outside over strings and they looked like giant spiders because all the thin strips would curl up toward the middle as they dried. Sometimes we stayed the whole summer at Dewdney, or moved on to Hatzic or Mission to pick strawberries for the local Japanese farmers.[3] But the moment the big runs of [sockeye] salmon came upriver, we were back at Devil's Run. It was so nice to be home again in that big spacious house with Mama's mats and blankets and baskets everywhere. And I'll never forget the smell of the open fire.

During the fall and winter in those Depression years, many home-less people stopped with us and begged for food. The CNR ran behind the smokehouse, and I suppose those poor men "riding the rails" could see the roof as they passed. There was a rail station at Murphy's Landing, about three or four miles downriver from us. Mama, like all the old people, would never turn away these ragged men. Of course, she would always have them do chores, too, like splitting wood and hanging fish high up on the driers. She used to save old clothing that we had been given by missionaries or by people who traded clothing for our cedar-root baskets. She always made sure these hungry men had enough clothes to keep them warm.

I remember one man in particular. He had long stringy hair and a beard. His clothes hung from him in tatters. Instead of boots, he had burlap sacking covering his feet and tied onto him around the ankles. This was his only footwear. Mama gave him a bar of soap and pointed to the river. While he was washing, she dragged out a musty-smelling cardboard box and took out some clothes and a pair of used boots. After she had fed the man and he had left, she burned his old clothes, muttering away in Halq'eméylem that if she didn't burn them and their lice, they'd just crawl away by themselves.

3   Today, the Xa:ytem Longhouse Interpretive Centre is located beside Hatzic Rock, near Mission, British Columbia. The site is somewhat downriver in rela-tion to Devil's Run, and on the opposite bank of the river. The rock is a sacred "transformer site": it is said to be three *sí:yá:m* who were turned to stone by Xa:ls the Creator for having refused to teach their language, songs, and writing to the coming generations. Next to the stone are the archaeological remains of a large dwelling that dates back six thousand years, and some items at the site have been radiocarbon dated to nine thousand years (Simon Fraser University Museum of Archaeology and Ethnology 2008–9).

Spring was always a beautiful season at Devil's Run. As soon as the weather warmed up, Mama and I would take long walks down the CNR tracks. We picked all kinds of Indian herbs and medicines, as well as early greens like thimbleberry and salmonberry shoots. We peeled these and they were sweet and juicy. Sometimes we mixed these with fish eggs that had been matured in the ground, or else they were hung outside in a flour sack until spring came. The buried fish eggs tasted strong, like limburger cheese, but we didn't mind. We were used to it. We always ate what was provided for us. We picked Indian liquorice ferns, peeled them, and chewed them thoroughly to make our teeth clean and freshen our mouths. We also scraped the sap that oozed down the cottonwood trees and ate it on the spot. We picked buds from the cottonwoods too, but I forget what they were used for.

When summer came, we picked berries—wild strawberries, blueberries, thimbleberries, and salmonberries. In May, we'd paddle down to Dewdney Slough and the water level would be high and swift. As we paddled along the slough, we could reach the salmonberries hanging over the edge of the water. We filled our berry baskets in no time at all. And we did it without even having to get out of the canoe.

There were field mushrooms and morels in the same area, but to gather these, we had to climb out of the canoe. We scrambled through woods and fields looking for mushroom treasures. Once our baskets were filled to the brim, we'd be *so* happy and very cheerful as we made our way back to the canoe. I remember nearing the heavily laden canoe on one occasion and noticing hundreds of little grey frogs moving around in sets of hoof prints left in the mud along the edge of the river. They were hopping in every direction. I shrank at the sight of them and ran to Papa. In Halq'eméylem, he said, "Don't be afraid of them and don't hurt them. They have just as much right to be here as we do. They belong to the Great Mother (the earth and the river). To her they are just as beautiful as we are." I have never forgotten his words. No matter how strange I find other people or the other beings who are God's creatures, I tell myself that they have a right to be here too. That was my first lesson in tolerance toward other creatures and other ways.

When fall came, Mama had us picking late berries like salal and wild brambleberries, wild crabapples, Indian tea—such as Hudson's Bay tea, or swamp tea, as it's sometimes called. We call it *móqwem*. This was also the season for gathering medicines. We took strawberry leaves; wild rose leaves and the rosehips (when rose leaves are chopped and simmered they turn pink); the bark of alder, cascara and barberry—oh, there were many more. They all have their medicinal uses.

In the winter months, I helped Mama with her mountains of wool and with cedar-root baskets. I did odd jobs and served as her legs. I learned to help with the cooking too. Mama would sew my dresses by hand, even when she wasn't well. She suffered from pleurisy, so she never was really well. I remember her being in Abbotsford Hospital many times. Then, we'd be alone with Auntie Jean and her family. There really wasn't too much to remember. I just felt that at that time there wasn't much of anything available to us. Papa and Mama were very strict with me. I had to learn to work with wool.

The long winter evenings were spent listening to Papa. He was a superb storyteller. It was during those winter nights at Devil's Run that my brother and I learned our history. Papa would start a story as he whittled wood shavings and cut kindling to use as firelighter the next morning. We heard the stories time and again, but I would become spellbound every single time. We sat enchanted as the tale unfolded. Papa was the greatest storyteller I've ever listened to. Peter and I were getting our Xwélmexw education right there at Devil's Run, and we didn't know we were being raised any differently from anybody else.

As far as learning the ways of our people are concerned, there was very little teaching. We learned by watching and working, doing little jobs and getting better at them. I learned through the years from my grandparents and Uncle Ambrose. (He was my mother's brother David, but everybody called him Ambrose.) And, to some extent, I learned from working around my mother. My grandfather Pete was not from Kilgard. He came from Skw'átets and so the stories he told about my Semá:th family came by way of his mother-in-law, Mrs. Henry Vedder [Th'etsimiya].

I remember the smokehouse days at Devil's Run as being a lot of fun. We worked a lot and there were lots of stories while we worked. Our elders would remember the old days. They'd say, "Remember such and such old Indian names that were used by Old So-and-So?" All those stories!

There's something about childhood learning that sticks in the mind. It gets caught there—maybe because my fingers were always busy and I had a good memory. Some stories were told to me, and others just happened. I remember one day we'd finished working with the sockeye and we could see my stepfather, Alfred Phillips, paddling toward us from across the Fraser River in his canoe. There was something big and long and white in his canoe. I kept guessing what it was, but it wasn't until he got close that we could see it was a huge sturgeon. It got rolled up in his net. It's really amazing that he didn't tip over pulling it in. It was the biggest sturgeon people had seen. Men who were working on the railway came and took pictures. They measured it, and it was nine feet nine inches long.

Another time, the train got derailed and a load of green silk fell into the river. There were skeins and skeins of green silk. We thought it was a kind of wool. Grandfather brought some of it home. Grandmother knit him a green silk sweater, but he didn't like it much. Said it was cold. It didn't keep him warm. That silk train was derailed somewhere between Devil's Run and Chilliwack. We didn't have a clue what they would use that green silk for. I still don't.

While we worked, the old people told us so many stories about what life was like before the whites arrived. But when you look back on those times, and then forward to today, those stories drained away, just like Semá:th Lake. I remember some of them, and my brother really remembered a lot. I was only little at the time, and when the stories were told at night, I would fall asleep before they were finished.

Nowadays, the art of storytelling seems to have died. What a tragic loss this has been for my children and grandchildren. The only storyteller today seems to be the television. When you listen to a storyteller, your imagination goes into high gear. That doesn't happen with TV.

I used my imagination to visit Semá:th Lake. I'd heard so much about the lake. My grandmother talked to me about it, about the little wee canoe she had. She'd go out in it and cut those long rushes. She'd take them in to the shore and lay them on the ground. And they had another, very old canoe. It lay on the beach there, and they would fill it with water and drop in hot rocks, and they'd put the rushes in the warm water and cover everything with old mats or blankets or whatever, and then they steamed the rushes. And once they'd been properly steamed, then they would lay them out in the hot sun to dry. Once they were dry, they turned white. After that, the ladies would work on them. They would pick them over and measure them and cut them to lengths they wanted. Then they would weave them. So it was a big project. I watched her when she worked. I saw that canoe sitting there. It was like that old canoe was part of the lake that had gone. Of course, the lake wasn't there any longer, but they used to talk a lot as they worked, about how they would go out there and dig these roots, you know. They called them "potatoes" and "carrots" and "wild celery," and things like that. I would hear them talking and I would imagine the lake with all kinds of things growing around the edge. They said that the reeds, the rushes, they grew up to twenty feet tall. They must have been really, really long. So I always imagined what it would have looked like, in my mind—with the canoes all around.

Canoes were part of our lives every day during those years at Devil's Run. There were tiny canoes, ten or twelve feet long, for women to pick rushes and gather foods, especially before I was born. They used them all along the edge of Semá:th Lake. When they got old, they would be used to boil rushes in. They dropped heated stones in those old canoes full of water and boiled their food in them too, for big events like feasts. Then there were the shovel-nosed canoes for use on the rivers and in lakes, mainly by the men. Then there were freight canoes, long and with a hole through the seat so we could fit a pole like a mast and hoist a sail when we were moving up and down the Fraser River. That's all I saw in my childhood, and we used various canoes to move between the village and the smokehouse at Devil's Run. Finally, there were the war canoes. They were a bit like today's racing canoes, forty-five or fifty feet long. Great-grandfather Jacob Milo was the last to make them, real ocean-going canoes. They had the Nootka [Nuu-chah-nulth] type of stern, sort of sweeping up sharply. They were wide and deep. In the later years, people paddled them down [to Puget Sound] to around Seattle and beached them there and travelled overland to Wenatchee [Washington State] to pick fruit. Then, at the end of the picking season, they would paddle home again. There were some families among the Stó:lō who probably went on raids to Vancouver Island, but I wouldn't swear to it. I will say, though, I never heard about our family going out looking for trouble.

Mama made sure my fingers were always busy. I learned to operate that spindle whorl, the *sélseltel*, when I was very young, at Devil's Run. I learned to use that, and later, I learned to spin on an old spinner. By the time I was nine, I could spin like an old pro. I learned to knit and to weave a blanket or a robe. And I was also learning to do basket weaving at that time. And as I grew older, I learned to do a lot of the cooking, with my Aunt Jean—my Uncle Ambrose's wife.

Peter "Speedy" Bolan

Because Peter was crippled at the age of five, my first duties, from the time I was three, centred on serving as his legs. My mother, Annie Silva Bolan, became frantic when the accident happened and he was paralyzed. She decided to move us back down to Kilgard, because if Peter were to die, he would have to be buried with his mother's ancestors. Kilgard was where her children belonged. As I explained, Peter survived but he was paralyzed down the left side and he couldn't walk. He would sit all day in a chair and had to be carried to and from bed, and to meals, and anywhere else he wanted to go. Between these trips, my job was to be his legs. As a result, we became very close. Sometimes, his quick, overactive mind became bored, and I realized I was really in for it. He would send me to fetch Dad's matches. He lit every match in the house—a real fire bug. Or he would send me to rob the cupboards for raisins, prunes, dates, or any goodies that Mum had on hand for baking. One day, he got it into his head that we would make butterscotch. I was ordered to fetch a can of Rogers Golden Syrup and a whole pound of butter. He fired up the syrup and butter in a pot, and it boiled over, all over the stovetop. Boy, did we ever catch it! Mum came running in from the garden when she smelled the smoke that was pouring out of the house.

One day, we were taken down to Kilgard from where we lived just off reserve. We were left at the home of our grandparents while Mum and Dad went into Abbotsford, about six miles away. It was a warm Saturday afternoon, and Grandfather Pete was outside helping Grandmother mend fishnets for the salmon season. Peter and I had been told to stay indoors until Mama had finished her chores. Peter grew restless. He surveyed the room and spied Papa's wine bottle. He said, "Can you fetch it, Sis, and bring a cup, will you?" I did my best to hurry because I knew he was getting bored. I handed him the wine bottle and the cup. With a mischievous glint in his eye, he filled the cup up to the top and handed it to me. He said, "Taste this, Sis. It's real good. Tastes just like soda pop."

I hesitated. He prompted me again, several times. I took a big gulp of the wine.

"Hmm," I said, "it tastes good."

I handed it back to him. He drank some and handed it to me. We took turns sipping. We finished the whole cup!

Peter laughed and said, "Sis, will you get me some water? I feel thirsty."

I took the empty cup and turned toward the kitchen area. Suddenly, the floor came up and hit me in the face, full force. Laughing like the dickens, my brother kept telling me to get up, get up! After falling back down several times, I hit on the idea of using the wall for support and navigation. I wobbled my way over to the water and filled the cup, but there wasn't much left by the time I got back to Peter. I was staggering along on my third trip when Mama came in. She saw water all over the floor and me holding a half-empty cup. She figured out what had happened in a flash. For the first time in his life, Peter had his bottom peppered. I got off scot-free, except for the worst hangover I've had in my life. I didn't take another drink again until I was twenty-five—and that was at a wedding.

Peter learned to whittle on pieces of driftwood and the thick bark of fir trees. We used to pick up pieces of wood on the gravel bars and bring them back for him. He loved to carve little canoes from them. He also made weather vanes from cedar that we put up on windy days to watch them spin. He carved old-fashioned cars like the Model A Ford, the touring car, and the rumble seat coupe. He even made all the little wooden spokes for each of the wheels. Papa showed him how to make a whistle from a willow stick, a slingshot, bows and arrows, a wooden comb, and a spinning top from an empty spool of thread. He taught Peter all kinds of games you could make from string, like cat's cradle—and there were stories that went along with all the string figures. My brother quickly learned all the history, songs, and Indian names that belonged to our family. He also learned to speak a high-class form of the Halq'eméylem language. Me, I'm limited to the everyday basics of our language. If we had been born a generation earlier, my brother would be known as a *híkw' sí:yá:m*, a great chief or a hereditary chief, because he was the eldest son of a hereditary carrier. But he was born in 1924, at a time when the government was applying new laws to the Indian peoples. He lost all traditional rights and jurisdiction over his people because the government classified him as a "non-status Indian," and wiped out his real identity with the stroke of a pen. However, within our family, Peter has always held the supreme title and has all the knowledge that goes with it—even though he lived a long time in "exile" in an Okanagan nursing home.

After his accident, Peter got therapy at the Hospital for Crippled Children. They operated on his left side, and he could walk, at times, with his braces on, swinging one leg. But he tired very easily. So he mostly sang, but towards the end of his life, he was mostly just in a wheelchair. But he was a singer. He used to sing for different radio stations. He sang for CJOR in Vancouver; he sang at Osoyoos. He married a German woman. They travelled a lot. He had a pretty good life. He sang a lot—at different "dos"—nightclubs . . . and he never did go back to the reserves.

He just was not a reserve person. But he did retain a lot of knowledge that he learned from my grandfather. He spoke our language fluently. He spoke German, French, and Spanish, as well as English and three dialects in Indian: the Thompson, the Douglas, and the Halq'eméylem. He lived in Penticton and then he came home to die, which was the old way. The carriers of the lineage had to be buried at their old place of origin where their old people are. He came home, he passed away, and we buried him at Kilgard—because he would have been a hereditary chief, although he never carried it out in life. He had two names, a Sxwóyxwey name and a hereditary chief name, which was the brother name to mine—he gave one name to Steven and one to Tim. So today, these two boys carry his names.

The Sxwóyxwey name he gave Tim is Xwemxwemíleq, which means "the fast one" or "the quick one." That is, when you're dancing, you know, for the mask. And the one he gave Steven was Xwelíqweltel, "the speaker of the house"; -qweltel means "speaker." "The hungry flesh-eating speaker of the house!" Xwemxwemíleq—it's like, quick movement. Running fast. It's like saying "Speedy," and that's what they called him. They called him "Speedy" because he had that name. When he was five, he was a very fast runner. My mother had a hard time keeping up with him. But even after he became paralyzed and couldn't walk anymore, he used to tell people, "My name is Speed Bolan." They'd look at him and smile, and he'd wink at them. So he had quite a sense of humour.

FIGURE 10

Silva family portrait, ca. 1929–30. Clockwise, from the top left: Margaret Silva Lorenzetto (Mrs. August Jim), David Ambrose Silva, Francis Bolan (Rena's father), Pete Silva, Rena's brother Peter ("Speedy") Bolan, and Sarah Vedder Silva. Photo courtesy of Rena Point Bolton.

He's sitting on my grandfather's lap up there. The little boy that's sitting there, that's my brother Peter, he has dark curly hair.[4] My grandfather Pete Silva had curly hair. He was part Spanish. And my grandmother, Sarah Vedder, she's sitting there beside them, on the left. And Margaret, Mrs. August Jim, is up above. And my mother's brother, David Ambrose Silver, is there. The man that's sitting with the cap is my father, Francis Bolan. My grannie, Annie Jamieson—she was married to George Phillips in Lytton before she died, she held onto that picture for many, many, many years. She had it put away for me. She phoned me one time and said, "You better come and get your picture before I lose it." So Mark brought me up to Lytton and she gave me that. And the writings on the back. That is important. You'll have to read them. The statement on the back tells how all these people are connected to me and what I inherited from them.

4   Here and in what follows, Rena is referring to the photograph of the Silva family reproduced in figure 10. The following information appears on the back of the photo (the spellings have not been altered, but the text was originally in capital letters):
    My Elders
    by
    Rena Point Bolton (written Aug. 26/84, by C. Bolton for Rena)
    Standing in back from left to right is:
        – Mrs. Augest Jim (nee Margaret Silva) she was Pete Silva's sister
        – Davis Ambrose Silva (son of Pete and Sarah Silva)
    Sitting on front row (l–r):
        – Mrs. Pete Silva (nee Sarah Vedder)
        – Peter Lewis Bolan (Speedy) little boy
        – Pete Silva (holding Speedy)
        – Francis Bolan (Speedy's father)
    Picture taken approx. 1929–1930 by Annie Bolan (nee Annie Silva) daughter of Mr. and Mrs. Pete Silva, and wife of Francis Bolan
        – Pete Silva was the son of Raefelito de Silva, a Spanish explorer from Chile (South America) owned a dry goods store in Yale B.C. in the mid-1800s.

    This picture was given to Rena Point Bolton by Annie Bolan Phillips (Mrs. George Phillips) of Lytton B.C. (nee Annie Jamison) daughter of William Jamison, first Scottish explorer to build an "inn" in the Fraser Canyon highway. Francis Bolan (on picture) is the son of Annie and (her 1st husband) John Bolan. (Or Puliann?)

Charlie Gardner

This is the story of one of my relatives. She was living in Matsqui with her grandfather. They were related to X̱éyteleq. I can't really say whether she was a grand-niece, or a niece, but she was related to X̱éyteleq. She fell in love with a white man. His name was George, I think his last name was . . . Gardner. And he was the one in charge of putting the border through our land, marking Canada from the USA. His father was a Philadelphia lawyer. They had a huge law firm. He was a young lawyer, I guess, but he wanted to travel, so his dad let him go. But when he finished with the border, he was to settle down and start his life as a lawyer. In the meanwhile, he had started on the border. He had a crew of men working under him. They were charting the border, surveying it, all the way from the Pacific Ocean to the Atlantic. And while he was going through there, he fell in love with this woman from Matsqui—oh, I had her name on the tip of my tongue. I can't remember it.

Yeah, he began to live with her. I don't know if they got married, but whenever he could get off work for a while, he would come and live with her. She had a child by him, a boy. She named him Charles, Charles Gardner. When his dad got too far away to come back home to stay with them, she had the boy on her own and raised him herself. When the boy was five years old, two men in suits arrived. She could feel in her bones that they were coming for the boy. She asked her grandfather to take the boy away immediately. So the boy and the old man left. They paddled downriver and then across to the other side of the Fraser. The two men in suits came to the door and said that they had come for the son of George Gardner. She began to cry and told them that he had died when he was still a baby. Those men left.

Meanwhile, the grandfather had paddled back up to Mission and registered the boy at St. Mary's Mission School. He was very bright, and later, he went on to chart all the rivers in British Columbia and the Yukon. He hired Indian pullers and they paddled the various rivers. They charted the Fraser, Stikine, Nass, Skeena—all the way to Alaska. In places the whites couldn't get into, he hired local Native people and relied on their local knowledge of the area. When he grew older, he became a steamboat captain. He was a descendant of X̱éyteleq, and in old age, he recalled a big feast at Sumas when a girl who was his relative came of age. The host family piled hundreds of blankets around her to give away. This was how they celebrated the girl coming of age.[5]

5 Rena brought my attention to Captain Charlie Gardner's own telling of his story, which appeared in several instalments in the *Vancouver Sun* (November 29 and December 6, 13, 20, and 27, 1941). Here is part of the story as reported by journalist Edna Brandon Hanson:

> Captain Gardner was born at Matsqui in the spring of 1860. His father was Lieutenant George Clinton Gardner, a civil engineer and astronomer surveying the boundary between British Columbia and the USA. George Gardner's own father was chief surveyor for Washington and Oregon territories. Captain Gardner's mother was Sela:miya, daughter of the chief of Matsqui and Sumas. She was said to be granddaughter of the last great síːyáːm on the Fraser River. The boy was given the name Qwotaseltil. For the last forty years he has been a legendary river captain on the Skeena, Stikine, Yukon—where he witnessed the gold rush—and Mackenzie.
>
> Weeks before Captain Gardner was born, his mother, who had returned to Matsqui after staying with Gardner, received a message from the boundary surveyors, who were at work behind Chilliwack Lake. She was told by Gardner to wait for his return. He would be a while because he had just been called away for railway work in Peru. He promised to return. A Mr. Peabody and a Mr. Roder from Bellingham were appointed guardians of the unborn child, who was to be called after his father, but Father Chirouse at the Catholic mission of St. Mary's later mistakenly christened him Charles Alphonsus Gardner. Sela:miya never saw Gardner again.
>
> She used to go down to Bellingham and get groceries from the guardians from time to time. In 1864 they said he was growing into a fine boy and they had decided to send him to school in Victoria. Sela:miya took the boy home, worried. She had lost her husband to the white world and now they wanted to take her son. She went home and sent word to the guardians that the boy had died and therefore she would no longer come to them for supplies. The boy now learned traditional river life from his maternal grandfather and, from his mother, the gathering of plants and weaving materials. He was present at the potlatch given by his grandfather's brother for the coming out of this man's daughter. She was called Slalhilluet and there was much food to eat and give away because the ceremony was in the autumn when the larders were full. Guests told the history of the girl's family, one after the other. Then the girl's father threw down money and gifts of blankets, mats and deer hides to where the guests stood below them.

My grandparents just could not get into their heads the idea of an international border running through the territory. About the people at Lummi, they said, "But they are family too." The border runs right down the middle of our old territory, right through our family. The government said we would never be stopped going back and forth between the villages. The government said, "The border is for others." Our people believed them because they were not used to dealing with people who seldom kept their word. Nowadays, the government stops my children every time they cross the line.

* ❀ *

School, Work, and Marriage

Coqualeetza

The missionaries came along next, after those years at Devil's Run. Dr. Raley was principal of Coqualeetza Residential School.[1] We were at the hop yards—the Sumas hop-picking camp—in late summer, and my grandmother wasn't well. I remember Dr. Raley coming and speaking to me. He called all the children together and asked us to talk to him. We gathered around him in a circle, but we stood back. Everybody stared at him. Nobody said anything. I was the only one who stepped forward. I must have been quite a sight. I had long braids and a long skirt.

---

1   After some years on the north coast, George H. Raley, Methodist missionary, was posted to Coqualeetza Residential School run by Methodists in Sardis. He was principal from 1914 to 1934. In 1937, he published a monograph on the totem poles in Vancouver's Stanley Park.

I was also very hot and dusty from our play. He asked me, "How old are you, little girl?" I told him I was nine, or eight—I guess I was eight— I don't remember too well. And he says, "Do you go to school?"

"No."

"No?" he said. "Why not?"

"I live with my grandparents," I said.

"You speak well. Can you write your name?"

"Yes, I can." We talked for quite a while.

"Well," he said, "I think it's time you went to school. Would you like to go to school where I go?"

"Yes," I said, "I would."

He told me, "Before I can take you to school, you must be baptized. Kneel down, right here. Have you been baptized before?"

I didn't know. So he had me kneel down, right there, down in the dust! I knelt down and he took something out of his pocket, like a little bottle or something. He sprinkled water on me, and over my head. And so he baptized me into the Methodist Church! I had been baptized a Catholic when I was born, but I didn't know about it when he asked me. My mother was visiting up in Boston Bar with my dad's relatives when the local priest, Father LePine, baptized me a Catholic. Then later on, Dr. Raley baptized me as a Methodist! Ha ha ha. So I was baptized good and proper—twice!

He talked to my Aunt Antonia and they tried to work out how old I was. She told him I was not registered on the reserve and therefore he could not take me to Coqualeetza, since it was only for registered Indians.

He said to my aunt, "And how much can one little Indian girl eat? I want to take her to school anyway because she is bright."

Anyway, Dr. Raley took me to the residential school at Coqualeetza in Sardis. This was in 1934 or '35. I was there for five years. I thought it was a wonderful school. Maybe the reason I loved it was because I had not been raised by my parents. My grandparents had always been very strict. Life was serious business and we were poor. I liked the school. It was so different and I enjoyed learning things.

There must have been a discussion before I went to school. My grandparents did not like the idea. My grandfather was a Catholic and

Coqualeetza was Protestant. My grandmother wanted me to be a well-trained, well-brought-up Indian lady. She did not approve of the white ways. She thought that girls with white education became too loud, outspoken, and rude. She didn't want me to become like that. But Aunt Antonia was younger and she talked her mother into allowing it so that I would fit into the new world. She said, "Look at her! Look how she's dressed. She's so different from all the others. She has to learn she's not part of that old world."

This was all going on in Halq'eméylem, which I understood. My grandmother wept. She cried and cried, but in the end she said, "All right. She can go."

Dr. Raley went around the hop yards baptizing a lot of children. But when I got to Coqualeetza, though, he was no longer there. He had left. It was Reverend Scott who was there instead. He was the new principal. They cut off my braids and confiscated my old-fashioned clothing. We all had the same clothing, the same shoes, and the same haircut. Everything was *very* regimented, but I didn't mind. I had been taught to accept life as it was and not to complain. I learned self-discipline and many things. I had already been taught to meditate as a child and to help myself when I needed help. I spent a lot of time at Coqualeetza reading. I read a lot, I meditated and I prayed a lot. Others found it difficult, but I didn't. I realized there was so much to learn, especially new things like science. It was a world of wonder to learn about the sun, the moon and stars, and the planet Earth. I was like a starving person. I just couldn't learn enough. I stayed after hours in the library so I could read more. Most schools, as you know, have a bookworm, and that was me. I took my studies seriously.

I soaked up the teachings like a sponge. I soaked up everything that was being talked about at the school. Quite often, it was cold and wet on Sundays, and they would herd us into the hall and show us slides. These slide shows were from missionaries and their travels. They were about life in the church's missions in other parts of the world. I was just fascinated, not just by the pictures of these other countries but also that missionary work spoke to my sense of wanting to be useful. I thought it would be a way to help the needy in this world. Most of the missionary operations were in Africa and India, and I decided maybe I could do something to help them out. I don't know why, but I was intrigued, especially by the mission in India. The principal, Mr. R. C. Scott, used to give inspiring talks, and he encouraged the children to go out into the world and spread the word of God.[2]

I was really taken with science. If I had been allowed to go on with my schooling, I would have studied science—but that wasn't to be, and in the meanwhile, there they were, all these poor people in need of saving from savagery and brought to the glory of God. They obviously needed my help, and it was something that seemed much more real than the dream of becoming a scientist. I knew all the teaching techniques and all the Bible stories. I was sure I could be a good missionary, even though I was still only twelve years old.

At the end of my school days, I came out—I guess it was the end of June—and Papa, my grandfather Pete, asked me about what I had learned at school. I told him I was all set to go off to India to help the poor and save their souls. He looked at me for a very long time. He had a kind of funny look on his face. It didn't change. Then he looked me in the eye and said, "Agh, goodness, Rena, you don't have to go all the way to India. There's lots of souls that need saving right here. And lots of poor wretches who could do with your help, here at home, right under your nose, among your own people."

So I never got to be a missionary. I never got to save any of those souls over there in India.

My mother came to Coqualeetza to visit when I had been there for a while. She told the principal that she wanted me to learn to cook and sew and keep house. These were important for my future. She did not want me to learn things that would interfere with being a wife and

2 Robert C. Scott began his mission work in 1913 at Gibson's Landing, British Columbia, among loggers, fisher folk, and Aboriginals. He was later posted to Hazelton, Cape Mudge, and Ocean Falls, where he had a mobile ministry aboard the Methodist ships *Thomas Crosby II* and *IV*, before joining Coqualeetza Residential School in 1933, where he succeeded the Reverend George H. Raley. When Coqualeetza was phased out between 1939 and 1941 and converted to a tuberculosis sanatorium, he became principal of the Port Alberni Residential School. For further information, see http://www.memorybc.ca/robert-clyde-scott-fonds-2;rad.

mother. So I became a good seamstress at school, almost a professional, and I could cook. But despite this, I did not neglect my studies. At the end of five years, I was awarded a prize as "most outstanding student of the year." When I left in 1939, I was still only twelve years old. But that was the end of my formal education. I was "non-status" and could get into no other school. Public schools were not integrated at the time. If I had been white, I could have continued with schooling.[3] My mother said, "You've learned enough to be a wife and mother. You don't need any more schooling. Anything more would just go to your head."

3   State-funded and usually church-run, residential schools were set up for registered "status Indians." When Rena Point Bolton was a child, Aboriginal children of mixed parentage were designated "non-status" and were not generally admitted to such "Indian schools," nor could they easily access the existing public school system.

School days could be sad and lonely at times, and a lot of the girls were very lonely. If there was any child abuse at school, I never saw it. I did, however, see some bad behaviour. There were some very naughty girls who were always getting into trouble. Some of them were strapped or made to stand in the corner during the lessons. Corporal punishment was not against the law in those days. We didn't think it was bad. We grew up with it and it was just part of life. We knew that if we did not do as we were told, we would be punished.

One Haida boy, Claude Davidson, ran away from school.[4] When they caught him and brought him back, they locked him up in a closet. I don't know how long he was locked in. I met him later in life and he told me about it. I thought it was inhuman, a terrible thing to do. I watched boys being strapped for stealing or getting into fights, but I did not see sexual abuse. And I didn't hear about it happening at Coqualeetza at all. Mind you, once the school closed and was converted to a TB sanatorium, the students were moved to Port Alberni, and I have heard bad stories from there.

One of the interesting things I learned at school was that there were so many different kinds of Indians in BC apart from us Xwélmexws or Stó:lōs. We were Haida, Tsimshian, Kwagiulth, Nisga'a, Haisla. I met these children from all over the place, and it sort of formed the way I was to become later. I felt a kinship with them all. I went to school with so many who later became leaders of their communities. We were like a loose network, I guess. This experience brought BC into focus for me as a family of nations and helped much later when I got involved in politics. I wouldn't say we were one people, but we were like a nation of peoples who had suffered a raw deal. All the other eventual leaders who came out of Coqualeetza felt the same way. There were no more tribal boundaries

4 Later in life, Claude Davidson was chief of the Haida Gwaii village of Dadens. He devoted much of his life to Northwest Coast First Nations culture: song, dance, carving, and general art work. His sons, Reg and Robert, are leading Haida artists who carry on the Haida aesthetic path blazed by their father. Ulli Steltzer's beautiful volume, *Indian Artists at Work,* contains portraits of them at work on their carvings (Steltzer 1976, 15–17, 23–25).

to our politics. No one said, "Oh, you're Haida, you're Nisga'a, you're Kwagiulth," etc. We grew up like kindred souls and the cultural barriers came down. We tried to comfort each other later in life when we were busy with Native politics. Lots of leaders went to Coqualeetza: Jimmy Gosnell, Bill McKay, Gordon Robinson.[5]

One thing that was sad for me was the fact that my grandmother died while I was in my first year at school, and they didn't tell me until summer vacation because they knew I would mourn.

During the time that I went to school, I lived at Coqualeetza Residential School in Sardis for ten months a year. Our life was school, meals, and prayers. We would wake up and have to say a prayer, get washed and dressed, and go to morning service for prayers. Then we would pray before eating breakfast, pray before we went to our chores and work, pray after we worked, before lunch, afterwards, before and after our lessons. There was praying before and after almost everything we did. We also fit in some hymn singing, but by then it was bedtime and we were locked in. There was neither place nor time for anything like social life. It was an institution and it turned me into a little adult.

Home for Summer

In the summers, though, my Xwélmexw education continued with Aunt Antonia and with my mother over at Deroche. Mother took me out into the woods and along the riverbanks gathering herbal medicines. She showed me the plants and the barks of the trees to use. When people were sick, she would ask me to go with her—whatever illness they had—and

---

5 From my years living on the northern British Columbia coast, I recognized these men as community leaders. James Gosnell was chief of the Nisga'a Tribal Council and the treaty negotiator for the Nisga'a with the provincial and federal governments. He was later elected president of the Nisga'a Nation. Bill McKay was a Nisga'a hereditary chief, educator, and treaty negotiator, and Gordon Robinson, born in 1918 at Kitamaat Village, Haisla Nation, was a writer, teacher, and cultural worker (who once, when I visited him, gave me fresh oolichans).

she would show me the kind of plant and bark to use. We'd take them home and she'd clean them and scrape them and cut them and boil them. We'd put them in jars or bottles and take them to the sick person. She never accepted money. She said it was wrong to ask for money for helping people who were ill. It was just our job and we had to do it. She learned about herbal medicine from her father, Pete Silva. She was also a midwife who delivered a lot of babies, but she never did introduce me to that work. Maybe because so many babies were born in the middle of the night and it wasn't easy for a child to take part.

She also knew how to prepare bodies for burial, after they had died. She bathed them, cleaned and anointed them. I never took up that calling because the undertakers were starting to take over. Undertaking and taking over—funny words, eh? We often say we are going to plant somebody. What we mean is we are going to a funeral! The old people, when they talked about burying, said that, because they never used to bury people long ago; they put them in death houses—in tombs like—or they put them in the trees, or in canoes, or they burned them, or whatever. But they didn't bury them. And when the white people came and told them that they had to bury their dead bodies, they were a little bit dismayed, because the only thing that you used to put in the ground was when you were planting something. What we called *pí:lt*. That means "to plant." So when they had a burial, they called it a planting!

So I did learn a bit about healing different sicknesses. When I really got into medicines—and I didn't really do it when I was young because I had too much work to do with raising the children—but after I was on my own, I got curious about all these things. So I started studying, trying to remember the things that my mother had taught me. I started using them on different people. Then, as time went on, I really took to Maria Treben, who was Austrian, and she wrote a book called *God's Own Pharmacy*.[6]

6 Originally from a German family living in Czechoslovakia, Maria Treben (1931–92) spent much of her life in Austria. She swore by the effectiveness of "Swedish Bitters," a concoction that dates back to the ancient Greeks but was reformulated, or reconstituted, by Swedish doctors. Rena refers here to Treben's perennially popular *Health Through God's Pharmacy* (1980).

I studied her book for quite a few years. And so I mix the medicines now, the natural medicines from here, from the country, with other medicinal plants that I can buy from the health food stores. I find it works, to make a mixture of medicines. Some of them work well together. So this is what I do now when I am called upon to help anyone who is sick. It took years— it took my whole life to develop what I know now. My early teachings came from my mother, when it comes to the medicines.

I dry a lot of medicines. I did a lot of drying this year. But also, if someone is sick and they need attention and it is summertime, and if the plants are out there, I use fresh ones. Fresh is the best if you can get it. But I do dry a lot of herbs and plants and barks for winter, if people should become ill in the winter. They are not as strong as the fresh, but they do help. I used to have a lot of dry medicines. Now I have gone down to maybe half of what I used to do. For one thing, we just don't have the room.

When you go out to gather, you should never take more than you need, because then it just becomes wasteful because you can't keep them for too long. Like, I try not to keep mine for more than a year or two, and if you take too much, you are just wasting. No, a lot of times when I go out, I don't expect to find anything. Sometimes I am just walking along and I run into some small willow herb, or some other plant I didn't expect to come across, and I'll pick them and give thanks while I am picking them. But if I am going out deliberately, then I ask my spirit guide to help me to find these things. And if and when we find them, then I will leave an offering. If I have nothing at the time, my elders used to tell me, just open a little hole in the ground and spit in it. You are leaving a part of you behind. This is a part of your body, and you are making an offering to help grow . . . It's like giving some of your body energy to help the tree or the ground where you took the plant. But you are giving something of yourself and leaving it behind.

I usually try to carry tobacco or other things that elders seemed to think were good. But there are many times when I come upon some really good medicine and I don't have anything to leave behind. Then I just offer my prayers and spit in a little hole and cover it—so I leave my identity behind. Giving thanks for what I am taking. When I went out to get roots, my elder, Elsie Charlie, told me to cut a little thin root and tie it around my waist.[7] Then I would become connected to the tree. I would become like a child to the tree. When I ask for more roots, she would allow me to have them. When we were ready to leave, afterwards, I would remove the little root from around my waist and bury it, and thank the tree for allowing me to have some of the roots.

We were always taught never to walk into a forest boldly—like, I guess what you do is knock and say, "May I come in?" You always ask to enter the forest. Of course, there are the birds and animals. That's their home and you don't want to disrupt them in any way, unless you are looking for food. You have to let the spirit know you are looking for food. My grandfather used to say, "Before you kill an animal, you always ask them to pray for you when they reach the other side. Tell them you were hungry and had to kill them. Ask them to pray for you on the other side, so that you will have a good life." He used to say, never throw a live fish in the canoe. It is like you being thrown in the water to drown. The salmon drowns in the air. He can't breathe, so it is better to club him on the head and kill him, *then* you throw him in the canoe. So we always did this, we always had a fish club. Clubbed them on the head and then threw them in the canoe. It seemed cruel, but that is what they taught us to do.

There are lots of people opposed to killing animals, but they want their beef in a plastic package from the supermarket. They want their McDonald's—Kentucky Fried Chicken, ha ha. I know! When I see ducks swimming in a pond, I always say they're beautiful, but then I think, ah, duck soup! It's just the Indian in me! Ha ha ha. I don't mean to be disrespectful to it or anything, but it's just food.

I think the training was the same for the boys. In the old way, all the specialty skills—canoe building, carving a house post, making fishing gear, like the girls with weaving and making mats—the learning was done in consultation with the old people. You would ask your grandfather or your uncle. He would be the master, whoever was doing it. Or if it was a different family, then of course, your uncle or grandfather would go and ask if the young person who was very interested could be included.

7   Steltzer (1976, 117) quotes Elsie Charlie as saying: "My mother used to tell the tree she would not waste any of it."

I think most men knew how to whittle, to make a paddle, or even just to make kindling, you know. You had to make fish spreaders and sticks for hanging fish. I mean, everybody had to know how to do these things. But if there was a specialty involved, if a family owned that specialty or took care of it or whatever, then you'd have to approach them to do that specific thing, to apprentice, like.

We had what you would call hands-on learning—one to one. There were no textbooks, no writing, no lectures. You learned as you did things with your hands. You watched others and then you were told to start doing it yourself. Older persons said, "Just do it and I will watch you." They watched and made sure that you learned to do it right. It was very different from learning with pencil and paper. For me, learning to do things was part of learning how to behave in general. They taught me to wait on my elders, be responsible, considerate, and helpful. If Grandmother was busy sewing, I would sit in the corner and thread needles for her or fetch things she needed. I was always helping, working, and seldom playing.

Uncle Ambrose and Auntie Jean

The first summer, I came out of school for the holidays and they told me my grandmother was gone. She had passed away while I was at school. So I had a very abrupt change facing me. My Uncle Ambrose's wife, Auntie Jean, had already taken over responsibility in our home before grandmother passed away. Things were no longer the same. But you know, children always learn from what goes on around them. I suppose I went on learning Stó:lō ways just by living, especially in those summer months when school was out. Oh, I don't think I mentioned Ambrose Silver's children, did I? His children with Auntie Jean? Their children were Ray, and Dalton, and David, and Alec, and Herman, Yvonne, Frieda, Mona, Diane . . . now what was that youngest daughter's name? Auntie Jean had a lot of children. Beatrice! Beatrice and Ike. I don't know what his full name was, Isaac or Ike. Those were the children of Ambrose with Mary Jean Shaw.

Then the youngest sister of my mother was Charlotte. She had one child and that was June. June is still living. She lives in Washington State. I don't want her to think that I have left her out deliberately. June Boome is her name now. She married into the Skagit Tribe. I think that's all. I've mentioned my mother's second family, my father's second family. They were children of my mother's brother and sister, Ambrose and Charlotte. But they are all from Kilgard even if they don't live there. The girls all had to leave and marry and move to where their husbands were from. The only one who's left at Kilgard now is Ray. His brother Herman married one of the Kelly girls. So they have family there. The rest are all gone, very few of the Silvas and Silvers are left there. Alec's dead, Herman's dead, only Ray is left. Dalton died when he was little. The girls are still living.

Canneries

When I got out of school, it was still the end of the Depression. When I was fourteen [1941], the war was on and I started working in the canneries at Steveston, just as my mother had done up at Port Essington. After my grandmother died, Grandfather Pete wanted us to learn to work. First, he went out and asked various Japanese farmers if they needed help. He said he was doing this to give us work experience—planting and harvesting and, in the fall, picking hops. When I look back on it, it was not hard work, but it kept us perpetually busy. We were too busy to get into any kind of trouble!

But in general, when I was young, I didn't know much about having fun. Of course those were the war years as well—World War II—and they were serious times. And there weren't many young people around, just children and the elderly. I became old at fourteen. One season, though, we went berry picking outside Seattle, on Bainbridge Island. We used to go into Seattle and see a movie on Saturday nights and then rush to get the last ferry back to the island. That was the high point.

I was looking for cannery work, and suddenly, there were vacancies. I guess it was because the government had removed all the Japanese

Canadians on account of the war against Japan.[8] My cousin and I found work at a cannery. It was at the end of cannery row down in Steveston [on the Fraser River estuary], at Great West Cannery. Our first job was on a herring production line. We had to place each herring headfirst in a little moving trough so they could go through a machine to have the heads trimmed off. We filled these grooves with herring all day long. I enjoyed it—mainly, I guess, because it was the first real job I had where I got regular pay.

After we'd done the supper dishes for the older ladies, my cousin and I would go for walks along the boardwalk. We noticed all these empty houses. They had belonged to the Japanese who had been taken off to concentration camps. They were allowed to take only a few things with them. I felt so bad when I saw all the stuff they left behind. We went into some of these empty houses—we didn't take anything but we were curious. They were neat and tidy. They were very clean. I remember the porcelain dolls, little Japanese dolls about six inches high on the windowsills. We didn't touch anything, but it made us feel so sad.

While I was still at school, Grandfather had taken us over to Mission on the other side of the Fraser River where we would pick berries for the farmers. I remember on one farm, we lived with a Japanese family, Mama-san and Papa-san. They were very clean and very kind people. They had us use their wooden bathing tubs in a bathhouse. It was very different. First, you went into a room and washed your body with soap and water and rinsed all that away; then you could enter the wooden bathtub. They had a son called Tadoshi. He was the one who cracked the whip and got us to work. I must have been twelve or thirteen.

So we saw these empty houses that looked like somebody lived there and had been called away for a few minutes. There were sewing machines, beds, and chairs and tables. We wanted to know why they

8 After the bombing of the US naval base at Pearl Harbor in December 1941, both Canada and the United States interned (that is, imprisoned) Japanese immigrants and naturalized Japanese Canadians and Japanese Americans in camps located well away from the Pacific Coast. For the most part, however, nationals from the other Axis powers—Italians and Germans—were not consigned to camps.

were being treated so mean. Even after the war, they were not allowed to return within a hundred miles of the Pacific Ocean. Their old homeland had been bombed by the world's first atomic bombs, and many, many got burned and killed. The Germans, who were also our enemies during the war, they could just go free wherever they wanted. They were allowed to. After the war, Canada welcomed a lot of German immigrants without any restriction. It was different for the Japanese. There were restrictions because they were not Europeans. It still doesn't seem fair to me.

I worked down there at other canneries in Steveston for about three years. Three winters. I had to learn to live alone, and I remember I got real hungry. I didn't know how to save and I would run out of food. I remember coming home one night, so hungry! And as I walked down the boardwalk, I saw a big potato, just sitting there on one of the cracks of the boardwalk, smiling at me. I was so happy. In fact, I have never been as happy to see a potato ever in my life, not before and not after! I took that potato home; I washed it, scrubbed it, and cooked it. After that, I learned to be frugal. And I admit it. I am still very frugal. Everybody teases me that I might have a big dollop of Scottish blood in me that controls what I do.

We had lots of learning by doing as we were growing up. As I said, I picked up weaving and basket making and doing salmon for the winter. And learning to do women's work was another example, and canoe racing too.

By the time I reached puberty, my grandmother had died. Grandfather Pete talked to my mother. They decided to send me to an aunt at Deming, across the border, where I learned the domestic side of being a woman.[9] I was there for a whole month, learning how to behave as a

9 Ethnographer Bernhard Stern, author of *The Lummi Indians of Northwest Washington,* had lived in the Lummi community near where Rena was sent for the domestic side of puberty training. His book came out around the same time Rena was being inducted into womanhood, but Stern describes earlier practices explained to him by elders of the day:

   After the puberty ceremony, the girl is again secluded until arrangements are made for her marriage. During this seclusion, she is instructed in the

woman. I think I was thirteen years old. I had to get up early, make the fire, cook breakfast, do the laundry—fetch the water, heat it on the stove, fill the washtub, scrub the clothes with a washboard, and hang them out to dry. I had to wash the floors and clean the outhouse. I had to empty the wood stove and the heater and use the ashes for the outhouse toilet. Then I learned to bake and roast and boil and fry. I made jam and jelly and learned to put up preserves.

My aunt was very strict. It was thirty days of very hard labour. Then, at the end of it all, the women of Deming and Nooksack took me out to celebrate by picking berries up on Mount Baker. We picked buckets and buckets of blueberries. It was beautiful up there, and it was so joyful. There was joking and laughing as we mashed the berries with sugar. "You sit down and rest," they said. "You've earned it. We will wait on you." So we had a blueberry feast. Fried bread and mashed blueberries. They pronounced me a good girl who would make a good wife. My aunt took me home in an old Model T Ford. Everybody was happy, in good spirits and saying I had done a good job, and that now I was a woman. They said I had to reach marriage age without causing any problems, so after this, I was now chaperoned and watched.

In those days, when you had your first menstruation, they put up a screen and screened off a corner of the room in the house. I stayed in there. Papa, Grandfather Pete, had talked to my mother. She came to be with me and he got her to give him the first blood. He was a healer and he did something, some ritual, to ensure I would have many children and be strong and a good hereditary carrier of our culture and so that I would not fall down on the job. I don't know what he did.

---

various details of motherhood and infant care, by an old woman who is paid for these services. She is told to be patient in case of poverty, to endure cruelty on the part of her husband, to take married life for better or for worse. She is taught weaving and basketry and other women's skills so that even if her husband is never at home, she will be happy because she has her work to do. The seclusion of the girl, occasionally lasts as long as two years during which time she never leaves the house except to bathe in the evening when she cannot be seen. (Stern [1934] 1969, 26)

Marriage and Family

When I was sixteen, my mother said it was time for me to marry. The elders of the area got together to decide who I would marry. They included Mr. and Mrs. Dan Milo and Mrs. Julius Malloway. In addition, Mrs. Raymond Fernandez represented Musqueam and Mrs. Amelia Lewis represented Lummi. This was my first marriage meeting, called together by Grandfather Pete Silva. There were two candidates from Lummi, and there was Roy Point, Dan Milo's wife's grandson. Roy and I were both in the house, but we did not know each other very well.

Dan Milo offered the most. He decided he would give us the farm and the house and everything. In this way, I would have a home. The two from Lummi hadn't settled down yet. They were Amelia's relatives, and she was Frank Hilaire's daughter. So she was a relative of mine. Roy and I were fourth cousins. That was considered distant enough. And since he was descended from Charlie Point, it was considered a good match. Charlie Point had been raised by my great-grandmother, Th'etsimiya, Mrs. Vedder.

FIGURE 12
Rena and Roy Point with their first child, Tim, at Skowkale, ca. 1945.
Photo courtesy of Rena Point Bolton.

Roy was chosen to be my husband. His father was from Musqueam, and his mother, from Matsqui. Her name was Mary Edwin. She was the daughter of Agnes Edwin, and Agnes's husband was just known as Edwin. Mary Edwin married Abram Point of Musqueam. They had only one child, Roy. When Roy's parents died, his father's mother, Mrs. Charlie Point, raised him. But then she—who was also known as Emily Coutts—married Sí:yá:m Kwíkwetl'em, Chief Coquitlam, and moved to Coquitlam. When that happened, Roy was taken in by his mother's mother, Mrs. Dan Milo, at Skowkale, where Dan Milo adopted him.

They got the priest, Father Campbell, to come out and meet us. He set the date to marry us on his next visit. I think it was in April. It was 1944. I was terrified, because now the wedding was set. We got married. Roy was a logger and was usually away at logging camps. I was home at the farm with the children. We had kids almost every other year. In addition, I looked after a total of sixteen foster children on the farm, too. They fit right in and did their share of the work around our little farm.

I don't feel the need to go into the details of our marriage except to say that Roy was usually away working in logging camps around the Fraser Valley, up around Harrison Lake and down in Washington State around Mount Baker—many places. I saw very little of him. He helped out whenever he could. For the most part, we lived on the Milo farm, with the Dan Milos. Dan lived to be 99, and Mrs. Milo went on to 103.

FIGURE 13
Rena's "grandmother-in-law," Mrs. Dan Milo, outside her home at Skowkale, shortly before her death, at the age of 103. Photo courtesy of Rena Point Bolton.

I spent a lot of time alone with my children. The Human Resources Department asked me to take in foster children. I took in quite a few and I got along with them very well. I gave them support and encouragement, and they worked for me as extra hands on the farm. I couldn't afford to pay them, but we all got along somehow. I remember making a wedding dress for one of them.

My ten children all had their chores to do to make sure the farm ran well. Tim was in charge of the milk cows. Jeffrey was responsible for the pigs, Mark the white-faced beef cattle, and Steven the chickens and the eggs. Brian was just a wee fellow, and he didn't have the same responsibilities. The girls all had to help with cleaning and washing and cooking and canning, putting up fish, basket weaving. The children all married young and started families of their own. Some really went in for education, and others weren't interested. They all took their different roads in life.

Suddenly, the family was grown, and today, even my grandchildren are having grandchildren! At that time, since Roy and I had been living mostly separate from one another anyway, we decided to separate, divorce. By then, I was up to the ears busy with the promotion work for the arts and crafts of our people. I really felt deeply that if we lost our arts and crafts and languages, then we would only be poor carbon copies of white people. This work was at the top of my agenda in the late sixties and early seventies, and since the children were gone and busy having their own families, Roy and I decided to separate permanently. I will say that throughout this period, I followed the teachings of my elders.

Child Rearing

In the old times, our grandparents raised the children, passed on knowledge, and made a lot of the local decisions. Younger adults, our parents, were out doing the heavy work on the river and in the forest, fishing and logging, and before that, putting up various foodstuffs for winter time. But time doesn't stand still. The generations roll on. That all changed when I was having children, and it has changed again since then.

I tell you, things were different when I was raising my children. We were running a farm, and I sometimes had to be The Enforcer! Once, when Wendy was a year old, I asked Charlotte and Steven to take care of her and not play on the other side of the road because she would want to cross over and follow them. A while later, I heard the screech of car brakes. I went running out to see what had happened. Wendy had come darting out of the tall grass and had run into the road. Steven and Charlotte were across the road, playing down in the creek. They'd forgotten all about their little sister, and so she was running to join them. The driver had got out, all pale and shaking. He was really upset. I called the children up from the creek. They had cut themselves some willow sticks. I said, "Come here, both of you, and bring your sticks." They came up to me and I switched them on their bare legs. That is the only time I ever hit them, and they still remember it to this day.

Today, nobody can tell anyone what the right way is to do something. Any kind of punishment is a foreign idea. I raised ten children by myself. If they disobeyed, they were punished and they had to apologize. I worked together with the teachers and tried to find out if they misbehaved at school. This was the same discipline I was raised with. Today, children are out of control, even though parents only have two or three these days. Still, they can't control them or teach them to behave.

These days, there is the problem of drugs, too. And if you don't have a dynamic relationship with your kids, they can very well fall by the wayside. I see this as a result of the loss of respect, all around. There is now too much emphasis on money as the solution to all problems. Parents give their children too much and do not encourage them to do more for themselves. They don't encourage them to earn money and do things under their own steam. Some even go out and look for easy street, the easy road to money, selling drugs, for example. They abuse their own bodies and their souls, just to get what they want. I really do not understand anything any longer.

When I was raising children, I had so very little to give: a cup of cocoa or an apple. That was all. The children would work in the summers and get two dollars a day. They worked for what they needed. Today, kids seem to be rootless. And they don't eat proper food. The early behaviour that children are encouraged to develop teaches them an attitude toward life—toward people, animals, and the whole environment. This early behaviour can be good or not so good, but it stays with you for life unless there is a big effort to change it. For example, our family learned always to ask permission of the Creator before going into the forest, or into the mountains where they bathe as part of the *mi'lha* training, or if they are going to get medicines or food. It was just part of the training, of being respectful to all the living spirits around us.

I think when you have children, you can't wait until they are a certain age before you start teaching them who they are. You have to start teaching them as soon as they're born. You carry on through your lifetime, setting the example of never forgetting who you are and teaching them the old ways, the traditional beliefs. And the trainings, of always doing what you are told without question. Of course, you have a right to think what you want, but you do not display that. It could create embarrassment for your elders, and that is something that is simply not done in our culture. As well, they must always honour their elders and serve them obediently. This will show how great a person they are—in the long run—that they have always done the right thing.

Sometimes, it's difficult. It might be humiliating, but these are things you have to learn. It helps your character grow when you're tested and you are made to do things that you might not want to do—but when an elder sees that you are a good person, and not a troublemaker, then they will trust you and help you through your lifetime by giving you advice and encouraging you. But if they see that you are stubborn and hard to handle and that you are disobedient and you answer back, then they won't waste their time on you. You will then probably go through life never knowing how to behave properly, saying and doing the wrong things to other people—both in public and at home.

So I tried very hard to raise my children—right from when they were little—always to be ready to help, always to be pleasant, never to be angry all the time. I tried to train them to be willing to help others as well, outside the home—people who needed help. I would always tell them, "When you are at home, you are Stó:lō, you are Native, Indian, Xwélmexw. When you leave the home, you might have to put on a different face and go to school so that you get along with the white children and the teachers. You have to do what they ask you to do, but when you come home, you remove all of that, and you are just a Native child again, obedient and subservient to your mother and other elders who may be around. When you are told to do a job, you do it without complaint. The sooner you start it, the sooner you are finished."

This becomes a habit with children. If you make sure they are doing what they are told—if you stand there and make sure they do it, instead of just giving it lip service, then they become used to it. They do what they are told, in jobs, self-discipline, or whatever it is. They will do it and it becomes a habit throughout life, the early teachings that you give to them. If they are allowed to slough off and be lazy, to become a backbiter and gossiper—and you allow them to do that, then this also becomes a habit and they think that this is the normal way to live. But if you correct them and let them know these are not nice things to do—and of course, you must not do them yourself—then, if you've done all that, they realize as they grow up that they just don't do those backward kinds of things. It's not proper. Whenever they would want anything, I would tell them that they had to earn it, to do extra work or go out and work for whatever they wanted. They must not expect to be given everything. And of course, they were not allowed to take anything that wasn't theirs.

I don't think they were perfect. They had normal growing pains like anyone else. But the early teaching, and me being at home every day to watch over them, it had an effect.

Down through the years, I have tried to pass along the feelings of responsibility that were put on my own shoulders when I was a child. It hasn't been easy. We had to break trails into a lot of new territory. The white society didn't accept us interfering, or helping or handling our own people. There were times when we came upon officials who felt we were interfering. And yet there were also times when they came to us to get support or help, like with the teenaged foster children. Human Resources didn't know where to place them. They used my home as a halfway house until they were able to place them.

So we worked openly with different government offices. Today, I have retired, as much as I can, from all of this, although my family is still involved a lot in it. I think the younger people—the teachings they receive in the smokehouse [mí'lha híkw'lalém], associated with the winter dancing, with learning to live well and to help other people, to feed them if they are hungry, to shelter them if they have no shelter—in this way, the teachings are being carried on.

When you learn these things, respect comes automatically with everything that I just told you. You have to instill these things in them early in life. They must do what they are told, and they must honour the person who is telling them what to do. In the end, all of these things boil down to respect, and as well, they get praised for the things that they do, after a job is well done. Of course, they don't know they are building self-respect as they learn to respect others in what they are learning at home. It isn't until they grow up that they realize they do respect other people, because of how they treat them, how they behave with them. If elders scold them, they feel embarrassed.

The old people used to say, "Never work when you are upset, when you are angry or when you are sick, because you don't put forth your best job." So I still follow that rule, because when you do a poor job, you kind of lose respect for yourself, thinking, oh, no, I should never have done that. I wasn't feeling well and it shows. And again, this shows up when you have to take the initiative when you go out into the woods, when you take the children, when you take them out, you show them and tell them about the land, about the trees and the animals, and how they are to behave toward them. Never, ever cut anything down unnecessarily. I used to take them fishing and I would tell them about the fish, how they came up the river to spawn, how they had the little fishes that hatched from eggs, how we'd watch them and let them go so that they could grow and come back again and feed the people. This is what the Creator expected them to do. My oldest son, Tim, for many years, he took care of the hatchery, and when the fish went out, he would say goodbye to them. These were his babies.

And I'd take them out when I went digging roots for basket weaving and peeling bark, and show them how they were only allowed to peel so much off a tree. How we mustn't harm the trees and how the trees, too, had spirits. Everything else does, too: the little frogs that we might step on—they have a right to live, too. Everything deserves respect. They understand all of these things when they are little. It just depends on your manner, how you are behaving with these things. If you speak ill of them, then this is the message they get. So you must be careful how you speak to animals, to small children, and to everybody else, to the environment—how you don't litter the place, throw garbage all over, and so on. They follow your behaviour and parents don't seem to realize this. They dump stuff out their car windows and then they expect their kids to respect the environment?

And I always tell them, before you go into a forest, you ask permission. This is where the trees live. You don't go wading in there and start hacking away or doing things in the woods you wouldn't do at home. Well, the forest is where the trees and the animals live. It's their home. And so, to this day, when they go up into the mountains to bathe, they always ask permission and talk to the spirits that live in the mountains. They go swimming up there every day when they are in the longhouse [when involved in the spirit dancing] in the winter months. They are very close to nature.

I took time out, many, many times, to tell them stories about the woods, the little animals, the birds . . .

Another almost automatic part of upbringing is sharing. We shared almost everything. It's a wonderful feeling when you have something good to eat and you can share it with the rest of the family. We divide everything up and go house to house with things we can give to others. It's the big *sí:yá:m* who can share whatever he has, whether it is fish or meat or berries—any little thing whatsoever. He can take it door to door and share his wealth. If he can do this, he is considered a very rich man, and a good man, or woman. That was one of the big things that our people did. They enjoyed sharing. It was a satisfying part of being a *sí:yá:m*, to be able to give and share. That was more important than having a lot of things that others didn't have.

Taking care of people who were not strong enough or well enough to take care of themselves—that was a good feeling. So the strong people took care of them. I did a little writing on this. I wrote that it was the big man who shared, and the man who was stingy and kept things hidden for himself and his family, he was looked down upon as being *ts'a:s*—poor and pitiful, and other people felt sorry for him because he was not a big man. He was poor in spirit. I wrote this for the Gitxsan students, for a speech when they graduated years and years ago. I still have that speech here somewhere. In their language, the same thing is called being *gwa'ay*. You're small and *gwa'ay* if you are not generous with what you have.

A man or a woman who hoarded stuff, they were considered to be very *ts'a:s*. If you shared what little you had, you showed you had an open heart, but if you had a little bit and you hid it for yourself, then you were really poor. You were pitiful, because what it boils down to is this: you are so unsure of yourself that you do not believe that the Great Spirit will take care of you. You don't trust that the spirit world and the world around you will provide, so you hide things and hoard them. This makes you *ts'a:s*. You're insecure, I guess that's the word. If you're insecure, you become like a pitiful person. It's kind of hard unless you understand the culture. It's different from the modern culture. In the modern culture, security is the individual having a lot of money in the bank and piles of stuff.

FIGURE 14

The children of Rena and Roy Point. In the top row are Mark, Brian, Steven, Jeffrey, and Tim, and in the bottom are Gail, Sheila, Wendy, Charlotte, and Rena. Photo courtesy of Rena Point Bolton.

I guess in the old days, food was so plentiful, it never dawned on you to hoard anything. You just kept what you needed. But of course, for winter supplies, you had to put up your winter food, but you also helped everybody else to make sure they had ample winter supplies, too. So it was up to the *sí:yá:m* to make sure that everybody had enough for the winter.

As far as the children are concerned, well, whatever they have done in life, they have done by themselves. I stood on the sidelines and did my best to support them. If they got too much off the track and bogged down, I tried to steer them back on track, but that's not easy, of course. They're a good bunch, but they certainly weren't angels.

Tim, my oldest, followed his father's footsteps into logging. He married and had two sons, and another son from a different marriage. He went on working in the woods until he had an accident and smashed his ankle. That put an end to his years in the bush. He was born in 1945, so he's getting on in years now. He stays around home and helps Jeffrey run the smokehouse and keep tabs on the rest of the family. He helps keep things together. He also ran the fish hatchery at Skowkale.

FIGURE 15
Rena's son Mark, wearing a Salish robe that his mother made when he graduated with a master's in education. The photograph was taken at the University of British Columbia's First Nations House of Learning. Photo courtesy of Rena Point Bolton.

My next, Jeffrey, trained as a cook. He learned to be a chef at the army camp. He was a good cook, but he eventually got married and went into carpentry. He stayed at it until he fell off a roof. He's in his sixties too, and retired. He is very busy conducting affairs in the smokehouse at Skowkale.

Mark finished school and took business management at Simon Fraser University. He worked for a while for Manpower, and for different bands, too. Oh, he's worked everywhere. He is a teacher now. He went back to his studies and took a Master's of Education at the University of British Columbia, and he'll soon have his doctorate in education. He's been teaching many years now. He was principal at Seabird Island School and the vice-president in the School District of Agassiz and Hope. Now he has switched to working at Coquitlam, and when he's down there, he is helping them with canoe building and bringing back old ways, because the people there have lost so much of their culture.

FIGURE 16

Rena and Steven on the occasion of his graduation from law school, outside the Faculty of Law at the University of British Columbia. Photo courtesy of Rena Point Bolton.

Steven, as you know, went to law school and practiced law and got involved in local politics and social things around Skowkale. Later, he was appointed as a judge and worked up here in the north. He taught Aboriginal law in Saskatchewan and looked into those Prairie peoples' indigenous issues. He taught Native law at UBC too, about the Indian Act. His students were mostly Native law students.

My youngest boy, Brian, was a chef in a restaurant, and now he works on cultural programs for the Abbotsford School Board. He used to work with programs for young offenders. The mother of his son is a descendant of a well-known Nisga'a family, the Calders at Greenville on the Nass River. She's the grand-niece of Frank Calder. Frank was the first Native who got elected as a member of the legislative assembly in Victoria.[10]

My daughter Wendy went to Simon Fraser University and took a degree in Native studies. She specializes in teaching Halq'eméylem. Gail went to school for years and years, and she has much experience managing and operating child care programs. Rena works for the Stó:lō Nation and is busy being a grandmother. I think you would call her a cultural consultant. She gives advice and she helps the sick with herbal medicines. I lost my youngest daughter, and her death has left a lot of questions. She was troubled but had planned to be a marine biologist. Charlotte married Jerry Wesley here at Kitsumkalum and lived up here.

10 Frank Calder (1915–2006), a Nisga'a chief, House of Wisinxbiltkw, Gispud-wada/Gisgaast Killer Whale Clan, was the first First Nations person elected to a provincial legislature in Canada. He represented Atlin, British Columbia, from 1949 to 1979. In 1972, he was BC's first minister of Aboriginal Affairs. His case on behalf of the Nisga'a (Calder et al. v. the Attorney-General of British Columbia [1973] S.C.R. 313) established the legal recognition of Aboriginal title in Canada and was one of the first of the present-day round of Aboriginal title cases before the Canadian courts. I recall watching as Frank Calder accepted a beer on board my father's troller at Namu in the 1950s and then invited the local RCMP officer to arrest both him (he was already a member of the legislative assembly) and his host for violating the Criminal Code—the act of supplying alcohol to "Indians" was as illegal as supplying it to children. The police officer did not rise to the bait. He smiled and walked away.

Now they are divorced and she is back down south working as a teaching assistant in Sardis. She was deeply involved in caring for the deaf, for the hearing impaired, but then she suffered a burnout. All of my girls are the motherly type and I am proud of them. And the boys' wives are helpful and supportive women, too.

It seems very strange to me, but my own children are getting white hair and turning into grandparents. I have many grandchildren, and now my children do, too! They all married young and raised families. They have also been very hard workers.

I used to wonder why my grandmother was so strict with me, and my grandfather was, too. I wasn't allowed to play with the other children. I was isolated most of the time. They kept me away from other families a lot because they didn't want me to be any kind of example that wasn't right for my upbringing. So I was alone a lot. I thought a lot. I thought a lot about everything. I wondered why I was having such a strict upbringing, and why I had to learn so many things. As time went by, I stopped thinking about it, and I was busy learning, you know—academic things—and fitting into the white society, learning about Christianity, about the Bible and everything else that the modern society demanded of us, and the fact that we had to throw all our ancient ways away because they were looked down upon.

At that time, I really didn't care about the old teaching. It was just something that had happened in the past. It was part of the knowledge I had, but I didn't see how it was going to fit in anywhere in my adult life. I guess I almost forgot about it. I put it aside. I worked in a hospital for a while, in the tuberculosis hospital at Coqualeetza. I learned the value of sanitation—or at least, that's what we were told, being clean—and I worked with the dietician for a while. I worked in the kitchen and I worked with the patients, so germs were a great fear. So with this background, I was always on top of everything with my children. I made sure that they ate properly and that they had rest, and they had to be obedient. They had a stiff training, almost like I had myself when I was at school.

Canoe Racing

I had children already when I joined the canoe racing. I must have been close to thirty, I guess. I can't really say, but I did have three or four little ones at that time. I was raised in a canoe, up and down the Fraser, when we were living at Devil's Run in the smokehouse. The only way of transportation, the only means, was the canoe. So the canoe was just a vehicle to me. When they started picking up the canoe racing in Chilliwack, the Mussel family, who were distant relatives of my grandmother, they asked me if I would like to train, to try out, as they called it—they try out a lot of pullers, but they pick only a few. So I tried out and I was chosen. I raced with them on a canoe called the *Golden Arrow*. It was owned by Jones Mussel and family.

But it just became too much. I had to garden and do a lot of other work on the little farm. It was just too much, so I quit. And then the boys, as they grew older, they started training on a canoe called the *Chinook*, which was owned by Burns Mussel. Later on, I think they trained with the Jimmy boys from Sx̱woychá:lá [Squiala Village]. So it's just grown from there—Mark started making his own traditional canoes. He's been building canoes for most of his life now.

FIGURE 17

Dugout canoes created by Mark Point and Cliff Bolton from red cedar logs: a Salish canoe, on the left, and, on the right, a North Coast canoe. Rena's son Mark learned the Salish tradition of canoe building and later combined his skills with those Cliff Bolton. As a team, they built canoes in both Tsimshian and Salish styles. Photo courtesy of Rena Point Bolton.

The kids were always in canoes. They went out on the river setting the net, picking up the net, checking it, you know, for salmon. So they were always in a canoe, and with their dad when he was at home. And as they grew old enough, they were in a canoe by themselves. They knew how to handle the canoe on the Fraser River.

And I think as far as canoe building is concerned, Mark inherited the genes—because we had canoe builders in our family. Jacob Milo was the last canoe builder in Sardis, from around the Skowkale area. And my grandfather built canoes too, although it wasn't something he did for a living or anything. He did understand the making of a canoe. He used to make a lot of paddles. And whenever the canoes needed repairing, my grandfather did it. That was Pete Silva. Canoes were just part of our daily lives. We never thought anything extraordinary about them. They were like having a car today, ha ha!

When I was training, it was under Mr. and Mrs. Jones Mussel at Chilliwack Landing, at Skwah [Sqwehá] Reserve. They were the elders, the parents of all the Mussel family. As I said, they owned a canoe called the *Golden Arrow*. This must have been . . . probably in the early sixties, I would say—late fifties and early sixties. I trained under them for six years, and they were still carrying on with a lot of the old training. Mrs. Mussel, the elderly woman, she did all of the cooking. She wouldn't allow us to eat a lot of heavy foods. She didn't allow us to eat pastries. We ate a lot of fish and fish soup.

We had to go to bed early when we were in training; when we were actually attending canoe races, we had two huge tents. One tent was for the girls and the other tent was for the boys. And she would sleep with us in the girls' tent, right at the door, and we couldn't go out anywhere after a certain time. Then, at five in the morning, she'd get us up and we'd have to go out on the water and train. We'd have to pull maybe two miles or so, and then we'd come in and she'd have breakfast ready for us. We were not allowed to mingle with other people, to have much conversation. We weren't allowed to eat sweets or drink pop. I can't remember all the "dos" and "don'ts"—it was so long ago, but we were watched very closely. We couldn't wander all over the campgrounds. We had to stay very close to the tent, and before the actual canoe race, she would make us lie down and rest for a while. Totally relax. We weren't allowed to eat anything before the race. Then, when it was time to go down to the water, we would carry the canoe down, each one of us helping. We weren't allowed to talk to anyone or have anything to do with anybody else. We just put the canoe in. Mr. Mussel would stand there and give the captain instructions. And that was it. We entered the water then. We didn't win every race, but we did win a few—in Lummi, at Cultus Lake, and over on the Island, in Victoria. Gosh, I can't remember.

There are eleven pullers, yes; well, for the girls there were ten pullers and then the captain. Then, with the boys racing it was eleven [pullers] —they call it "eleven-man." The captain calls the stroke, and he counts, and then we switch. He'd count so many strokes and then we'd switch sides paddling. His instructions were mostly in our language, and which way the canoe was going to turn, he'd call that out to the "strokes person." That's what they call the one at the front, isn't it? Yes. I don't remember the words. It was men's language anyway. So all I can seem to remember is that we were watched very closely. We weren't allowed to mingle or to go out at night. The Mussel family used to race from Hope—I don't know how far—down the Fraser River. They were very powerful pullers. The Mussels, the Williamses, and the Jameses. They were the really heavy-duty canoe pullers. Then they would end up back at Hope, at the finish line. I remember going up to Hope and watching the canoes coming back up the Fraser River against that rushing current, and back up to the bridge. That's where they started and that's where they finished. That was years ago. I don't remember when. Those were the old canoe pullers.

Lehál

You asked me about "lehál." I'm no expert, but my kids play it. They say *slehá:l* or *lehál*. It all depends on who's saying it. They have two teams facing each other. They used to, in the old days, have a board in between and they would all have sticks with which to hit the board, what we called *q'ewétem*. Then they would have one or two drummers who would lead the singing. I don't see them with that anymore. They don't have the big boards. They just have the drum. And usually it was one tribe against another or one village against another—or if it was just for fun, one family against another, or men against women. It can be anything, you know, anybody. Sometimes, the betting would get really heavy and a lot of money would be involved. Other times, it was just for fun. But they have—how many sticks? Yes, eleven sticks. And they have king sticks. No, one king and another a little bit smaller than the others. I don't know what they call them. If Mark was here, he could tell you what their names are. Anyway, there's about eleven or twelve sticks on each side. Then they have two sets of bones, one plain white bone and one with a black circle around it, a mark. They have two sets of those.

The side that has the bones, they have two people shaking the bones and hiding them, and the opposite side has to guess which is the white one—that is, which hand is holding the unmarked one. And if they guess right, they get the bones, and a stick. And if they guess wrong, they lose a stick. So they could lose two sticks if both bone shakers . . . you know, if they guess wrong. With two bone shakers, they could lose two sticks if they are wrong. If they guess them wrong—it's hard to explain. But if each team member who is a bone shaker doesn't know what the other one—which hand his partner is hiding it in—and the other side guesses, then they could get both sets of bones instead of just one. The sticks are all in front of them. The object is to win all the sticks. But I forget what you do with the king sticks.

There's usually a lot of taunting, and some women try to distract the men on the other side by flirting. Sometimes, they get carried away a little. It makes it real funny. Everybody starts laughing, you know. But the object is to divert the opponents' attention and to win all the sticks from the other side, from your opponents. If you win them all, you win the pot. I guess in the old days, they used to get so carried away they'd lose their canoes, a lot of their belongings. They could lose their meat, if they had dried meat or whatever. I heard say that some men lost their wives, but whether that's true or not, I don't know. Maybe that's just a joke. People played everywhere. On the Plains, they would lose their horses. All the Native people play versions of this game, all over the place. It could be very high stakes, you know.[11] A man could lose everything he owns—if he was a gambler—maybe even his wife and children!

11 For an example of *lehál* played at gatherings in the Chilcotin region of British Columbia, see the video *Lahal: A Close Look at the Bone Game* (http://www. youtube.com/watch?v=_BBHge8wzRO, accessed August 22, 2013). The game as it is played there is very similar to the game played in the Coast Salish area.

* ❀ *

Life of the Spirit

Syúwel

As I said, I went to the Methodist residential school at Coqualeetza, and a lot of what I learned was Christian. I learned to love the Christian faith and I love to sing hymns. I used to sing in the choir at school. To this day, as I sit here and work, I sing "The Old Rugged Cross" and all the other old favourites from my childhood. They became part of my nature. As the kids grew up, I took them to Sunday school, and at the Catholic Church, they became altar boys and we all attended church. The church played a big part in our lives.

But then, after ten children, my health began to fail. I talked to the priests about trying to have surgery done so that I would not have any more children. But the priests refused to talk about it. I told them the doctor said my life was threatened. They said that only God knew when I was going to die. They said the doctors had no right to tell me I risked dying if I had more children. It was in God's hands. They refused to allow me to have surgery that could save my life. It was like the old mushroom story, the way the churches used to treat the Indians . . . You want me to spell it out? Well, the mushroom story is keeping them in the dark and feeding them . . . well, to put it politely, horse manure!

Well, I did what I had to do. I went ahead and got the surgery done. The doctor said to me, "The church means well and I know how strong your faith is, but the church won't raise your children if you die. They'll probably put them in foster homes. And if you survive and are seriously ill, you will not be able to raise and care for them as you would like."

This hit me very hard. I went ahead and had them do the surgery. I had to go to confession eventually. When they found out what I had done, I was refused the sacrament. I was excommunicated. The children were growing up now, and some of them were already married. They became very upset and angry because I had practically run the local church single-handedly, our little St. Theresa's. The children and I kept the church clean. We raised funds to buy oil for the heater, and we did a lot of church work. We even kept the priest. We fed him whenever he came on his trips to our village. We always had him over for dinner, and we looked after him on all those visits. When the children saw the way the church had treated me, they all quit going to church.

About this time, my son Jeffrey started to get seizures, and we didn't know what was wrong with him. We took him to the doctors and they couldn't find anything wrong. They checked his brain, did X-rays and everything. So James Point, one of the elders visiting from Musqueam—my first husband's uncle—James Point looked at Jeffrey and saw his dilemma.

Uncle James diagnosed him as suffering from an old Indian spirit sickness. In the winter months, after the growing season, the power of living things comes out into the human world. Those who are receptive can get sick when this power is not controlled. They are taken, according to the elders, by the powerful *syúwel* spirit forces. This is old, ancient Indian spiritualism. Uncle James said, "They've come for him. They are going to reclaim your family now."

So we took Jeffrey to Musqueam, where his father was from. Vincent

Stogan and his brother Walker took care of him there.[1] And there was an elderly Penelakut man from Kuper Island who came over and helped. I think his name was Brown. Jeffrey was the first to get these powers after years and years of it being suppressed by the churches and the potlatch law. For years, this had been done away with by the churches and outlawed by government.

But some of this spiritual life was kept alive, at a very low level, in those dark years, like in the 1950s. Richie Malloway was one who kept things alive. And there were a few others, like Annie Paul. She was one of those who kept the *mí'lha* fires burning—kept the smokehouse tradition going, quietly, without fuss. They held little dinners sometimes in the winter and kept the tradition going—a bit of spirit dancing. At the same time, up here in northern BC, people were quietly holding the feastings and potlatches, out in the bush, away from the public eye. Things were at a low ebb, but down underneath in the ashes of our way of life, the coals were still hot.

As well as Richie and Annie Paul, there was old Annie Jimmie from Kwaw-kwaw-a-pilt, and there was Charlie Douglas—Albert Douglas's father—from Cheam, and Hank Pennier's wife, Maggie. She wore the paint, too. And so did Ida Insley. She used to dance. She was very old and she could barely walk, but when the spirit took her, she got up and danced. She was married to Captain Insley, who was on the old river-boats, and she lived in Tzeachten. And one of the last besides Richie was Annie Paul, as I said. She was from Yakweakwioose and her father was Antoine George. He was a brother to Jimmy George of the Georges who live at Aitchelitz now. He married a woman from Nanaimo. I never heard her name, but Annie was their daughter, and she had a brother named Alphonse George, and they lived close by where St. Theresa's Church is now, at Yakweakwioose. She was an initiated and experienced *mí'lha* dancer, and so, every winter, wherever she happened to be living—her daughter married at Nooksack, so she would spend winters over there with her--but every winter, she would come home for visits to Sardis. She

1 Vincent Stogan (1918–2000), "Tsimalano," was a much respected healer, cultural ambassador, and activist at Musqueam and, more broadly, across the Lower Mainland. Among other honours, he received a doctorate of laws from the University of British Columbia in 1996.

and Richie Malloway and the others, they would put up a little dinner and have, I guess, a mini *mí'lha*. They'd have it in just a small house, part of it. So between the handful of them, they kept the fire burning. And every winter, those who still carried the *mí'lha*, they would get together at least once during the winter. But after they all passed on, then there was just Richie left. That was toward the end—about when the boys started up.

In those years, we were not allowed to practice any kind of ancient rituals like the *mí'lha* without the risk of going to jail. Everything was done away with, including the Sxwóyxwey masks. We were not allowed to use them. They had to be put away. In those days, the church controlled people's minds—until, that is, Jeffrey got sick and was the first to be brought back to *syúwel* again. Beginning with Jeffrey, we went back to the old ways. There was only one last spirit dancer left in the Fraser Valley at that time. It was Richard Malloway. He came and helped my children get back to the old ways, the ancient way of doing things. The rest of the family started to join Jeffrey, and Richie spent many winters teaching them. Other people in the valley were beginning to do the same thing. They followed suit. They began to leave the churches and return to the *mí'lha*, to *syúwel*, again.

Mí'lha

My children got into the *syúwel* traditions, into winter dancing, the spiritual dancing, after we broke with the Catholic Church. I'll tell just a little bit about how they train them. I couldn't tell you personally about what they learn, from the inside, because I have never been initiated myself. I just go by what little they tell me. When people come to be initiated, those in charge keep the initiates away from everything and everybody for four days. They work on them. A group of people who've already been initiated will work on them. They keep them in a tent, a so-called tent of blankets at the smokehouse, and they have what we call a babysitter with them so they won't leave, or have second thoughts, or harm themselves. The initiation is quite excruciating. They aren't allowed to eat for four days. They give them herbal teas, and they aren't allowed to bathe or anything. They have to stay in the state they were in when they were taken.

When they start, they have to be born again as new, because then they have received new power to help them in life. Three days after the babies are taken in, people are invited into the house to witness them being sat up. They are covered with blankets and you really can't see them. This is for the new dancer—they call him or her a "baby"—it's like being reborn again into the spiritual world. This first ceremony is so the baby can get used to people, because now, after the seclusion, his or her life is going to be together with a lot of people.

On the fourth day, they put a hat on the initiate, according to the colour of paint—if he sings a strong song, it will be black paint, and if it's a beautiful slow song, it will be red paint, generally. The older dancers can tell just by listening to these new songs what the colour will be. So they put on their paint and they put on their hats. If they are red paint, with the red ochre, they wear a cedar-bark hat that has been braided, with a long tail, and their garments are mostly red. If they are black paint, then they usually wear a woollen hat made out of spun wool, or it could be feathers, depending on what the family wants. They have to wear these hats for the duration, the rest of the winter in the smokehouse. Our smokehouse is very strict, and we keep them in the hats for the duration, until the season ends, February or April.

After four days, the babies are taken into the mountains, and there, they bathe in the icy cold creeks. They wash away their former way of life. Then part of the training is to bathe in the creeks every day. Gradually, they are introduced to other things. They are taught to scrub floors, to cook, clean, because a lot of young people who go in don't have any domestic skills. They have no timetables set for living their lives. A lot of them are found wandering the streets and they never had homes.[2] They are taught to live with other people, how to structure their lives.

2 A considerable number of the young people encouraged to become initiates are those who have at least a glimmer of desire to reclaim their lives as healthy Salish people after succumbing to street life, along with dependency on alcohol or narcotics. For any reader who understands the power of addiction, it is a testament to the *mí'lha* that so many former addicts find their way back into Salish, and Xwélmexw, cultural practices and healthier ways of living.

They have to learn to get along with other people; they have to learn dis-cipline, self-discipline, and learn to take discipline from elders without answering back rudely. Now they are going back to the old, ancient ways of doing things when young people were never allowed to answer back to elders in a bad way. They are being taught how to be born afresh, grow up the old way, all over again.

Our smokehouse at Skowkale is very strict. We are considered the most strict of all the smokehouses. Even on Vancouver Island, they say our smokehouse is very strict. We don't allow drugs or drinking in the smokehouse by any of the dancers or by any of the participants who come in and help out with cooking and cleaning, or even among people in the audience. They are not allowed to bring in cameras or tape recorders or to smoke inside anymore.

There was a word for a place to hold these events, and it was sacred, but I don't remember that word. The word we use now is *híkw' lalém*, which means great house or big house. *Híkw' lalém*. But everybody just calls them smokehouses. I guess that comes from the open fires. Sometimes, it gets pretty smoky in there. People actually lived in them years ago, and what they did was take down the partitions inside when they were going to have a *mí'lha*, a winter dance. Many families lived in them and unrolled long rush mats like we had at Devil's Run. These were unrolled for the night and rolled back up in the daytime, up to the beams again. At *mí'lha* time, when they were rolled up, this made a large area for the ceremonies. Today, people live in regular homes and they use the longhouse just for ceremonial purposes or dinners or other gatherings. They also use them now for funerals. At Skowkale, the priest will come and have mass in our smokehouse. But it is not being used for political meetings, not yet.

At the end of the season, they call it "removing the hats," and the initiates are allowed to mingle. Of course, the handlers are being very careful with them still, as they are new and inexperienced. They are allowed to talk to people and to their families for the first time since they started. Now, they are able to leave the smokehouse for the first time. In our smokehouse, if the babies who come out have no job or place to live, they can go on living at the smokehouse, but during that time, they must work in the village and help out. The initiates from the last winter often participate in the summer season of canoe racing. By that point, they would now be training physically. One of my sons makes caskets for the poor who can't afford the undertakers. He has the young initiates help him make these, the carpentry work. The aim is to strengthen the initiate and see that they come out healthier and more able to interact with people in a positive way. They have come out clean after an earlier life on the streets with drugs and alcohol. And their minds are totally different. They are no longer alone and feeling useless. Now they know they are needed. In *syúwel*, they now have a family, with the other dancers. They belong somewhere now—to the community of *stlaqwem* [the community of initiates who have been gifted with spirit powers]. People treat them very kindly when they are initiated, and they go back the next winter and participate again, for four years—they are considered babies for four years and are under observation by their elders.

They have meditation and other activities, but I have not been through it. As an outsider, I do not know all the teachings they get—spiritual healings—and they have their minds opened to this. Many young people go in not believing in anything. When they come out, they are very aware of the spiritual side of life. They are given an awful lot of spiritual training. They come out poised, dignified, quiet, sure-footed, and alert. They are like the old-time Native persons. Their minds are highly tuned. Men especially, who never showed their emotions or cried or showed any weakness, they now come out of this with emotions, like anybody else.

It was wonderful to see one of my grandsons who went in, who was very troubled. He had a mind like a steel trap, and he would never ever shed a tear for anybody or anything. When I saw him after he was initiated, he literally wept. I thought, "How wonderful! My grandson is a human being now." He is very tender and gentle and giving now. Before, he expected everybody to be perfect all the time, according to his idea. Now he's learned to think like a Native person. I have seen wonders.

I have also seen a few who come out feeling pretty cocky because they think that now they have been through the initiation. But soon they come back and realize they have to get along with everybody else or they are not going to make it. They come back and are subject to their teachers. There is a whole new lifestyle there for those who are initiated, for the people of *stlaqwem*.

Now, after the elders dealt with Jeffrey, we decided to build a long-house, a *híkw' lalém*, for the ceremonies. This was at Sardis. I went over to visit the First Citizens authorities for British Columbia, over to Victoria. I visited them and applied for a grant. I sat in their office and told them what was happening. They said, "Sure, we'll give you the money, as long as you get somebody to build it."

I talked to Richard Malloway, and he said, "Sure, we'll help." Everybody pitched in and helped. We built the big house at Tzeachten. Tzeachten had been set aside for a cemetery, a longhouse, and I forget what else, by Old Pierre.[3] He gave this piece of land for this purpose, but it wasn't long before somebody burned it down. Everybody kept quiet about it. There was just no point making an issue of it.

I told the children, "You've got to realize now you can't depend on other people to do things for you. You have to do it yourself. Build your own longhouse for your own ceremonies and look after it yourselves." And that's what they did. They got together—Steven, Jeffrey, Tim, and Mark—and they went to see their aunt at Soowahlie. They asked her for permission to take some small trees so they could start building the skeleton and some larger trees for planking. She said, "Sure. Go ahead."

It must have been around 1970 now. I don't remember the date. They built a little A-frame with teeny little poles, but at last they had their own longhouse right there at Skowkale. They started off with this little build-ing, and later on, they built the bigger one. They got more organized as they got older. They realized this was going to be their life from now on, and they put more into it. Now, today, they are trying to build an even bigger and better one again. The existing one has been used for quite a few years. It's become very strong with the family. We've inherited our masks, and we've trained the boys. Agnes Kelly held the songs for us all those years. We've trained the boys to dance and the girls to sing. It wasn't easy, but we did have some guidance.

3 Old Pierre was a spiritual leader of the Katzie First Nation, who was interviewed extensively by ethnographer Diamond Jenness in the 1930s. See Suttles, Jenness, and Duff (1956).

Spirit Guides

I already told about the importance of the grey wolf to my family at Kw'ekw'íqw. And we have other crests, too, that have helped our ancestors in the past, like the cedar tree. I've never heard anything about the power of a spirit guide being passed on from generation to generation, but we feel it is good to have these guides—like old traditions belonging to the family. It almost seems more like a myth, a legend, or whatever. But it's good to have them. It is good when your family owns a story like those that go along with the guide and how it first came to your ancestor. The Uslicks of Chilliwack have the beaver. The Wealicks of Kilgard have the brown bear. My grandfather Pete had the brown bear and the cedar tree. That cedar sings beautiful songs. They would hang cedar branches up over the door for good health and protection. I know my grandfather, when he worked with sick people, he filled a vessel up with water and he would have a little cedar bough to sprinkle water on his patient.

Other families had their spirit guides too. The Wallaces of Soo-wahlie, they were the giant lizard. Old Joe Punch, Joe Phillips, he had what he called "the cayoose power song." Cayoose was the name of his horse. The horse died, and Joe lay down beside it and dreamed. He dreamed the horse's song, learned it and sang it in all the smokehouses during the spirit dances at *mí'lha* time. Dan Milo's crest and song was the eagle. His grandfather's name was Xlok'weleleqw, "the man who flies like an eagle." Dan Milo's mother, her family had a crest with a story, too.

She was from Chilliwack, down—oh, I don't know the name of the village, I don't remember, or if it had a name—right on Wellington [Road], as you're heading down to the Skwah Reserve; there used to be an old courthouse there—just on the edge of town, of the city, like. There used to be a swamp there, Dan said. His mother's elder—I don't know if he was a grandfather or a great-grandfather—but the story goes that when he was young, this man was walking along the swamp there. This was before there were any Europeans. And he saw this, like, a great big huge worm come out of the swamp. It had a head on either side of its body, and he became frightened. He didn't know which way to go. He almost became paralyzed with fear. This creature, the Si:l'hiy, then said to him,

"Do not be afraid of me. I am your power. If you . . . if you kill me and take my bones, my ribs"—he had ribs—"and burn them, and with the ashes you make a paint, and if you paint me over your doorframe, then you will have my power. The rest of the paint, you use on your mask, and I will sing my power through you." That young man prayed and fasted. He went out and killed that Si:l'hiy. He took the ribs, burned them, made the paint and painted the likeness of that creature over his door. He went into *mí'lha* and became that two-headed worm, Si:l'hiy.

So this was the story that was handed down to Dan Milo's mother. She was generations down, I guess. The young man did as he was instructed, and he did become a very powerful man. He could do a lot of things that other people couldn't do. I wasn't told exactly what he did except that he became a powerful man.

Dan Milo's mother, before she passed on, she gave this to her son. He carried the spirit guide, or crest, or whatever you want to call it. And when he passed on, he gave the crest to my first husband, the father of my children, Roy Point. Dan told him, "Because you don't seem to have a spirit guide, you may have my mother's and your children will have it after you."

And so it's just been kept in the family. Roy was Dan's wife's grandson, and my children grew up on their farm. I nursed both Dan and his wife in the time before they died. Dan gave his eagle name to my youngest son, Brian. So we hold a number of these crests: Cedar Tree,

FIGURE 18
The Si:l'hiy crest, painted on a drum. The double-headed snake image belongs to the Milo-Point family of Skowkale, and the crest was passed down to Roy Point by Dan Milo. Photo courtesy of Rena Point Bolton.

FIGURE 19
The Si:l'hiy crest, knitted into a sweater by Rena. Photo courtesy of Rena Point Bolton.

Grey Wolf (that's mine), Brown Bear, Eagle Man, and Si:l'hiy (which was held by Roy Point and which I used as a design on sweaters for the boys).

In our family, whether all this has given us power, I don't know. We just seem to be ordinary people, as far as I'm concerned, who have been trained to do the work that we do, and yet other people seem to be in awe of the things that we are able to do. Now, whether this comes from these old spirit guides, I don't know. I never thought about it. It seems kind of coincidental, eh? My family members have been involved in canoe racing. I was involved in it for six years when I was younger, and then my children carried on. They have canoed on rivers, on lakes, on oceans—out on the seas, even on the Pacific Ocean out in the Polynesian area. They've been all over the place canoeing, and luckily, we have never had any fatal accidents in the water. But we have always given credit for that to the Sxwóyxwey, because it was a strong water spirit. We pray and ask for protection before the canoe season starts—so I guess maybe they do give us the help we need.

A Personal Experience

Now, this is something I do not discuss much, but I want to say I got a spiritual guide, too. It happened accidentally. I was down at Port Angeles, Washington, visiting my cousin June. June said, "You know, there's a lady who lives up the hill. I'm sure you'd like to meet her."

She felt very strongly that I should meet her. She took me up there and I met this lady, Dora Carlson. She was an elderly woman, and she embraced me as soon as I walked in. She said, "I've been waiting to meet you. I have so many things to tell you. But first we must have tea." We had tea and then she took my cup and read it. "Yes," she said, "you are the lady. You have a lot of work to do and you must do it right now. You shouldn't waste any more time."

She told me what I had to do. We sat and talked for hours. June and Cliff were there. Dora was not Native. Her people were from New York. Many generations ago on this coast, there were tall people here who did not look Native at all. Those were her people, spiritually. On the inside, she was a Native person.

Through the years, I kept in touch with her and she told me what I had to do. You might say she told me what the spirits wanted me to do. I can honestly say, you know, when that happened, I wasn't a particularly strong believer. I had been totally Christianized. I was sort of half-hearted about finding my way back into Indian culture and believing and trusting in spirits. I did it more or less to keep my children busy, to give them a goal to fight for. But inside myself, I still had this little Christian feeling. I still felt close to God, and that was before I realized that God, the Creator, and the Great Spirit were all the same. After meeting Dora, I came to accept that. As she was talking to me, I came to realize that I couldn't opt out any longer. Up to that point, I just went along with life and felt foolish. I felt that my grandparents had taught me everything for nothing. Now, I saw I was brought back to complete the circle. It was Dora who did it. She helped me see things as they were.

Some years back, Dora communicated again. My son Jeffrey, who is also a very avid sweat-lodge person, got a message from Dora. It came to him in the sweat lodge in his mind. He could see her there, and she told him, "I have to see your mother again, one more time. Please tell her to come and see me."

This was now years later. It was wintertime—cold, with snow on the ground. But Cliff drove me back down to Port Angeles. We were tired when we got there, so we stayed overnight. The next day, we went to visit Dora. Her elderly daughter was there. She said, "Oh, my mother doesn't know anything anymore. She's very old and she doesn't know anyone and doesn't talk to anyone. She doesn't even know me, but we keep her at home. She's no trouble."

I told her, "My son has said she wanted to see me."

"All right," she said. "I'll make tea. Maybe this visit will bring her out of the state she's in."

So we had tea all round. June was there again, and June's daughter, and Cliff and myself. She wheeled her mother over to the table and gave her a cup. She said, "Your friend Rena's here. D'you remember her?"

Immediately, her eyes came to life. The brightest possible light was coming from her eyes. "Of course I know Rena," she said. "I sent for her. I'm glad you came."

She then spoke to me as though there was nothing wrong with her. She read my teacup again, and the cups of the others, too. She said, "You must support this lady. She's getting older and there are people out there who make things hard for her, but she must not give up. She must not quit. You have to speak out and support her. Don't be afraid because the spirits are with you. She's the person who has to carry on this work. She was chosen years before she was born, and she's got to carry on this work. It's got to be done."

She talked to us for quite a while. Then, all of a sudden, her head dropped and her eyes went vacant again. Her daughter said, "Oh, she's gone again and she doesn't know you."

When we were leaving, I went over to the wheelchair and hugged her. I said, "Thank you, Dora, you know, for everything."

Her eyes lit up again, and she said, "If you want to talk to me about anything, pick up the phone and phone me." Then she went out again. I have never called her.

This actually happened and I have witnesses. Cliff was there, and my cousin June, formerly June Silver, and her daughter Lisa, plus Dora's own daughter.

Down through the years, the spirit has moved me very strongly. I live each day intending to be more strongly connected to the spiritual side of things. I am approaching the end of my time on this earth, and there is still so much to do! Producing this book is part of it, too—leaving a legacy for my descendants so they can carry on the work.

Sxwóyxwey

RICHARD DALY: On a hot summer day, June 20, 1988, my colleagues and I stopped our vehicle beside Kawkawa Lake, just north of the town of Hope. Seated in the front passenger seat was our guide and teacher, Agnes Kelly. She rolled down the window and nodded toward a cliff off to the left where, in the heat of the afternoon, the dry moss glowed straw-yellow. "That," she said, "is where that boy jumped."

This small lake, with the Fraser River to the west and the Coquihalla and Hope-Princeton highways to the east, nestles against the foot of a cliff, and behind it are the Coast Mountains. It is one of the most sacred locations in Xwélmexw country.[4] Yet on that particular day, it appeared to be anything but sacred. The air was laden with the boisterous sounds of summer vacationers whose moods were far from spiritual—picnickers, dads bent over gas grills, youngsters with frisbees and beach balls, mothers in foldout aluminum chairs smearing on the suntan lotion, small swimmers splashing and shouting against the roar of speedboats with water skiers swaying to and fro in their wakes. It was a sunny day, dry and hot, but there was a pleasant light breeze. Sonnie McHalsie, Randall Paul, and I had driven Agnes Kelly up to the lake from her home at Ohamil. She had agreed to give her own account of the Sxwóyxwey story at the site where the events happened.

She told the story without wasting words—she was not in good health and had decided that she would not live to see another winter—but what she did say certainly reflected the heated discussion in the Xwélmexw community about access and legitimacy to the secret knowledge and healing procedures of Sxwóyxwey. For me, her words were proof of the continuing spiritual power, political power, and cultural legitimacy of Sxwóyxwey—both in theory and practice. Hotly contested, the origin, history, and practices of Sxwóyxwey are constantly under debate and review in the Coast Salish world, and they remain an integral and vital feature of present-day Xwélmexw society. The advancement and protection of rights and duties associated with the Sxwóyxwey have inspired cultural training, special upbringing of children, moral teachings, intense competition, and far-reaching negotiations between families. This activity is highly important to the culture's ongoing vitality and dynamism. In what follows, Rena explains the legitimacy of Sxwóyxwey descending through blood and

4 Mohs (1987) considers Kawkawa Lake and the nearby Fraser River bank, Lhi'hletálets at Iwówes, to constitute one of the most important spiritual sites in Xwélmexw territory. His study cites many elders that he, or previous researchers, had interviewed.

marriage in her family, but, first, here is the story as told by Agnes Kelly; in this account, Rena's family is referred to as "the Points of Chilliwack."[5]

5 The following story is taken from my field notes of July 20, 1988, which were later filed with the Alliance of Tribal Councils, Lytton, British Columbia. Let me also provide some background information about Agnes Kelly. This account is drawn from notes made by researcher Gordon Mohs (a copy of his notes is in my possession), on the basis of interviews with Kelly conducted by Mohs, Sonny McHalsie, and Linda Louie:

Agnes Kelly, Síyameyot, was the daughter of Patrick Louie [Yámyétel] and Amelia Joseph. Her paternal grandparents were Lí:luwi Sqw'átets and Agnes Herman [Lhakw'emlomet] and her maternal grandparents were Jimmy Joseph [Koqweet], known as Jimmy Church, and Isabelle Sam [T'elixwelwet]. Agnes was raised by her grandfather, Lí:luwi, from whom she learned the Halq'eméylem language and much about traditional Stó:lō ways. She was very knowledgeable about family histories and spent much time with Stó:lō researchers recording this information. Her own ancestry traces to Xapé'lá:lexw, Lí:luwi's grandfather. Xapé'lá:lexw was born on Greenwood Island in the Fraser River and was the first in Agnes's family to be a direct descendant of those possessing the original Sxwóyxwey mask, recovered from the pool in the Fraser River above Hope. Xapé'lá:lexw's name is tied to the origin of the Sxwóyxwey at Lhi'lhetálets and means "coming to the surface at this spot." Xapé'lá:lexw made two Sxwóyxwey masks, which were passed on to Agnes's grandfather Lí:luwi (Louie) Sqw'átets. Agnes herself owned a song, which she passed on before her death. Of the two masks made by Xapé'lá:lexw, one was burned up by Catholic priests and the other was lost. Agnes's great-great-grandmother was from Sq'ewa:lxw and was one of the wives of the warrior chief Xételeq. Agnes believed strongly in Native spirituality and in the sanctity of the old ways. Her knowledge of the Halq'eméylem language, place names, customs, traditions and legends was unfathomable. Although reticent to impart this knowledge casually, she spent considerable time with Stó:lō researchers, recording a wealth of information. She once said that she was reluctant to talk of these things, not only because they were so dear to her but also because of punishments received as a child by the clergy whenever these matters were spoken about.

AGNES KELLY: That boy, he jumped from the cliff over there to kill himself. He landed on top of a house under the water, on the roof. He looked down and there sat a baby. He spit and the baby shook. That's where the Sxwóyxwey mask came from. After that, one lady, from up the cliff top, saw the roof underneath the water, when she looked down.

My grandfather told the story. It is a long, long story. I sing the Sxwóyxwey song and I cry. I just can't take it. It makes me all shaky. The Points are using it now. Frank wanted it but didn't get it yet.[6] Parts of it are related to my grandfather. I told Frank, "Ask your father. He has a Sxwóyxwey song in the family, too. It sounds like a dinner song."

One thousand people lived on the island just off of Hope. That priest come along and saw the masks and costumes. That priest told them it was against the law. They had to burn it all. My grandfather's great-uncle would not burn the mask. He threw his mask into the river. So it got down the river [underwater] to Chilliwack. It comes from up this way, though, but Chilliwack uses it now.

That boy lived at Union Bar [on the bank of the nearby Stó:lō, upstream above Hope]. He had sores all over his body and wanted to kill himself. He was called lazy. He got the sores from eating coho when he wasn't supposed to. Only old people should eat it.

The boy was under there in the water for a whole year. They cured him, asked him where he lived.[7] He told them. Beaver drilled a hole from the bottom of Kawkawa Lake all the way out to Iwówes on the main Stó:lō [in the direction of Union Bar] so he could get home. The

---

6 Sí:yá:m Sí:yá:mches, Frank Malloway, son of Richard Malloway, is a tireless defender and promoter of Xwélmexw culture and interests. He has devoted much time to answering the questions of the curious, whether from schoolchildren, academics, or others interested in First Nations cultures in British Columbia.

7 In most versions of this telling, the boy's affliction is cured as a result of him curing a similar affliction infecting the underwater people. This is a normal feature of shamanic learning around the world, wherein the new greenhorn shaman learns to cure others as he or she gradually recovers or gains health after suffering a serious affliction.

first time, Beaver missed and he had to do it all over again. That's why the steelhead and the coho get through there, too, and on into the lake. He went through and he got home.

He told his grandmother he could get a gift in four days' time. After four days, he told his sister to fish in the creek there, at Lhi'lhetálets. She fished and she got the mask, and the man was inside it. She fainted. The boy pulled it in to shore. It was a male mask. It happened a second time and they got a female mask.[8]

RENA POINT BOLTON: The Sxwóyxwey follows the female bloodline. When you're in Stó:lō country, the name is Sxwóyxwey. On Vancouver Island, they call it Sxwaixwai. The true home of Sxwóyxwey power, the mask, the costumes, is Kawkawa Lake near Hope in Xwélmexw country. It was imported later by the [Vancouver] Island people when they married girls from our area.

Mrs. August Jim used to talk with Agnes Kelly, her grand-niece. They discussed the bloodline and the passing of the Sxwóyxwey. Agnes's grandfather Louie Sqw'átets had wanted to pass it on to my grandfather Pete Silva, because Louie's own sister's [Mrs. August Jim's] people had joined the white world, but Grandfather Pete died long before Louie Sqw'átets did. Louie lived to be 115. Mrs. August Jim decided to pass the Sxwóyxwey to my mother, Annie Silva, because the other descendants were not in a position to handle it. For a long time, it was held in trust by Louie Sqw'átets.

8 Other accounts of the story are found, for example, in Jilek (1982) and in Duff (1952b), who gives several versions, the most extensive of which is an upriver account similar to that of Rena and Agnes Kelly. For archaeological and ethnographic support for these narratives at Kawkawa Lake and the adjacent Fraser River, see Mohs (1985). Other Indigenous tellings have located the Sxwóyxwey story in other settings, which to me indicates the power of family knowledge and history to situate features of Xwélmexw culture (and aspects of Coast Salish culture as a whole), locally. People root stories of origin in their immediate physical surroundings with links to specific families.

The mask names go with the Sxwóyxwey. They are called the human faces. They do not look like animals or birds. They are faces of human beings. They are the oldest masks on the face of the earth, in the Stó:lō Nation, at least. They were the first ones ever to be taken. Then, later, the birds and the animals came.

Agnes Kelly carried those for us until we all grew up.[9] Ha ha! I remember she was telling me, "I am so tired of carrying these masks! I want to leave but I can't leave until you take them." And you know, right after we took them, she passed away. True to her word.

Yes. We stopped on the way upriver, and I told her, "Well, we're coming back in a month or two. We're going to the Kamloops powwow," and she says, "Well, don't take too long because I'm not going to wait for you anymore." And she laughed, "Ha ha ha." So we stopped in after the Kamloops powwow and somebody came and told us that she'd just passed away. And I thought, oh my goodness, Agnes didn't wait. We got to the house and her daughters said, "She said to tell you she just didn't want to wait any longer." We brought the masks out then and we did a farewell for her.

She had taught us a memorial song and an ownership song. In fact, she taught us five songs, but we had no tape recorder and we didn't remember them all. In the "Human Face," there are twelve masks, six male and six female. I have a granddaughter and great-granddaughter who are organizing a coming out in Chilliwack at the end of September this year [2009]. We will bring out the masks to honour the girls and their reaching puberty. When you bring out the masks, you need other families there to witness it and acknowledge what you are doing.

Anyway, we brought out the masks in the early morning before Agnes's funeral. She had been carrying the masks for us for a long time, and her spirit needed to be lifted up out of her body, along with the masks, so it could go on its way. So we did this on the fourth morning after she passed away. The girls lined up and sang at sunrise on that fourth day. And the spirit was lifted up to the four directions.

9 By "until we grew up," Rena means until Rena's family members were culturally and spiritually mature enough to assume responsibility for the ceremonies and the healing.

We brought the masks up to Ohamil where Agnes had lived. We had her daughter instructing us on what she wanted done for her mother. They had the casket outside. The girls, who sing the Sxwóyxwey songs, lined up, and the dancers who were to bless her and send her spirit up, they came out—I can't say it in English, but it's like a blessing—we call it *telset*, like a coming together [palms up and arms raised], yes, they do that, I think they do that four times. Anyway, after that's done, the girls sing and the boys dance around the casket. The song is—there is one verse that they repeat four times. Then they take a break. Then they repeat the verse four more times. They do this all four times so that there are, like, sixteen verses done. When they were finished, they and their spiritual presence, they took their leave and Agnes had gone, so then they buried the remains. Our people believe this releases the soul. And so, this is how we gave thanks to Agnes for taking care of the Sxwóyxwey for us all those years while my children were growing up.

At naming ceremonies, as well as at puberty rites and bringing out new babies [the initiates from the winter dancing *mí'lha*], my daughter comes out and greets the people and introduces the dancers. They have to be brought out and introduced to the public. When this happens, before the ceremony starts, the girl who is wearing the female ownership mask, she comes out and *tets'eets* [welcomes] the people. She goes right around the smokehouse and raises her arms. She praises the people for coming and paying their respects to our family. And then she stands at the head of the line of the singers. Now the boys come in, and after they have danced, after their four rounds of verses, they go out. After them, the ladies, the female part leaves.

The boys are dancing while the girls are singing. And we have one drummer, too. It's usually my son Jeffrey or his son, but it has to be one from our family. Then, the lady who welcomed everybody, she departs; then it's over. The masks enter, one at a time, and they leave, one at a time. After the masks are finished and have gone, the lady mask withdraws and the whole ceremony is finished. All the ladies who were singing, they go around in a single line and they *tets'eet* the people and thank them for their attendance. And then it's finished.

Only the lady representing the female line wears a mask, when she's greeting everybody. The rest of the masks, that's the boys. They're out back. She's the only one—the lady—who can go out there with a mask, but it can be any one of my granddaughters or daughters who wears the mask. This is with the mask of the human face. We are the only "human face" mask in the world where the women have total control of the masks. Right now, my daughter Wendy represents me while I'm up here [northern British Columbia]. She still phones me and we talk about whatever work we are going to do. She pretty well has a free hand to do whatever she thinks is best, unless she has a problem. The boys are always concerned. They phone and consult with me if anything comes up.

FIGURE 20

The large basket that Rena made to house the female Sxwóyxwey masks and other ceremonial regalia. Photo: Richard Daly.

FIGURE 21

The large basket, also made by Rena, that houses the male Sxwóyxwey masks and associated regalia. Photo: Richard Daly.

The masks are made of wood and they are usually put on a flat piece, almost like a board. Then the face is carved. It's a human face. We don't have birds or animals. It's just a human face with the tongue protruding and with the four directions on the face, in red paint. Like, on the forehead, on the chin, and on each cheek. And those are the only markings. They don't have a lot of colourful material on them. They have reeds with puff feathers, and on certain occasions, they use those long fronds that grow up in the mountains. They are long fronds that grow like ferns. They attach them to the headpiece so that they trail behind while they are dancing. They don't wear bright colourful things. They only wear the pounded cedar-bark robe that comes down to the knee or a little past the knee, and they have a *swo'hwa* apron. Then they have leggings. They carry shells—a hoop of shells, I should say—in one hand and a cedar bough in the other. They are from the shellfish where you see just the one shell. The scallop, yeah, like the Shell Oil sign. I don't know what they stand for. It just seems like something the Sxwóyxwey—maybe because the masks came from under the water. I don't know. When the whole regalia was first brought out of the water, the shells were there, and the cedar bough. No one has ever explained to me what they stand for, but I notice that the medicine men all seem to use cedar boughs, so it must stand for power, the power of nature, of the trees. And the shell is the power from the water, the sea. That's what I would think anyway.

Water is a powerful medicine among our people. My grandfather Pete used a grail of water to cleanse a house if something bad happened there, or when somebody died.[10] The souls of people travel at night and the medicine man, the *shxwlá:m*, he keeps a pot of water beside the bed so he can draw the soul back. Water brings life and food to us and because of this it has a power of its own. A bowl of water is very important. Louie Sqw'átets was very powerful with water. He was a good healer and he

10 Raised as a Roman Catholic, Rena understands the Holy Grail to be the name of the cup that Jesus used at the Last Supper, but here she is using the term *grail* in a generic sense to denote the spiritually imbued stone bowls, some carved, some plain, that were important to shamanic activities along the lower Stó:lō, as she goes on to explain.

used it for any kind of sickness. A healer can put a current through water and it gets good healing powers. Water is very powerful with the Sxwóyxwey people, too. It is the source of their power. They take their power from the world around them and they put it into the water. When we are young, we are taught to go out in the early morning and warm our hands in the first rays of the sun, then rub our sun-warmed hands on our arms, our chests, and then our legs. After this, we run, we breathe in the fresh morning air, and we come down to the stream and jump into the cold water. This way, we share the power and the energy that flows from the ancestors.

Responsibility for the Masks

Then there is the responsibility for the masks. I was very troubled when Dora Carlson down in Port Angeles told me I must not shun my responsibilities. I was asking myself, "Why me? Why do I always have to be responsible for everybody? Why can't I be free like normal people?" So now it is the masks, something again I have to be responsible for. I knew the responsibility that went with them.

I went to a Hindu woman, a very powerful channeller. It cost a lot of money but I wanted to talk to somebody who didn't know me. I went to this woman. She went into a trance. Before that, she asked me to form some questions and said there was a man who usually came out to her during the channelling and answered clients' questions.

She went into a trance and then she said, "Good afternoon. I'm Mr. So-and-so"—I can't remember the name. She talked more sternly, but it was still her voice. The voice asked, "What can I do for you? You have questions."

I asked him quite a few questions. I asked him, "What is the Sxwóyxwey, the masks that the Salish people used? What are they for? What good do they do? Why do we have to have them? What is their purpose nowadays? They might have been good in the past, but why do we need them today?"

He said, "The masks—the masks of centuries ago?"

"Yes."

"All right. Your people were a holy people. Your people believed in doing good and living a good, clean, holy life. The masks were to keep you civilized. They were an ancient form of discipline. They were used at birth if the couple who had a child lived a good life according to the laws of the land and the people living there. Their newborn child could be blessed by the masks. So then the woman had to carry her child properly and live according to the old laws, or if she did not, then she could not bring her child out with the mask. Using the mask this way was a great blessing from the Great Spirit. This would show that she had lived a good life so far and followed what she was taught.

"The second time the masks were used in life was at puberty. Only the children who lived according to the laws of the land and the elders were brought out for this. Other children who were not taught properly could not be brought out with the mask. The third time that the masks brought them out was when they received a name. This was not their baby name but the name they would keep the rest of their lives, the name they got when their character was formed. In order to receive a name, you had to have been a good citizen, a strong person who set a fine example for others.

"The fourth time you could be brought out was in marriage. If this marriage was done properly and was looked upon as a good marriage by the people, then the masks could bring the couple out. The next time that the masks came out was at their death, when they had lived a good and holy life. The masks would now send them on their way.

"All I can tell you is that the masks were used to keep the people civilized. That is all I can tell you. You must know this yourself but you just wanted me to clarify it."

I said, "Thank you. Now I know." I knew the Xwélmexw people were civilized. They were dignified and they were holy. I was very happy when I heard that. I went home and told the children, "We must be very careful with the masks. We must not use them to exploit people. We must be humble when we wear them. We must never ask for money because these masks are only given to people who will take very good care of them, who will set a standard for other people to live by."

And, you know, it has been difficult. We have had the masks for many years now, and it hasn't been easy, but most of the family though, they abide by the rules. We have a few who drop out and say, "Oh, Mum, I'm not going to be told what to do." Gradually, they come back.

Then there are others, competitors who make a mockery out of the masks, people who use them to hold themselves up high and act superior to everybody else. The masks are not supposed to be used that way, but that's what they do! People are selling them and selling the names for thousands of dollars—which is very wrong. But here again, we are not allowed to pass judgment on what others do.

I have talked to my children many times. I've told them it is not up to us to decide what is wrong and what is right. The people in our community are adults. If they have been trained by their elders, they must know what they are doing. If they are doing wrong wilfully, well, this is on themselves. It is not our duty to tell them what to do and what not to do. If they come to us for advice, we will do our best to tell them what we think of what they are doing. We must do this without hurting their feelings, and we must be diplomatic. But we cannot condemn them. We are only here to set examples.

FIGURE 22

One of the Point family's racing canoes. As Rena explains, a women's team customarily has ten pullers (plus a captain), while a men's team has eleven—but, as this photo illustrates, teams can also been mixed. Photo courtesy of Rena Point Bolton.

Our canoes have been winning in the canoe races for many years. We are the Five Star Group—and very few others have beat us through the years because we live with a very high standard of training. Other canoe clubs have been envious and jealous and have wished that we would quit for a while and give them a chance to win, but at the same time, they respect our canoe club. When the children's father passed away, and also their sister who was a puller—she passed away—as much as I hated to shut down the canoe club, I did. I said, "This is to show respect to your father and to your sister."

Some of them were very angry because some of them are star pullers. They don't want to give up their standing and the sport that makes them what they are. But my sons, who are older, they agreed that Mother was right. So we shut down for one year, as is the ancient way. The people from the island and the coast and Washington State, they were totally in awe. They could not believe that the winners of so many years would quit because somebody passed away in their family.

Now that the family has gone back to training and racing, the others say, "Now we know why you are so strong. You are obeying the laws of the elders." Many, many are coming to us and want to join our canoe club. Mark phoned and said, "Mother, we have so many pullers, I don't know what we are going to do with them all."

I said, "That's nice. They will learn the correct way to handle themselves and be gentlemen pullers."

Many times through the years, we have had to prove ourselves. The people are ready to condemn us. They criticize us, but in the long run, we are the ones who come through and adhere to the old ways. So I feel the masks are giving us the strength and the power we need for living today. It isn't easy for any of us. Every child must be counselled about what they are getting into in our family, how they are expected to learn and to teach the old ways of doing things. The new ways around us are often easy to follow and very attractive, but they are often full of corruption. To me, it all leads to losing your soul. I lost a daughter because of the new ways.

I think the reason why we had to take the masks was so my family could get back to the old ways. It's been difficult, but we are doing it. If we can do it, others can too. I'm sure of it. We have to continue to set an example for others to do the same. Mama and Papa, my grandparents, they always instructed me to hold myself as an honourable lady because *sí:yá:m* people always had to show strength and dignity. They had to be examples for their people, because if they lived right and then the people did the same, things worked well. That was the main form of government. Living the laws was at the centre of things.

The white people came and said we had to change. Other families around us liked the new ways, the fun and the parties, and it was easier than the old pecking order and the old laws. So they gave way to the new Department of Indian Affairs and its way of governing, and they gave way to the churches. To them, the new was modern and civilized. They didn't really like the old way, which they called backwardness and poverty. But my grandmother believed in her role as a very high lady who had to keep to the old ways as much as possible. She saw the changes coming to the valley, but she told me over and over to keep some of our old ways, keep our past and our dignity. We must not lose our identity, we the Wolf People, the Semá:th *sí:yá:m*, who governed in this valley.

Passing on Sxwóyxwey

Going back further, I went to my grandfather Pete Silva's funeral together with my son Tim. He was about six months old. Actually, it was my grandfather's burning.[11] Louie Sqw'átets was there, and he said to my mother, "Your father [Rena's grandfather] did not claim the masks, so you can have them." The custom is that the woman is their owner and her brother is their guardian.

---

11 The "burning" refers to a ceremony associated with the funeral at which beloved objects and foodstuffs, among other things, are burned in a fire by a ritual specialist such that they may be enjoyed by the deceased in her or his new surroundings. This specialist has the ability to communicate with the deceased. The aim is to send the deceased into the afterworld surrounded with good things to eat and familiar daily objects that will remind her or him of those left behind.

But my mother said, "No. I lost the right by leaving home, so my daughter will take them as she was trained by her elders, Pete and Sarah." You see, my mother left to work up at Port Essington and her older sister Margaret, who had been properly trained by the old people, she drowned.

So my mother, Annie, declined and the Sxwóyxwey came to me. Louie blessed Tim, who I had sitting on my knee. By doing this, Louie meant that Tim was to be responsible as guardian of the masks. I stood him up in front of a thousand people some years ago and Agnes put everything on him. When I die, the mask will go to my eldest daughter, Rena Greene, who's married to the carver Stan Greene.[12]

In the years before her death, Agnes advised my sons in the carving of the masks. She protected and guarded the boys so that they could handle the power that is in the Sxwóyxwey. A lot has to do with fasting and burning. They can't have any food for twenty-four hours before they dance. Food would be a danger to them. Tim keeps a low profile, but he is responsible for the behaviour of my other sons.

FIGURE 23

Mark Point and his wife, Brenda, with Rena, in her home at Kitsumkalum. Standing on either side of Brenda are the two large baskets that Rena made to store the male and female Sxwóyxwey dance regalia (pictured in figures 20 and 21). Photo courtesy of Rena Point Bolton.

12 To her unending sorrow, Rena's eldest daughter, Rena Greene, passed away in the spring of 2013, following a long illness.

Steven learned the upriver Tii:t type of burnings from Agnes Kelly. This was also inherited from my grandfather Pete Silva. Mark has been trained as our canoe builder, and, beyond that, I have been teaching the girls to weave and do basketwork. They will do more of it as they get older and they don't have so many responsibilities with small children. They all know how to make cedar-bark capes. We use these for our dancing. The techniques involved are special family knowledge. This knowledge belongs to us. Usually, we don't even teach it to girls who marry into our family.

The Steqó:ye Wolf side of my family specializes in types of weaving in wool; the Tii:t side of the family from upriver made fine, fine weavings of mountain goat wool mixed with dog hair. They also did beautiful work with cedar bark. The Wolf women of the family in Semá:th have specialized in a kind of twill weave called *swox'wath*. *Swox'wath* is not just the twill weave; it is also the way the fibre is prepared. Small feathers and feather down are mixed with mountain goat wool and dog hair. This is all then mixed with fine white clay and a bit of water. Then it is spun out on a spindle whorl while it is still wet. The wool strands were sometimes strung out across the big house, or up to the smokehouse and back down. It took two women to do this. Then, when the strands have dried, you would shake out the clay dust and have a beautiful feathery yarn. This was the work of Semá:th Steqó:ye people. They also made fine robes because of their close association with the wolves.

FIGURE 24
Wool, after the carding and spinning, that has been treated with natural dyes and hung to dry, at which point it can be used for weaving. Photo courtesy of Rena Point Bolton.

Burnings

Burnings are just offerings to the deceased, to the ancestors and to the ones who have just passed on. It could be food, whatever it was they ate and they liked. It could be a bit of clothing, perhaps, that they left behind or that their relatives think their daughter or son or whoever it is may want, so they offer this. It helps the deceased and the mourners by giving food and things that might be appreciated on the other side.

FIGURE 25
Rena at her loom, weaving a Salish swéqeth *blanket. She is wearing a mask because she has an allergy to wool. Photo courtesy of Rena Point Bolton.*

And especially for the living, the ones who are offering these foodstuffs and what not. It must make them feel better. I know it makes me feel better when I burn for my friends and my relatives. I feel like I'm still connected to them. So it's kind of like a good way to stay . . . healthy, ha ha. I think it's a balance. It's a good balance for you. You are not just mourning the loss and trying to forget. You're keeping the person alive in a way. It's a loving gesture that you do, and it's not meant to be a gory [morbid] thing. It's just a gesture.

If there is any one thing that a mourning person might want to keep as a treasure or a keepsake, you pass that object over the fire three times, and they say that the deceased gets the essence of it, and then you are allowed to keep the hat or bag or box, or whatever it is. And that way you are sharing the object with the person who owned it. They have the essence of it on the other side but—what do you call it—the physical? That stays with the descendants and the essence of it goes with, with the other, because you are sharing again, between the living and the deceased.

6

* ❀ *

Breaking the Silence

Weaving My Way into Political Life

In 1952, the potlatch ban was lifted finally and we were allowed to go back and speak our language openly, and do our arts and crafts—to teach it again. This was quite difficult because several generations had already, well, gone by without knowing anything about the weaving, the medicines, the carving, even the giving of the potlatch—the songs, the dances. We decided to revive as much of it as possible.

I had always been weaving and making baskets and thinking about the power of our culture. That's what got me involved in going around promoting Native arts and crafts everywhere. It started long ago when the children were still small.

Oh my goodness, when was it? We heard that there was a contest going on at Brockton Oval in Vancouver's Stanley Park. They were going to have judges come out and give prizes to the best tables showing Indian crafts. And people said to me, "You should go out there and show your work—your basketry, your knittings and your weavings."

I said, "Oh no, who'd want to see my funny work?"

The ladies of our homemakers' club—Wigwam Homemakers, we were called back then—they encouraged me. They said, "You go. You're the only one left who knows how to do all these things. And you know the stories that go with everything. So you should go there and meet the public."

I was really nervous because I wasn't used to being out in public like that. I had always thought I had a quiet life, hidden away from the white world. I was a real homebody. Anyway, I told the kids, and they said, "Sure, let's go, Mum, it'll be fun."

My boys were young teenagers, like twelve, thirteen, fourteen, fifteen—around that age—and the girls were little. Well, I thought, if I'm going to enter a contest regarding Indian crafts and Indian artifacts and stuff, I'm going to do it up right. So I went over to Mrs. Malloway. I asked her if I could borrow some of her baskets because I didn't have too many at the time. I was too busy raising kids right then. She said, "Sure, go ahead and borrow."

She had one nice large basket. I had a few smaller ones. And Richie Malloway said, "You can borrow my *kwóxwmal*." I was afraid of his *kwóxwmal*. It's the stick [staff] with the deer hoof rattles on it, you know. But I took that along too, and I took down a load of smoked salmon, and the boys cut a bunch of cedar boughs. We drove down in our little truck, and we took along a hammer and nails and stuff we might need. I had seen other displays, you know, and I kind of had an idea of what I wanted. We were lucky. We found a sort of shed out there, and we just put up our stuff the way we wanted it.

I told the boys, "Take your shirts off and just wear your shorts." And so they did, and I put on my regalia. I had a woven headband with a feather in the back. I had my Indian dress on. So I had a whole display. The wool and the yarn that was spun, and some sweaters, and different foodstuffs—dried soapberries and other stuff that people don't see too often. I can't remember everything we had, but we had a really good display of our food and all those things that we had made. I had some cedar bark and roots, and different bundles of wood that we use, like for fish, when we're smoking salmon. We had things stacked around in that little area. I had my spinner there and I was spinning wool. People were coming in droves! The kids were hanging around and our salmon was hanging from the rafters—ha ha—we had Salish Indian blankets that I had made. They were hanging around on the posts and what not. We weren't very artistic, but we did our best to display what we had.

This elderly woman—we didn't know who the judges were—she came by. She was with a man and she looked at me. She started talking to me, asked me who I was. She asked me about my spinning—oh, she asked me *many* questions. She really wanted to know about me. She became so enthralled about everything. She didn't move around very much—she did check all the other tables—they had some beautiful plates and dishes there that had Indian designs on them—pottery and what not—but they weren't Salish, they weren't from our people. They were different, from different areas. Some people had leatherwork, which was nice, you know, with beads and buckskin and what have you. Anyway, when this was over, we won the bursary. We got first prize. I was so surprised!

And the lady came back, and she said, "My name is Mrs. William Rogers. We own the Rogers Golden Syrup and Sugar Company." I was so shocked. Here I had been talking to her freely like—I hadn't been one bit afraid to speak to her. And then when she told me who she was, I kind of got tongue-tied. But she said, "I am very interested in you. There aren't many people like you today, and you're just a young lady."

That was how I met Mrs. Rogers. So after that, we kind of continued to meet and talk. She would phone me now and then, or if she found out that we were going to be in town for a meeting or something, she—I don't know how on earth she kept in touch, kept track of me—but she always seemed to know where I was going to be. And she wanted me to come and visit her, down on that street, I think it's Southwest Marine Drive, getting out toward Musqueam on Point Grey in Vancouver—she had a great big mansion there. She wanted me to come down and visit her and bring the children. She was a widow by then. But I felt intimidated. You know, I didn't feel right about visiting such really rich people like her. I just didn't, but she was relentless. She didn't give up on me. When she found out that Trudeau was coming to Vancouver to dine with a few people and plates were going to be—people were going to have to buy the plates of food to raise political money—she got in touch with me and told me that she was going to sponsor me. She said, "I would like Mr. Trudeau to meet someone like you." I don't know why, but that's what she said. And so, that's how I got to meet him.

So I said to her, "Heavens, no. I haven't got the clothes, and I can't afford the money"—I meant the sum of money per plate that they were asking for that dinner!

"Don't worry. I'm going to sponsor you, my dear," she said. "You are to dine with Mr. Trudeau and I will buy anything you need to wear, or whatever."

I couldn't figure out why on earth she wanted me to dine with Mr. Trudeau. Anyway, I told Steven. He was at university at the time. He said, "Go to it, Mother. You should go. We'll help you."

So, you know, everybody got busy and I got a new dress and a new coat. I got a new hairdo. Steven brought me down to dine with Mr. Trudeau. We went in and Prime Minister Trudeau walked over to me with his security man. He said, "Madame LaPointe!" He clicked his heels and he bowed.

"Good gracious," I said to myself, "was I afraid of meeting this tiny little man?"

This was in Vancouver. He was very nice looking. He was very, uh, what do you call it now? He was the kind of person who was like . . . imposing, dynamic. He had a very strong presence and I had a feeling that if I didn't watch my Ps and Qs, I'd be ending up with Mr. Trudeau—so I behaved very properly. Then gradually—he took my hand, you know, and I thought he was going to kiss it, but he just took my hand for a moment, then he spoke to me about—I don't even remember—I was so overcome, I don't remember what I said, but I remember thinking he seemed such a small little man but at the same time he could generate this huge power.

One day some time after we went to the exhibition in Stanley Park, I went to one of my elders, she was Mrs. Albert Cooper from Soowahlie, and I asked her if it was all right to weave the old Salish skirts out of cedar bark, and capes. I wanted my daughters, my children, to get involved in the old Salish dancing, the exhibition dancing. She said, "Certainly, go ahead. But just be careful that the girls wear something underneath the skirts because then the policeman will pick you up if they don't." And she kind of tee-hee'd about it.

I went to Oliver Wells and we had a talk about it. He said, "Well, I'll help you to get the cedar bark or the bulrush, whatever you're going to use."

It was the tradition that we used the bulrush, too. It would have to be processed in such a way, but I already knew how to do all of these things because I watched my grandmother making the mats. So he did help me. He cut the bulrush for me and we dried them. I went out and picked the cedar bark and cut the lengths. And then I hung them on strings and wove the skirts. Every day, Oliver Wells would come and we'd chit-chat and have tea and he'd watch me weaving. Soon Richie [Richard Malloway] would be coming over and watching—they were so surprised, you know, that I remembered! All of these ancient things that had died so many years ago! They didn't know there was a living soul who remembered. And I was young yet, very young. When was it? I remember when the canoe races were started at Cultus Lake, so that must have been about '58 or '59—somewhere around there. My children were still quite little yet. They were just coming into the teenage years.

I managed to weave about a dozen skirts and capes. And I made my boys velvet jackets with paddles on them and made them woven head-bands.[1] I wove the woollen tumplines. My great-auntie, Mrs. August Jim, she taught me how to weave them out of stinging nettle fiber or just ordinary yarn. So I wove those too, and the girls wore them for head-bands. The boys wore them also. Everyone was in total surprise when I brought my children out in the old traditional garb. Earlier, I had gone to Mrs. August Jim and asked if I could use some the Tii:t songs. She said, "Go ahead. Nobody uses them anymore." So I got two songs from her. I got one song from Uncle James Point from Musqueam and one song from Uncle Ed Leon in Chehalis. I can't remember where I got the others from—but I know I asked everyone, all the elders, for songs. They said, "Sure, go ahead and use them."

---

1   In figure 8, the early-twentieth-century photo of Frank Hilaire and the Coast Salish dancers, it is possible to see the dance paddles and the tumpline-style headbands, although the latter are partly obscured by the feathered headdresses.

We were taught never to use songs without asking permission because they belonged to somebody. So this is what I did. I got them to sing into the tape recorder. Some of them did. One fellow who did was from the Island. He did sing a song for me and he gave me permission to use it. To this day, I still sing it sometimes in public. I was very enthusiastic. I put up this big exhibition dance at Cultus Lake. Everybody was enthralled. They couldn't believe that in this day and age, we were having something like this, in these outfits. Some were afraid that the police would come and stop us. But nobody did.

Indian Homemakers

THE INDIAN HOMEMAKERS' ASSOCIATION: SOME BACKGROUND

The following information is provided by way of background to Rena's participation in the revival of Native arts and crafts in British Columbia. Because Dr. Rose Charlie was not in good health while we were completing this book, we were unable to interview her directly about the social and political climate around the Indian Homemakers' Association in the late 1950s. The account that follows has been taken from a history of the Indian Homemakers' Association available on the website of the University of British Columbia at http://indigenousfoundations.arts.ubc.ca/?id=547, and we are indebted to researcher Erin Hanson, who kindly granted us permission to use the material, as well as to those scholars on whom she has relied and consulted.

As early as the 1930s, the Department of Indian Affairs provided small grants to fund homemakers' clubs on reserves across Canada. Here, women would gather to sew, knit, and share skills and knowledge related to raising children, cooking, and other domestic tasks. But since poverty was so severe and pervasive on many reserves, it was almost impossible to find adequate facilities for carrying out even the most basic domestic tasks. As historian Cathy Converse (1998, 170) notes, "Many women did not even have the basic essentials of life; hunger was a more immediate problem."

Homemakers' clubs thus hosted clothing drives, craft sales, and bazaars to raise money to help those most in need in their communities. Gradually, the "Indian Homemakers" became more politically motivated. They began to put pressure on the DIA to provide the support and infrastructure that their communities so desperately needed. As Mary John, former president of the Vanderhoof chapter of the IHA, explained:

> In those early years, we were not political. We called ourselves the Busy Beavers and we were just what the name of our club said—we were busy homemakers, looking for ways to make life better for our families and our village. All of us were having babies and raising small children and we believed that we didn't have time for politics. We were still content to let the Indian Agent and the priest and the chief do our talking for us. All this changed in 1976! We discovered in that year that we could no longer knit and crochet and quilt and leave Native politics to others. [. . .] Here was our chance to talk, and talk we did, about the poverty of our reserve, the lack of opportunity for our people, the racism that we had to deal with day after day, the stranglehold that the Department of Indian Affairs had over our lives. (Quoted in Moran 1988, 135, 142)

The DIA stopped funding the Homemakers in 1968. Together with other Xwélmexw women activists, Dr. Rose Charlie, of Chehalis, then president of the Vancouver chapter, managed to incorporate the clubs into a single independent organization across British Columbia. They were now constituted as the Indian Homemakers' Association, the first in Canada, and Rose Charlie became the association's first president. Here is how Erin Hanson, at the time a researcher in the First Nations Study Program at the University of British Columbia, explained the development of the organization in the 1960s and 1970s:

> During this time, the IHA moved beyond promoting homemaking skills to more extensively improving the well-being of Aboriginal women, and, by extension, Aboriginal families and communities. The IHA established the *Indian Voice,* their monthly newsletter, which quickly became a major media source for Aboriginal peoples across BC. The *Indian Voice* was a significant force in communicating between First Nations across BC and spreading awareness about conditions on reserves, and, more specifically, giving a voice to the perspective of Aboriginal women.
>
> The IHA became one of the only First Nations organizations in Canada that had successfully managed to unite First Nations province-wide. This inspired organizations such as the National Indian Brotherhood (now the Assembly of First Nations) of which Dr. Rose Charlie was a founding member, as well as the Native Women's Association of Canada. [. . .]
>
> In 1969, the White Paper was proposed by the federal government. The Indian Homemakers' Association opposed the government's assimilation policies proposed in the White Paper. President Charlie set out to unite First Nations chiefs across BC in order to discuss and strategize how to approach the potential implications of this policy. This was to be the largest gathering of chiefs in BC's history. In November, 1969, 140 bands were represented at a conference

in Kamloops. At this meeting, the Union of B.C. Indian Chiefs was born—an organization which would go on to become one of the most influential Aboriginal organizations in Canada. [. . .]

The IHA continued to advocate for the human rights of Aboriginal peoples, particularly women. They attended UN conferences in Geneva and worked with Amnesty International, while simultaneously maintaining a direct involvement within their own communities. Along with other women's rights activists, the IHA successfully campaigned for the repeal of Section 12 1(b) of the Indian Act, to restore Indian status to Aboriginal women who had married non-Aboriginal men. Over the next few decades the IHA also worked to support and improve Aboriginal women's health, self-government initiatives, education, child and family services for the prevention of child apprehension, a culturally sensitive model for female Aboriginal inmate rehabilitation, and so on. [. . .] The Association created the Aboriginal Mother Centre Society (AMCS) in Vancouver's east side, a drop-in centre where Aboriginal women could gather and receive support including childcare, training, and hot meals.

Early in the 2000s, the Indian Homemakers' Association dissolved, largely owing to lack of funds. Although there has been talk of reconstituting the organization, it remains dormant. In Hanson's summation: "The BC IHA provided advocacy and outreach work in response to issues experienced by many First Nations communities, particularly in respect to women's rights, and gave much-needed representation to Aboriginal women who continue to be underrepresented in Aboriginal political organizations."

Evelyn Paul and Rose Charlie came and asked me if I would start a group or an organization where I could teach the other women to do these things, or anyone who wanted to learn to do these ancient things.[2] I said I'd love to. They said, "Do you know you're one of the last people on this earth who knows how to do these things?"

I was surprised! I didn't know. At that time I was weaving a Salish, Stó:lō-Xwélmexw type of basket with the wood inside the plaiting. Somebody from the *Sun* paper in Vancouver got wind of it and they came up with the reporters and they took a picture of me weaving my basket.

FIGURE 27
A Coast Salish basket, woven of red cedar, wild cherry, and grasses.
Photo courtesy of Rena Point Bolton.

2 Evelyn Paul and Rose Charlie were two of Rena's fellow artists among the Xwélmexw women activists of the 1960s and 1970s. Both were leaders of the BC Indian Homemakers' Association: Rose Charlie was the organization's first president, and Evelyn Paul was executive director. They both lobbied on behalf of Aboriginal rights, taking their demands to Victoria and Ottawa. For a useful discussion of the role of women during the formative years of Aboriginal nationalism in BC, see Barkaskas (2009).

This was probably 1968 or 1969. Here again, I got some more publicity. I was really so naïve then, I didn't know that people were going to make something out of it.

What it all came down to was they asked me to become the president of an organization called the Indian Arts and Crafts Society of BC. Those were the times! We seemed to have so much energy, and we really fought hard. We were with the Homemakers, and it was a powerful women's group, the BC Indian Homemakers' Association. And the Indian Arts and Crafts Society was under the same Homemakers' umbrella. We were registered with the federal government, as well as provincially. We were a nonprofit body.

I didn't know what that entailed. I had no idea, but they told me, "Don't worry. We will be behind you. You will be up front because you are the teacher. You know about the crafts. You know the traditions and the culture. If there is any political organizing in the background, we will do it. Don't you worry about it."

So I got into it and one thing led to another. The Homemakers women worked well together and supported one another. We had been actual homemakers and did not have much experience with doing things outside in the world. The Indian Agent and the church, they had spoken on our behalf, but they did not represent us and didn't really know what we faced. Our men were mostly away from home, working in the city or on fishboats or in logging camps. They didn't face the poverty that we women and children had to live with day after day. Often, especially in winter, a woman with children would have no water in her house, or no electricity or heat. Services were very poor and nobody seemed to see us and how we were living. Someone had to do something. We women in Homemakers were the ones who had to find the food and shelter to keep bodies and souls together. But now when the government cut our funding, that's when we realized we had to stand together, raise money and raise our voices.

Women have a special way of working together. We had our own separate chapters in all the villages, and each had its president. We took up our own issues, but if ladies in other places were having trouble, we would send a delegation to give help and moral support. Because we weren't used to the ways of the world, we sometimes got overwhelmed, and one or another would break down and there would be lots of tears—sometimes we were so naïve about the world. We thought we were a lot tougher than we were. But others would be there to give a hug, help with the children, and make suggestions about what to do next. I guess it was different from the way men go about things, but it worked for us.

We didn't have many resources, but we learned how to make noise. We brought the issue of illegal adoptions into the light. Children from our communities would be apprehended and sold for four thousand dollars each to American families and sneaked out of the country. Later, many of these people got completely lost and ended up on the streets. Some came back to Canada and some of them lived on the streets here, too. They went into drugs and alcohol. We couldn't really help them as individuals, but we got the news out and the practice was stopped. Native organizations on the Prairies helped on this, too. I forget which ones.

We kept in touch around the province with our newsletter *Indian Voice*, and it helped us feel stronger. One thing we did early on was to set up hostels for Native people in the cities like Vancouver, for people coming from their home areas to visit sick family members in hospital, or for other things. Some of the chiefs in the north proposed this and the Homemakers made it happen. We weren't forgetting our artistic side either. We set up the Indian Arts and Crafts Society of British Columbia, where I was very active.

What else? Yes, I remember there was the idea that Native leaders get together and begin to organize for change. The plan was to have a founding meeting in Kamloops. It was planned for November 1969, and the agenda was to set up a Native political party so that our peoples could have representatives in the legislature in Victoria. Well, it didn't happen like that. What they managed to set up was that Native association, the Union of BC Indian Chiefs [UBCIC]. The party idea suffered from too many different approaches, and if I am allowed to say so, too many egos with different agendas, but the UBCIC is still working for the rights of Natives today. It seems to be more effective in the interior than it is on the north coast area.[3]

3 Headquartered in Vancouver, the UBCIC is involved in many projects. Its main aims are improving intertribal relations; fighting repeated attempts by government to extinguish Aboriginal rights; supporting the interests of First Nations

But anyway, we Homemakers in the Lower Mainland had the task of raising money so delegates could get to the Kamloops meetings by bus from wherever they were coming from and so they could afford a hotel room. We raised thirty thousand dollars, and that was a lot of money in those days. What we did was launch a campaign called "Moccasin Miles." It was a walk from Vancouver to Hope, about a hundred miles, and those who joined in had to get sponsors who would pay for so many miles walked. And there was even one fellow who ran the whole way. I forget his name. I think he was from somewhere in the interior.

We learned how to get publicity and we learned that publicity could lead to better conditions for our women and children. We took up the question of social welfare for the poor and old-age pensions for the elders. They were only getting seven or eight dollars a month! We really went all out. And child care: we fought for free medication. We fought for the rights of women who lost their Indian status when they married—that Bill C-31 business.[4] We got a system of Native court workers set up, like legal aid. Like I said, we fought for our children, the ones being adopted without the family's knowledge and brought down to the States. They were being smuggled over the border, and nobody knew anything about it. So we had a lot of clout when we went public, and at times we would appear at the Parliament Buildings in Victoria, protesting—right where Steven is presiding now![5] Before this, our people got very little. Gradually, things improved.

---

locally, nationally, and internationally; defending Aboriginal title through the revival of political, social, economic, and spiritual ways of First Nations life; and continuously promoting healing, reconciliation, and decolonizing processes in the wider society. For more information, see http://www.ubcic.bc.ca.

4 Bill C-31 was an amendment to the Indian Act of Canada, ratified by Parliament in April 1985. The bill was intended to address gender equality in accord with the Canadian Charter of Rights and Freedoms and to give band-governance bodies control over their membership lists.

5 At the time of this interview, Rena's son Steven was lieutenant-governor of British Columbia. His official residence was Government House, and, among his other duties he received official visitors, toured the province, and presided over the opening of the provincial legislature.

So I got involved. That led to a whole bunch of other province-wide things I got involved in. I went for it, and at first it seemed like I was in over my head. But I kept as cool as I could. I had to hire babysitters. Good thing that my sister Joyce was at home at the time and she stayed with the children while I was travelling. Later on, I travelled throughout BC, encouraging the older people to teach the younger ones the weaving and the carving, or whatever it was they did in their areas.

This led from one thing to another. I got so much publicity. It went up so fast, you see. It was something that I couldn't handle. It just seemed as if everything went out of control. I was young at the time and it was too much for me. I hardly saw my family, and my marriage, which had not been on a strong footing, fell apart, too. I sort of had a nervous breakdown, almost. I couldn't take it any longer. Sometimes, I wonder how it was my children managed to grow up in those years! I was gone a lot, to meetings, often in Vancouver or Victoria, and sometimes a Homemakers chapter would call on us for help and we would send somebody to advise them and give support when they were being ignored or exploited.

I guess my approach to life was changing at that time. I gradually started to come out of my shell and do a bit of teaching. There was a basket-making workshop at Harrison Hot Springs Hotel. I was instructing there and got sort of known. I came forward and let the world know there was this strange person around, someone left over from the past. I was being called on to leave home more and more.

At the same time, I felt bad about the children. I was falling down where it really counted as a culture carrier—as a good mother and wife. I was being torn in half. I wanted to throw up my hands and just quit, but people encouraged me to go on. They hauled me out of myself. That's also when I first met Dora Carlson down at Port Angeles in Washington State. She told me I had been given a heavy set of duties and that I was capable of carrying them out.

This encouraged me. I decided I would carry on. I knew I had to do it. It was a job put on my shoulders by the elders. I started cutting the old home strings and moving out in the world.

Alliances

Now, as I said, after the elders dealt with Jeffrey, we decided to build a *híkw' lalém*, a longhouse for the ceremonies. This was at Sardis. I went over to visit the First Citizens' Fund authorities for British Columbia in Victoria. I had learned about them from a visit to the University of British Columbia. I was mostly behind the scenes at that time, unless I had to approach the government for funding. Then I would do it myself. I would go to the university. I met with Wilson Duff and Dr. Hawthorn and all the old professors and anthropologists who were working there. We had long talks about subjects and about how to get funding. Before I knew it, I was getting into politics. I won't go into that. It was just something I did not enjoy doing, but there were times when I had to get political.

I met so many people at that time, and I was totally unafraid. I don't know how I got that way, but I was not afraid of anyone. I remember walking with Dr. Hawthorn, the head of anthropology, on the grounds out at UBC.[6] There was Dr. Hawthorn, and with him—you know the guy, the

---

6   Harry B. Hawthorn (1910–2006) was the first professor of anthropology at the University of British Columbia. With his wife, Audrey, he specialized in studying and promoting a better understanding of Northwest Coast cultures. He was the principal author of *The Indians of British Columbia: A Survey of Social and Economic Conditions,* a groundbreaking 1955 report that was highly critical of existing government policy, rejecting assimilation as the driving goal and advocating instead a needs-based approach that would emphasize the right of Aboriginal peoples to equality and self-determination (Plant 2009, esp. 18–22). (The report was subsequently revised and published under the title *The Indians of British Columbia: A Study of Contemporary Social Adjustment:* see Hawthorn, Belshaw, and Jamieson [1958].) A decade later, he authored the two-volume "Hawthorn Report" (*A Survey of the Contemporary Indians of Canada: A Report on Economic, Political, Educational Needs and Policies,* 1966–67) for the federal government. The Hawthorns were also the prime movers behind UBC's Museum of Anthropology (designed by Arthur Erickson) that sits on the tip of Point Grey in Vancouver, with Hawthorn serving as the museum's first director and his wife as its first curator.

one who did the rocks? What was his name? Oh, yes, Wilson Duff.[7] And there was this other fellow, Kew, Michael Kew.[8] The three of us—there was the three of them and three of us, Evelyn and Rose and myself—we were walking on the grounds at UBC and Dr. Hawthorn and I were walking on ahead. I said to him, "Why is it that you can get a longhouse—you've got a longhouse here at UBC, at the Museum of Anthropology. We're the people who owned the longhouses and we can't even build a longhouse because the church won't let us, and the government officials won't help us with the money, won't give us the grants to start them—the law—everybody is afraid. We want our longhouses because this is our parliament building. This is where we make our laws. This is where everything happens. How come you guys get the money to build one and all you use it for is show? It's very sacred to us and we can't get the money to build it."

Dr. Hawthorn stopped and stood there, looking at me. "Gosh, Reenie," he said, "I don't know why not. I could talk to Mr. Dan Campbell, an MLA in Victoria. He's the one sitting on the First Citizens' Fund."

Dr. Hawthorn suggested this. He asked me, "Would you like to go and see him?"

I said, "Of course I would, if you would endorse something for me."

So he said, "I'll phone him and tell him you're coming in." And you know, I got the money! The first longhouse in Chilliwack in the Fraser Valley! And I wasn't afraid. Afterwards, Wilson Duff said to me, "You

7   Wilson Duff (1925–76) was the first curator of anthropology at the BC Provincial Museum in Victoria before becoming a professor of anthropology at the University of British Columbia. He was an avid ethnographer with a long series of publications covering Indigenous cultures around the province. See, for example, Duff (1952a, 1952b, 1956, 1959, 1964, and 1975).

8   Michael Kew (b. 1932) was also a professor of anthropology (now professor emeritus) at the University of British Columbia, but he began his career as assistant to Wilson Duff, after completing a doctorate on Coast Salish ceremonialism at the University of Washington. For a summary of that work, see Kew (1990). With Wilson Duff, he worked tirelessly to preserve totem poles and other cultural items at Haida Gwaii and elsewhere, as well as writing on coastal cultures and their relationship to salmon and taking a keen interest in cultural continuity and Aboriginal rights.

know, your people used to build beautiful longhouses. They didn't only build the longest of longhouses, but they built these square ones with the funny roofs. You know?"

And he said, "Your people were very unique. Why is it that none of the Stó:lō will talk to us?"

I told him because Stó:lō people are not allowed to. We're not allowed to talk about things. It's just our way. You don't hear about us because no one will tell you anything. He said, "Well, that's no good. The world should know about you!"

Anyway, we had a little talk. Afterwards, when we got back home, Evelyn Paul and Rose Charlie says to me, "Gosh, I don't know what we'd do without you. You're so brave!"

"Well," I said, "why not? They can only say no. If you want something, you have to ask for it. If they say no, you know at least that you have asked. You've tried. You're not going to get anywhere if you just stand around, hemming and hawing and hoping that somebody will notice you, take pity on you."

So after that, you know, the girls became braver. They became outspoken and they were good leaders. Evelyn Paul was our executive director, and Rose Charlie was for many years our president. And I was sort of the cultural consultant, hiding back behind in the bushes. We just had to start getting political, even to support our Aboriginal arts.

And so, about building a longhouse, I visited the people in charge of the First Citizens' Fund in Victoria. I applied for a grant. I sat in their office and told them what was happening. They said, "Sure, we'll give you the money as long as you get somebody to build it." As I have already explained, I talked to Richard Malloway, and he said, "Sure, we'll help."[9]

---

9 Richard Malloway, Sí:yám Th'eláchiyatel (1907–87), was the son of Julius and Mary Malloway. Throughout his life, he was a powerful source of Xwélmexw culture and tradition, which he defended and endeavoured to transmit to younger generations, including his neighbours, the sons of Rena and Roy Point. His son Frank, in turn, has also been a tireless communicator of the culture. Richard Malloway cooperated to some degree with anthropologists such as Wilson Duff and Claude Lévi-Strauss.

Everybody pitched in and helped. We had the grant and we built the big house at Tzeachten because that piece of land had been set aside. We built the longhouse there to serve the whole community—Skowkale, Yakweakwioose, and Tzeachten. It was a big house with three fires. Then that crazy fella who was on drugs got angry and burned it down and we had to start to rebuilt on our own, under our own steam.

Later, after I'd met Trudeau, I met Jean Chrétien. He was minister of Indian Affairs at the time. One of my distant cousins, Billy Mussel from Chilliwack, was his assistant. So Billy brought him over and introduced him to me. I got into the car with him and we sat in the front seat. We chatted about everything. Of course, I was very political at this time about Aboriginal rights, and he was young, you know. A tall, skinny, young guy. I really gave him an earful. I sure did. He was a smartass of a kid, I thought, but he was fun, you know.

We didn't always agree, of course. When I was president of Indian Arts and Crafts, we already had the doors open to send handicrafts to Disneyland in Germany and to Japan.[10] But things didn't come to fruition because Jean Chrétien, as minister of Indian Affairs, turned down my proposal to do a huge arts and crafts marketing board, with districts and warehouses for cottage crafts and training programs. We did present it to Jean Chrétien, but they turned it down, but later on "the Blue Book" came out, which was the same thing. They used a lot of my ideas, but kind of watered them down. We knew at the time that all the resources would be finished—like the trees and the salmon and the oil—everything, everything else was going to be finished—and that the Indian people were going to have to somehow pull their culture back together—or bits and pieces of it—for tourism, if for nothing else. This was one of the reasons I fought so hard to pick up the crafts. Because we were so unique, so different, from any other Indigenous peoples around the world.

So my whole [Blue] Book's presentation was based on the fact that once the country goes broke, they were going to have to depend upon Indian culture for their tourism, to bring the people here, to keep our country going. One of the main reasons that people would come here

10 Disneyland Europe did eventually open, not in Germany, but outside Paris.

would be to see our people, to see them dance, to hear them sing, to have performances, to buy their crafts. But we just have to go at it in a big way.

I was helped by Dr. Karl Peter, a sociologist at Simon Fraser University, and by the Western Consultants of Vancouver—who were associated with the Liberal Party at that time.[11] This was going to be a huge thing. Some of our people went to Hawaii and saw the cultural thing in Hawaii where they promote all those Hawaiian crafts. We were looking to do something like that—only we wanted a place in Vancouver to show the work from all over BC. We wanted to get hold of buildings down there at Jericho Beach by Spanish Banks, and we saw it as important to the tourism boom we knew was going to come. But Chrétien didn't go for it. He turned me down, and at that time, I was moving up north and thought, well, I can at least try to get this going up around Terrace.

Oliver Wells

Oliver Wells also got busy with revival work among the Salish weavers, around when we were beginning to do a few things for our culture.[12] Actually, it was the Musqueam weavers who got together with him and started that. The very first person who started the [revival of] Salish weaving around us was Oliver Wells. He started a long time ago. He put a book out and he visited the old people, like Mary Peters, Mrs. August Jim, and Mrs. Lorenzetto—Adeline Lorenzetto. And Mrs. Henry, I think.

---

11 Dr. Karl Peter (1924–98) specialized in Hutterite community organization and society.

12 Oliver Wells (1907–70) was a non-Native resident at Sardis who took a great interest in the Xwélmexw culture around him and wished to see it preserved. To that end, he recorded interviews with many members of the local community (including Dan Milo, Albert Louie, and Lena Hope), which were published after his death in *The Chilliwacks and Their Neighbours* (1987). He took a special interest in Salish weaving: see Wells (1966, 1969). For more on Salish weaving, see Gustafson (1980).

He visited them. I kept giving him the names of these people and how to approach them. I worked in behind, in the background. I told him, don't mention my name. I'm too young. They will get insulted if they hear that I recommended you speak to them. They're our elders. So you go and talk to them but don't give them my name. So we worked together. He spent a lot of time—just like this. We used to sit in the house until the sun went down, and he'd be taking notes and the kids would be screaming for my attention. Oh, we did all kinds of things. And I told him, "I never, ever want to appear in any of your books along with the elders." He said, "Okay, I respect your wishes."

But years later, his daughter Marie phoned me. She said, "Could you come up to the house? I'd like to see you." So Cliff brought me to visit her. She was married to a doctor—and she took out a newspaper clipping, almost a whole page—and here I was, young as could be, and spinning away! And there was a whole story about me in this newspaper. I was spinning at the PNE [Pacific National Exhibition]. I was just demonstrating, and darn it all, that Oliver! He was doing this behind my back.[13]

Ollie was a good friend. He never used to frighten me. He never put me down because I was poor and I had a lot of kids. He used to bring me stuff—I remember once he brought me cattails. They were no good but I took them. I thanked him profusely. And he'd bring me stuff like swans' feathers—whenever they'd lose feathers, or if they died—he'd bring me a little skin, like, and so I'd keep them. We were good friends—really, really good friends. And he lived in a big mansion, and every now and then the kids and I would go and visit him. His wife would put out high tea for us, ha ha ha! Tea for us poor little Indians!

But he said, "You know, Reenie, I feel like we owe your people something. My grandfather, A. C. Wells, he came here and he took this choice land from the Skowkale people, and we never, ever paid them for it." He said, "I've always felt guilty, and now, whatever I can do . . ."

13 Rena still has this clipping, which is from an unidentified paper. The article, by a writer named Gay Neale, is titled "A Craft Revived: Salish Weaving" and features a large photograph of Rena at work at her loom. She is a young woman, with her dark hair in short braids.

The Wellses adopted Dan Milo, my husband's step-grandfather, to be their relative. Mrs. A. C. Wells was the one who named Dan's dad "Milo"—she named him Jacob Milo, Jacob from out of the Bible and Milo for her favourite cousin. And so when Dan Milo was young, he used to go and work for them on the farm. They adopted him into their family. They were one of the leading pioneer families in the valley, or in the Chilliwack area, anyway. And so we were always close to the Wellses, and through the years, whatever I could do to help Ollie, I did what I could. I told him some things I never told other people. He would sneak into the longhouse every once in a while because he wanted to watch the *mí'lha*.

Ollie wanted desperately to revive some of the things that were lost. So he took it upon himself to dedicate the rest of his life to reviving the Salish weaving. And he did. He did all he could. He was so happy—he went to Scotland to visit relatives—and that's where he was killed, him and his wife, in a car accident.

He started out writing a book on Halq'eméylem, our language. And he got that going.[14] So he did a lot! Grandfather Dan Milo worked a lot with him regarding the language and the history. Oliver and Dan were like brothers. And there was another anthropologist named Jimmie Harris. He worked out of Seattle and he used to come and pick up Grandpa Dan Milo and take him to Seattle and keep him for a month or so, and

14 Casey Wells and Marie Weldon, the children of Oliver Wells, gave the language tape recordings gathered by their father to the Halq'eméylem Language Project of the combined Coqualeetza Elders' Group and Nooksack Elders' Group. These groups, together with linguist Brent Galloway, used the recordings of elders' reminiscences in their own Halq'eméylem tongue by transcribing these texts and categorizing them to prepare a basic grammar and what he called a classified word list, with words grouped into categories: number, nature, river and marine terms, animals, birds, fish, other aquatic creatures, insects, reptiles, other amphibians, plants, the body, the non-human body, body functions and sicknesses, and so on (see Galloway 1980). A number of the people whom Rena mentions in her explanations of family trees appear in photographs at the beginning of Galloway's publication.

he has field notes that I sure would like to get my hands on.[15] The past has a lot to say about what comes next in life.

Yes, politics and art go hand in hand. Even today, I burn for a better world, but the feeling is strongest when I'm sitting in my workroom, weaving. We should have done this book when I was forty and still had lots of energy!

I didn't get involved in putting the Salish weaving group together. I remember Ollie wanted to have a canoe built. So we went to see John Wallace, up at Soowahlie. After that, I stepped back and let things happen. John did build him a canoe. It was a beautiful canoe. I guided people into doing things, propelled them along, got them started, then I'd back off and let them do their own thing.

Revivals

One thing seemed to lead to another. I was busy with my family in those years—which I now call my young years. But soon British Columbia started having celebrations. The centennial year came up. Was it in 1958? The priests decided to have—I forget what the church called it—it's like a pageant, where they dress everybody up and parade everybody around with different things representing the work of the churches, you know. Father McKinnon suggested we should do this pageant as part of the centennial year, showing how the church participated in "civilizing the Natives." We would have scenes representing the different stages in the life of the Native people, but of course, the pageant would be controlled by the church.

I guess you can imagine it: the child-like Indians were saved from themselves by the church. The pageant had scenes that showed how the church brought the savages to God and to a decent "civilized" way of life.

---

15 Evidently, Dan Milo told a set of stories, myths, and histories in the Halq'eméylem language, which James Harris recorded and transcribed. Steven Point (personal communication, February 5, 2013) provided this information after having reviewed the Dan Milo transcripts.

But the content of that pageant, the actual practices and the art, that idea grew and it got bigger and bigger, and the canoe racing came into it. That's when we began to realize, you know, this is really turning into something. We Stó:lō started organizing events on our own. We had the first Cultus Lake Indian Festival, with Father McKinnon guiding, helping us, along with the Wigwam Homemakers, which was the Sardis women's handicraft group. The Homemakers did the arts and crafts and the lunches or whatever food was going to be served. Richie Malloway, old Sam Jimmy, and Albert Douglas and Burns Mussel decided that they would organize the canoe racing. And they did so.

Then different people said, "Well, we should have some Native dancing." But no one knew anything about the dancing. But I remembered the costumes. Oliver Wells helped me, as I already said, giving me ideas about putting the skirts and the capes together. I did all the weaving and some of the early teachings that my grandmother taught me—those things woke up and sort of came back to life again.

FIGURE 28

Family members dancing in Rena's cedar bark costumes at Expo '86, in Vancouver.
Photo courtesy of Rena Point Bolton.

That started a whole chain reaction, the importance of the teachings that I had had. Our people were throwing everything away, and we shouldn't do that, because we had a beautiful and unique culture, especially the singing and the dancing, the costumes and the canoe racing. So it grew, and my family and I, we created the Salish Dancers, with the cedar-bark outfits. Steven and Mark and Jeffrey and the girls, they all took part in the dancing and I did the singing. Then later on, as the boys grew up, they started to help me with the singing. The Salish Dancers grew, and as time went on, I got more involved. People started coming to me about the things that I remembered about the past.

Suddenly, I had become the expert, and I didn't realize that I knew so much about the old ways, because I had just lived it without thinking, out at the old smokehouse on the river and living with my grandparents. All these things came back again, and I began to realize that I had a treasure in terms of knowledge given by my elders. Because so many people were coming to me and depending on me to provide them with the knowledge of the costumes and the songs and the dances, and with the children helping, I realized, you know, this is what the old people trained me for. This was part of the teaching that I received, to carry on, as a hereditary carrier of our people and their knowledge. I was doing it but I hadn't realized I was.

From then on, I took on the responsibility seriously. I began to think about them telling me this was something I had to do. I had to pass it on to the children. So I did. I would sit them down and tell them about the old people and the stories—the government of the land, the care that was given to all the villages, the protection that was given to both sides of the river by X̱éyteleq, who guarded the river. He was the guardian of the river, and because he was, the people upriver, they were protected. They lived as well as they could, in security, knowing he was there—with his family living on both banks—protecting the river from invaders.

I taught these things to my children, hoping that they would carry on, you know, so that they would feel the responsibility toward the people. I didn't force anything on them, but I let them know what my responsibilities had been. Through the years, it all just seemed to grow and grow. As my children grew up and got educated, the responsibilities just seemed normally to shift to them also. When Steven was in high school, there was a riot there. He was the vice-president of the student council, and with the president of the student council, he was locked away with the principal when this happened.

The principal would not go out and talk to the students who were smashing things, and there were hundreds of them. It was at the high school there in Sardis. Steven, feeling responsible for these students and feeling that they needed someone to speak to them, he got on the PA system in the principal's office and he talked to them. He talked to them and he reasoned with them. Somehow, he got through to them, and he went outside and he spoke to them.

They stopped what they were doing and the police came in and took over. They took Steven home. He was in tears. He was upset, but the first thing he said to me was, "Mother, I managed to stop them." Now, no one made him do this. No one told him this was his duty, but he had an inner, a built-in feeling that if he could do something to help, then he just had to do it. It was just an automatic feeling, and he reached out to the other students. He reached out and he managed to stop them. This is the kind of feeling that most of my children have. If they feel they can help someone, anywhere, they do so. It doesn't matter if it is giving food or clothing, or listening to hard-time stories or family problems—they're involved in all kinds of things like this.

Meeting Other Activists

Gradually, I learned to take things in stride. I got stronger and I told my family that if it ever happens that they go into a land claim, or negotiate or something, and they need someone to stand up for them and speak, then I will do it and I will not be afraid. I will not be afraid to say what other, nicer Native people are afraid to say. If I have to lower myself and speak rather harshly to those who oppose our people and their future, I will do it. This is the job given me by the elders. Even now, after many years have passed and I am not young any longer, I managed to get myself transferred as a band member from here at Kitsumkalum back down to Skowkale, so I could do this—so I can speak out—if my people need my voice.

Back in the 1960s, as you saw, I started running into various political people and learning from them too, in different places across Canada. I met George Manuel. He was like our first grand chief of Canada. What do they call them now? He was the president of the Assembly of First Nations. I met him when he was just starting up the Union of BC Indian Chiefs about 1969.[16] We had a meeting at a little house on the Chilliwack Landing Reserve. Just a handful of us had gotten together there. I didn't know too much at the time. I was green as grass, but I really looked up to George. He seemed to know what he was doing and he wasn't afraid. I thought he was a great speaker, and he seemed to be fearless. I really admired him. And yet he was a kind, gentle man. He was strong and he seemed to know what he was talking about.

It was people like him who encouraged me to go on into the political world. I didn't know the ins and outs of the plight of Native people. I didn't really understand it, I guess because I was so involved with our own family's work. What was going on with the politics of our land and resources, I didn't really know too much about it. I had heard things here and there but they weren't priorities at the time, until I met people like George.

16 George Manuel (1921–1989), author of *The Fourth World: An Indian Reality* (1974), was an extremely influential Aboriginal political leader, who served as president of the National Indian Brotherhood (now the Assembly of First Nations), as well as occupying numerous other positions of leadership. In 1979, he became president of the Union of BC Indian Chiefs, in which capacity he played a pivotal role in the protests surrounding the adoption of the Canadian Constitution, leading the Constitution Express from Vancouver to Ottawa and ultimately on to the United Nations, Britain, and Europe. This grassroots action culminated in the addition of section 35 of the Constitution, which recognizes and upholds Aboriginal rights, including rights under treaty. For more information, see http://indigenousfoundations.arts.ubc.ca/home/community-politics/george-manuel.html.

And another influence was Chief Dan George.[17] He was related to my first husband. He was a distant relative. When I used to talk to him, he impressed me as someone who was doing something for the Native people. He was being seen and he was being heard, even though he was just acting in movies and things. He was bringing our peoples out in front of the footlights, from where they had been hiding or where they had been shoved aside for so long—people didn't even really want to see us until then. He helped to bring us out under the spotlight, stage lights, I guess. He brought the people out so others began to notice us. He brought us out into the sunlight and people had to look at us, even if they didn't want to. I told him I admired him for this. I think it was at one of our *mí'lha* events, you know. He used to attend them whenever he could and everyone would shake hands with him and talk to him. I think it might have been at Capilano [North Vancouver], I'm not sure. It was either at Capilano or Musqueam [Point Grey]. I think it was at Capilano.

That first meeting with George Manuel wasn't planned. It just sort of happened by accident. Someone said—it was at a little red schoolhouse, a little tiny building—someone might have said, "We're having a meeting with a big man tonight. You should come and meet him." You know, that would be enough to bring me out—I don't really remember the details of why I was there, but these things always interested me. My ears were always open. I always wanted to know why things happened! Science was a real interest to me while I was at school.

17 A man of many talents, Dan George (1899–1981) was a chief of the Tsleil-Waututh Nation, based in Burrard Inlet, North Vancouver, from 1951 to 1963. In 1969, at the age of sixty, he embarked on an acting career, almost immediately earning an Academy Award nomination for his role in *Little Big Man* (1970) and subsequently appearing in numerous other films, as well as in George Ryga's highly acclaimed play *The Ecstasy of Rita Joe* (staged in both Vancouver and Toronto). He also wrote several books, including *My Heart Soars* (1974), and was an influential figure in the early years of the Aboriginal rights movement.

Speaking of science, I met David Suzuki at one of our big meetings.[18] He asked if we would break up into groups and every group write something about what they thought about things, about the environment and the way things are going. So I very quickly wrote out on a piece of paper the laws of the Stó:lō—I very quickly wrote it out—I don't know how the heck I wrote so fast for twenty or thirty minutes—and then we had to hand in our papers and he checked them. He looked at mine, and he said, "Oh my goodness."

He said, "Where did this come from?"

I laughed and I said, "I don't know. I just wrote down what I thought." And so he signed it and I still have that today, somewhere. It was about the relationship we have with the land, the fish, the birds and the animals, and the rocks and the rivers and the trees, and how it came about. I had just gotten started on another subject—it might have been the civic laws of the people when our time was up, so I didn't write any more.

When he saw that, though, he was really, really impressed, that something like that had come out so quickly! So people like Suzuki, for one—he really impressed me about the environment, because he brought out years ago all the things that our people already knew—about what would happen to the land if it was abused, and that we are one with the land and if the land perishes, we will perish too. We knew that. We always knew that. My grandfather used to talk about it, and Dan Milo did. We often wondered why the white people couldn't see that. What are you going to do when the last gold nugget is dug out, the last drop of oil is siphoned off and the last ounce of drinking water—and the air

18 David Suzuki, zoologist, geneticist, and environmentalist, is well known for his many television and radio series, notably as host of the popular and long-running CBC science program *The Nature of Things*, now seen in over forty nations. He has also been an outspoken critic of governments for their failure to take decisive action to protect the environment and reverse global climate change. In 1990, Suzuki cofounded the David Suzuki Foundation, the mission of which is "to protect the diversity of nature and our quality of life, now and for the future," as well as to promote the recognition that "we are all interconnected and interdependent with nature" (http://www.davidsuzuki.org/about/), a principle well familiar to Aboriginal peoples.

and the last fish and the last deer? What are we going to do then? *They will not quit!* It's just on and on and on. They are going to fight over the last drop of water.

Anyway, Cliff was with me that time and he read aloud a poem that I had written called "A Call from the Wild," and Suzuki wept. Everything touched him so deeply. He said, "I went to school for thirty years to learn about the fruit fly, and here you people have known all about ecology and relationships from a long time ago." These were his words. Here are the words of my little poem, from 1986:

A Cry from the Wild

O, cry from the wild, my brothers!
No food, no trees, no free terrain
Run, run from the strangers:
To kill you for sport is their game.

O, cry from the depths, my brothers!
For others have come to pollute your home,
To slay you without prayer or fasting:
Unclean, you die alone.

O, cry from the air, my brothers!
Your wings meant power and sovereignty.
But where is there to fly to?
For radar and death now rule the sky.

O, cry my brown skinned brothers!
Should we lose control of our land
We'll fail to save our brothers
And perish beneath the dying sand.

O, cry for the earth, poor strangers!
For the waste that you have laid,
No longer a land of plenty,
A third world you have made.

Another thing was, I used to go to the elementary schools in Chilliwack and other schools. I talked about the Indian culture. I'd bring my little loom and some wood, roots, bark—basket-making material—and I'd demonstrate. I'd put on my regalia and talk to the children. I did this for quite a few years. I didn't have a vehicle and I used to walk. Then I started taking classes of children to the longhouse in Tzeachten and giving them tours and explaining to them the longhouse and what it was used for. The children were allowed so much time to ask questions, and the teacher would stand by and make sure everything was done properly, not too much excitement. It really worked wonders. I think it brought forth more understanding in the white students. They began to understand that we were people, like anybody else, but we just had a different kind of life. As you know, there is a safe, restful atmosphere in a longhouse. It is very different from the life outside. By the time those children left, they had a better understanding of the people, they knew we were spiritual people. Usually, the teacher would be kind of moved by the time they were leaving. So I think through the years I did reach a lot of people. We were able to give them a broader understanding of our plight. We weren't just "the lazy drunken Indian" who doesn't do anything. We had a different lifestyle, and it was totally different at one time.

When you talk to them about this in the longhouse, they feel it. They understand it. As they walked into the longhouse, I'd tell them, "Before you come into the longhouse, children, I'd like you to understand that the Earth is very special to our people. The ground is sacred because for many, many, many thousands of years, our people lived and died here and they went back to the soil. So the ground carries the remains of our elders, and of the birds and the trees and the animals. They have lived and died here, and their remains go back to the soil. So the planet's children have remained here, right in this building. The big trees that you see in here that span the building, they grew on these remains. So they carried the life-blood of these people in the veins of the tree. So when they cut down the tree, it became a very sacred thing to the people. As they laid out the logs on the building, they would have a shaman come in and bless the tree for having given its life for our home, and red dust [red ochre] was thrown on the logs of those trees. This was a way of thanking them for giving their lives to shelter our people. I want you children to think of this as you walk through the longhouse, that everything in here had life at one time."

Then they would become solemn and they would sit and listen. They would ask questions about the ceremonies and I would answer as best I could. But when the teacher was leaving, she would usually have tears in her eyes. She would say, "Thank you. I think I am the one who learned more today than the children did. And I will always remember."

This was just one of the things I did in my spare time, and my time was really not very spare at all. I usually had to neglect some chores to do this, but I thought it was important working with children, so that they would remember as they grew up. This is a taste of some of the things that ran through my head and heart in those years when I became political, active in the renewal of our arts, and when I moved to northern British Columbia.

Moving North

I told you about walking around the grounds out at UBC with Harry Hawthorn and Wilson Duff and those people, and how that led to a grant and to us building our first longhouse home for the *mi'lha*. Well, we got to know the people at the First Citizens' Fund. I went to see Dan Campbell, who was the head of the fund in Victoria. I told him our plight. I told him how worried I was about our culture being destroyed, and now our people were left with nothing. I told him, "There might be a few elderly people left in the villages who could help to bring back some of the beautiful work and teachings from the past, but I have no vehicle, I have no money to travel. I have talked on the radio and on the television, but I don't reach everybody personally."

So he sat there and he listened to me. He says, "All right. I know what you're saying. I will have a car for your use, and a chauffeur, and we will put it down as part of your program, the project you're doing."

Promoting Native Arts and Crafts

That's how the First Citizens' Fund came to sponsor me. I had a car that they bought for our project, and a chauffeur, and my auntie from one of the reserves, Martha James from Chilliwack Landing—she came.[1] She took along her little loom. She travelled with me all over. We travelled to as many villages as we could. She was beginning to get tired by the time we reached the north.

So, with her loom, we used to march into the band councils and ask if we could come into their village and speak to their members. They would give us the go-ahead and tell us who we should speak to—maybe an elder, or some prominent person. We'd go and so I'd get to meet the elders. We'd speak to them. Not in an authoritative voice, but in a pleading one: "We need your help. We need your help to save what your people knew. It would be wonderful if we could bring back the beautiful work that your people did. And we'd be willing to pay you a salary if you could teach younger people to do the work that you know."

They would listen to me, and there would be other women in the room who would agree with me. It wasn't the same in every village, but the gist of the thing was that the younger people agreed that it should be carried on. So the elders then began to teach the younger people. This is how we got started again, and the ones most receptive were younger. The elders were more cautious, but the younger people were really the ones we wanted to train anyway.

I don't think we saved all of the crafts, but we saved a lot that would have been lost otherwise. Some of these older women just managed to teach one course and then they passed away. They were just caught in time. One old lady, she was in her eighties, she got so excited when she found she could teach her work that she went out into the woods by herself. I think I may have been up in Shuswap [Secwepemc] country somewhere. She just couldn't wait. She was going to go and peel a birch tree for the bark, but she got overtired and she got lost. They couldn't

1   Martha James is pictured with one of her weavings in Ulli Steltzer's *Indian Artists at Work* (1976, 100).

find her. The next day the troops went out and they found her dead by a birch tree. That was sad. I felt terribly remorseful about it. But I thought her spirit was doing the right thing. She wanted desperately to pass her knowledge on. And because of that, her family made up their minds. They were going to carry on her work. So they did.

I talked to many men as well about their carving and woodwork. I talked to a man up here, at Hazelton, at 'Ksan. What was his name? He just passed away. Chief Ge'el! Yes, Walter Harris—I talked to him.[2] I met him somewhere on that trip around BC. I don't recall where, and I asked him, "Would you be willing to teach your knowledge?"

He had told me he was a carver. I said, "We could pay you. We could get the money for you."

He said, "Oooh, I'd love to do that." And so, I had his name down as a master craftsman. I had all the names from each village. I think I must have lost all those papers. That would have been really great to have, because all these people are dead now. Anyway, down through the years, I managed to see Walter about every ten years and remind him of what he was supposed to do! We'd kind of joke about it. Polly Sargent moved into this activity.[3] And they started up their own thing [at 'Ksan]

2 A leading Gitxsan carver, Walter Harris (Simoogit Ge'el) was the principal chief at the village of Kispiox. Photographs of his work are also available in Steltzer's *Indian Artists at Work* (1976, 146–49). He and Earl Muldon (Simoogit Delgamuukw) were the Gitxsan artists who carved the front doors of the Museum of Anthropology at the University of British Columbia, which now guard the entrance to the museum's gift shop.

3 Polly Sargent was married into an established merchant family whose founders settled at Old Hazelton in the 1800s. She and her husband ran the local hotel and promoted Northwest Coast arts among the general public and especially among artists, anthropologists, and museum officials across Canada. Together with the local Gitanmaax activists and interested professionals like George MacDonald, Wilson Duff, Duane Pasco, and Bill Holm, she was active in starting up the 'Ksan centre and museum at Hazelton to promote and teach Northwest Coast culture: dance, song, storytelling, and of course, Gitxsan carving (see Dawn 1981).

so they didn't really need our program.[4] But the thing was, they did start to do things, too. I talked to Polly. I used to stop at her hotel and stay overnight and visit with her from time to time.

I went to school at Coqualeetza with Claude Davidson—Robert Davidson's father. We did a show together once, at a science fair in the Terrace High School. He was carving this black stuff—argillite. I asked him, then, if he could get a class together and teach. He said, "Oh, I sure could and I would, but I'm just so busy right now I don't have the time." But we talked about our school days and things like that. A lot of the kids who went to school at Coqualeetza were later leaders in their villages, not only in politics but also in arts and crafts.

So you see, I had my network! Whenever I travelled, I looked for old schoolmates because there was a lot of them—in Kitimat, in the Nass and the Charlottes. I met Ken Harris and his mother from Gitsegukla.[5] It was in Prince Rupert, when I travelled throughout BC, and we talked. He told me this story. "A long, long time ago," he said, "there was a great famine among the people here on the Skeena and some of our relatives had to leave because there wasn't enough food. So they broke away and they travelled down south and they were called Salis'tsian." And he said, "You are from those people." He hugged me there in Prince Rupert, and he said, "Welcome home."

Cliff and I ran into that Salis'tsian later on, when we were coming from Oregon, along that coast, there's a big sign on one of the stores, or hotels or whatever. It says, "Welcome to Salis'tsian Territory." I said to Cliff, "Look at this! Here! That's what Ken Harris said we were."

That was right at the tail end of my trip. We didn't make it to the Charlottes [Haida Gwaii]. My aunt was getting tired and she was getting sick. I thought, "Well, I better get her home." I think my driver was

4   The history of 'Ksan and its foundation is covered in Dawn (2006). For examples of working 'Ksan artists, see photos in Steltzer (1976, 136–45).

5   Ken Harris (Hag'begwatxw)—a Fireweed/Killer Whale chief from the Gitxsan village of Gitsegukla—was a resident of Prince Rupert and was active in Aboriginal affairs. He is remembered for his translation of local legends, collected in *Visitors Who Never Left: The Origin of the People of Damelahamid* (1972).

getting itchy feet, too—a young fellow from Manitoba, Victor Pierre, a grandson of Aunt Martha. I think he was getting tired of driving me around.

I don't remember where exactly we started—probably from Musqueam—gosh, I threw away all my notes. I know we went through—what's the name of that road that goes—you go through Kamloops—you go all through the interior—that's where that lady got lost. I can't remember the names of these villages. We went through the Kootenays, then up through Kamloops, then north of Kamloops. Then we came through the Cariboo to Prince George. I remember Prince George because they had those newspaper people waiting for us, at the radio station—the media. Oh, I can't remember these things! We went through Gitsegukla. I think we stopped at Moricetown. We went to Hagwilget. We stopped at 'Ksan. I remember we went to Kispiox because Auntie Martha, she was really tired and was lying down in the back seat. I said to her, "Come out and see the totem poles, Auntie. They are really, really huge."

She said, "Oh, okay." She got out of the car and she was tired, really exhausted. So I helped her to the totem poles—the row of them down below near the river. She said, "E'wxw! I don't like it here. Put me back in the car. It's terrible here. I think somebody died here." She wouldn't go any further. So I brought her back to the car. She said, "Let's get out of here. I don't like this place." Right there by the totem poles, she just about spazzed out. We didn't stay long. We talked to a few people. We left papers behind. They wanted us to stop and lecture, but Martha didn't seem to like it there for some reason. I don't know why she had that reaction.

Anyway, we kept on going. We stopped at Kitsumkalum. We stayed there overnight. Then the next day, we went to Prince Rupert. We turned around there. On our way back, we stopped at other places we'd missed on the way north. We came down through the Canyon. I think we were in Penticton on the way up. I think we stopped there. The old lady—I can see her right here—she had invited us there. We didn't like to impose on people who didn't want to have anything to do with arts and crafts, so we sent out messages to people, and if they responded and were interested, then we stopped. We didn't go up the Sunshine Coast, but we took in Duncan on Vancouver Island. I know I spent time on the Island, with the knitters. Representing Indian Arts and Crafts, I helped them when they were having problems with the farmers, but I don't know if that was the same time or a different time. Those women were having such a bad time getting their wool from the sheep farmers.

The farmers would allow them to take a certain amount of wool. Then, for their pay, the farmers would take so many sweaters or knitted articles. As a result, those women weren't making very much money at all. They owed too much money for the wool they got and the farmers weren't helping them get ahead. That didn't make it any easier. The women got very little cash for the knitted goods they were making. So they came to me in Victoria. I had stopped there with the other Homemakers at the time.

We had a meeting with them, with all the knitters on the Island. I wasn't well. Oh, I remember now, I was lying down in a motel room, and they had to prop me up with pillows. We had the meeting with the knitters. They came into the room where I was propped up, and we had that meeting. We dealt with it. We went to the Parliament Buildings there in Victoria. We approached the MLA for that area, and he said he would put a stop to what was going on and promised to help the knitters. The farmers would have to sell their wool, instead of trading. Eventually, the knitters quit anyway 'cause there was too much competition from other sources. They kind of died out. So that was part of my trip there.

I had my picture in *Chatelaine* magazine when I was on that trip around the province. They had me standing there holding a little basket. I think I was lecturing, but I don't know where I was. I have a lot of newspaper clippings of that trip.

That trip was rich in experiences. We had to plead with the elders to teach the crafts and skills they had learned as children. It was very difficult work. The old people were so afraid to stand up. They were terrified of the wrath of the church and divine intervention. Long ago, the churches had declared our ceremonial goods and arts and dancing and music and carving to be the work of the devil. Our cultures were totally condemned as something evil and pagan. They terrorized the elders, and without the backing of their elders, the people were afraid to lift a finger. They were really terrified, first that they would go to jail and then, even worse, to suffer the wrath of the Lord.

As we went around the province and met with the elders, we would say our piece. They would listen to us and then they would hang their heads and say nothing. Usually, some of the younger family members would say that the elders could not even think about what I wanted since it was against the teachings of their church. None of them wanted to say anything at all against the church. It was the same situation in almost every village and reserve we went to, especially wherever there was no craft production at all. We would start by talking to the band council, making a presentation and asking, "Do you have any artists working here?"

They might say, "Well, Old X used to do something. You could ask her daughter. Maybe she learned some of it."

So we would buy a cake or buns or something and go for a visit to one of those families. We would chat with them a long time and gradually they started to open up. Someone would pipe up and say, "Well, I remember the old teachings, but the church really frowns on our ways."

I would ask, "Do you do any drumming? Do you make drums?"

"Oh no," they said, "that's what the heathens do!" They said they couldn't sing or drum because the priest or the pastor would never approve of such a thing. And right to this very day, there are churches whose teachings are dead set against our ceremonies and our herbal medicines, even. That is the case in Stó:lō country and up here too, in the northern area.

As we travelled around here and there, people came forward and had the courage to agree to teach. We found that a lot of younger members of families were eager, and maybe they would have some influence on the elders who were intimidated. The ones who agreed to teach what they knew, we arranged for them to get paid by us. I could say that because we had a grant. What we were doing was sponsored by the First Citizens' Fund and the BC Indian Arts and Crafts Society.

I just wanted to get Native people off their butts and standing up to fight for a better life. They have a lot to contribute. For instance, our philosophies and our ways of thinking and our beliefs—we could save the Earth. We could save the future generations of Indigenous people if they decided to go back and see that they are all brothers to the other species of the plants and the animals; also, we have to learn that plants and animals are not a resource in a monetary sense, but rather we should see them as our brothers. That is a good way and a healthy way. If the people who came to visit us five hundred years ago, if they could only change their way of thinking and think the way our peoples once did—that we *must* live in harmony with Mother Earth if we are to survive—then I think we could, we can, still save the planet. If we don't, if we continue to harm the atmosphere and to excavate the Earth, well, then we are all going to perish. There are a lot of poisons under the ground and the atmosphere is so polluted that it is unhealthy and is causing all the strange weather we are having. It is all going to explode one day. One day, if we don't change our ways, we will all be destroyed, and it could be thousands of years before the Earth can heal again and house more people.

I like to think the Creator will save some of our people who are worth saving, who will live in harmony with Mother Nature and who will not destroy in the future. Maybe the bloodlines of such people will go on into the future. I like to think this, but I am not sure it will happen. When we cease to respect nature and think that we are more powerful than it is and that we can dominate it, we then have to be shown that we are not superior over nature. That arrogance and lack of respect, it can only lead to disaster.

I have come around to thinking that instead of winning over one another, we have to learn to cooperate and share what is left, teach each other the best we have to offer. Our philosophy is very good and the white technology is good if it's used properly and not to damage and destroy people and the Earth. We have to learn to combine our philosophy and the white technology. We have to control these things. We can do it if we just try a little harder. People who think this way should stand up and make noise. They should come forward. It's time we got up on our hind legs and said our piece, instead of sitting and waiting for a saviour to come to us. We must come forward.

The North: New Threads

Things weren't easy for me right then. It was a hard time. Here I was, breaking up my home and being out on the road, trying to convince people to have the courage to pick up the threads of the past and move forward into the unknown. Sometimes, we made no headway, like right here on the Skeena River. Even when I had moved up here [Tsimshian country], I asked various people about the famous weaving of this area.

FIGURE 29

Mrs. Agnes Sutton, of the Gitxsan Nation, who lived at Cedarvale, on the Skeena River, and taught girls domestic skills, northern-style basketry, and Chilkat weaving. Photo courtesy of Rena Point Bolton.

You know the Chilkat weaving was actually developed here in the Tsimshian world! It was here just as much as it was up in the Chilkat country.[6] But no, the local people here did not want to even hear about it. It was too uncivilized even to think your way back toward the past.

But I asked around and I heard about an old lady up the river [upriver from Terrace] near Usk. Mrs. [Agnes] Sutton, at Cedarvale.[7] She was Gitxsan and a very religious lady. I went up and talked with her. She said, "I feel so bad. Our old people wove such beautiful robes but now the churches do not approve of it at all. I tried teaching at 'Ksan, up at Gitanmaax, but it wasn't successful."[8]

"Would you teach me?" I asked her. Yes, she would. So Nadine and Kojo Asante went with me to see her.[9] It was not easy and progress was

6 Chilkat weaving owes its name to the Chilkat Tlingits, who live in the area of Klukwan, Alaska (although, as Rena mentions, the technique may have originated among the Tsimshian). Chilkat textiles were once produced by many of the Indigenous peoples of northern British Columbia and Alaska, including the Tsimshian, the Haida, and the Tlingit, and were generally associated with families of high status. The traditional materials are mountain goat wool, dog hair, and yellow cedar bark, and the resulting textiles have an unusual shapeliness. The technique itself is complex and had all but died out until it underwent a revival in recent decades. There are now Chilkat weavers working in many parts of the world, but many do not follow the old pattern-board tradition, in which the men provided the crest designs and the women wove them into being. For more information, see the work of Cheryl Samuel (1987, 1990), one of the leading researchers and practitioners of Chilkat weaving.

7 The first child christened at Methodist missionary Robert Tomlinson's Cedarvale church, and the first woman married in the same church, Agnes Sutton was an influential matriarch, who, as several Gitxsan women told me in the 1980s, trained young Gitxsan women in disciplined living, Christian devotion, traditional crafts, and respect for old, pre-Christian customs.

8 Rena refers here to 'Ksan Historical Village (http://ksan.org), a museum and art school run by the people of Gitanmaax Reserve, in Hazelton, British Columbia.

9 Dr. Kojo Asante, a medical practitioner in Terrace for some years, became well known for his work with children with fetal alcohol syndrome in western Canada and the Yukon. Mrs. Asante was a close friend of Rena's.

slow. We did laugh a lot, I guess. But eventually, I went back to her on my own. I kept it up. I picked up techniques. I read books. I studied pieces in museums. Peter McNair and a woman called Marilyn—I forget her last name—they were very helpful at the BC Provincial Museum in Victoria.[10] With their help, I was able to take apart some weaving rows and analyze them. Then at Kitselas, I began to teach what I knew, working with Willy White.[11]

10 Peter McNair is a researcher of Northwest Coast cultures and a former curator at the Royal British Columbia Museum.

11 William White is a Tsimshian weaver and artist. See, for example, his "Raven's Nest" Chilkat woven basket, on the Spirit Wrestler Gallery website: http://www.spiritwrestler.com/catalog/index.php?products_id=4103 (accessed 23 August 1913). See also figure 30 in this volume, which shows William and Rena modelling one another's work.

Life with Cliff

Life just rushes along. From morning to night, Cliff and I are busy. It's like we're *racing* with time. We have to get this and that done before a certain time. And now, see, he has to get the potatoes out! Ha ha ha ha! And, you know, I'm in my eighties and he's in his seventies, and we don't have time to do everything expected of us. From the time I had children, or from the time Grandmother started whipping me into shape, I just haven't had time—you know, there are days when I don't even comb my hair. I don't even look in the mirror. Oh, my goodness, sometimes when I do look into the mirror, I think, what has happened to me? But that's the way it is when you are busy. Then I find that people say to me, why is it that you don't get old? Well, I don't have time to get old! Ten years is just nothing.

I met Cliff when I was travelling around the province that time, going to as many reserves as I could to talk the elders into continuing on with their crafts—whatever knowledge it was they had, and whatever had been taught to them, including the languages—I told them that we would sponsor them. There I was, going from village to village. When I came here, this is where my stepsisters from my father's second marriage were, and my half-brother Bill, too; he had married Cliff's sister. The Boltons had all gone to the residential school at Lytton in Nlaka'pamux territory, where my father's family was. Cliff went to school there as well.

So, through the residential school, there was this . . . this young people thing, about getting to know each other, even from other areas. Bill met Cliff's sister there, and they eventually married. When I came up on tour, when we were touring around the villages, I stayed with my stepsister Annette here at Kitsumkalum. She was married to Alex Bolton. She had a family and so I stayed with her. And my aunt, Martha James, she stayed with us too, at Annette's. This is how I met all of the Kitsumkalum people. We had a display, with my aunt doing her weaving in the basement at the House of Sim-oi-Ghets [House of the Chiefs] on the reserve, and the media had come—TK Radio and the newspapers were there. As a result, I was on a program called "The Hourglass" on TK.

The hereditary chief at that time was James Bolton. That was Cliff's father, and after I had spoken to them and talked to them about reviving the arts and crafts as much as possible, they served a lunch, with tea and sandwiches. James came over and sat with me. We talked and he asked me how far I was going on this tour. I said my trip was almost over, and we chit-chatted. I told him, "As a matter of fact, I'm just going to Prince Rupert now and I think I'll finish. I'll wind up there. My aunt is getting tired."

He said, "Well, when you are finished, would you consider coming here and staying with your stepsister—you know, for one winter? My people are desperately in need of reviving their old culture. They are losing their Indianness."

These were his very words. I thought, "Well, this is something I have never thought of!"

Anyway, as a result of our little talk, it turned out that Alex and Annette were happy to have me stay with them for the winter. When I went home, I told the children, and of course, by then, their dad and I had decided to separate, and Roy, after a life working in the woods, now wanted to move home. I said, "Fine. You stay with the children. They are grown up now and mostly on their own."

The younger children, I told him, I would come for later, when I had a place to live. I had decided that I would stay in Kitsumkalum for the winter. So I continued working up here with the local people. The first thing I taught them was beading, and then basket weaving, and spinning and knitting. We got into the button blankets—oh, we had everything going! They were so busy, and yet I still hadn't really met Cliff, because he was working for the Department of Indian Affairs in Prince Rupert. He and his wife and family were living there. Then from there, he moved to Vancouver, and he was working out of Vancouver for the Department of Indian Affairs. He lived there for quite a few years, and then his marriage went on the rocks.

He came home and he worked for Port Simpson for a while, and then he just got tired. A lot of things were happening at the time. The older people, his mother and his father, they talked to me and they asked me, in the old Indian way, if I would consider marrying Cliff, who was now on his own.

I didn't really know him that well. I thought he was a little bit loud . . . ha ha . . . and a little over-energetic, but, you know, we did get to know one another. I found a very kind and gentle person underneath all of the boisterous surface. And he was interested in Indian culture. He didn't know much. He said he had been raised at Lytton and their culture in the Fraser Canyon was different from up here on the Skeena. And also, a lot of the elders that he knew had passed away. So we kind of made this connection. He had been working with Ottawa, buying Indian crafts, the cheaper stuff. He was buying for them and travelling all over British Columbia, picking up these things. I began to talk to him, you know, about quality. I said we should get into really good quality arts and crafts, instead of just the cheap stuff done in a hurry, and which looked like it got manufactured somewhere in the Orient, you know. I never found out why Ottawa was buying that stuff.

So we had this common interest. It was the totem poles, the carvings . . . he didn't know anything about the weavings. We did a lot of talking. We talked sometimes for hours. In the end, we decided, "Well, we'll give it a try."

FIGURE 31
Cliff and Rena Bolton.
Photo courtesy of Rena
Point Bolton.

So we did. We got married. I had a home in Terrace by that time. I was working for the Terrace School District as a counsellor at the Junior High School. There are a lot of Native students living in Terrace. A lot of them come from the Nass Valley, the Nisga'a kids. So I was really busy. I had bought a home right in town. My younger ones, the girls, came and lived with me in Terrace. Anyway, after Cliff and I got together, I decided we had to make our own home. He was always worried about his children because his ex-wife wasn't up to taking care of them. So we decided to take the children and raise them. They were little. They were seven, eleven, and fourteen. So we took them in, and we raised them. Then we decided to get out of town and move out here.

FIGURE 32

Rena, during the Christmas season, ca. 1980, in what was then the newly built log house on the Zymacord River. One of her Coast Salish weavings decorates the wall. Photo courtesy of Rena Point Bolton.

In 1978, we bought a little cookhouse from an oil field in Alberta. We had it brought out here, and Cliff built a little Joey shack on it for our beds, and we lived in it for four years while he built this log house. Then we decided to put a gallery on and have space to do our work. He took a little course from Dempsey Bob, and I was teaching basket weaving.[12] By now, I had studied the Tsimshian tapestry weave and their basket weave for fifteen years, and I finally managed to understand it. I picked it up, and by then, I was teaching it back to the people here.

But the years slipped by, and I no longer felt up to teaching anymore. So we put up the little workshop on the side of the house, and that's where I have been working ever since. Cliff's been carving and gardening and continuing to finish the house. We often say, "Well, one day we'll finish the house and finish the canoe shed and everything will be so beautiful when we finish." But it just seems as though we don't have the time now. Time is of the essence.

Cliff was chief of Kitsumkalum—for twelve years, I think—and he did a lot of work for them, working with the township. And I went back to the Arts and Crafts Society, which was in full swing at the time. I was on the board of directors for maybe four or five years.

So we were busy through the years. He worked for Manpower for a while, and he was with the Native court workers. Then he became ill. He had a kidney problem and he couldn't work any longer. He just got too sick. They put him on steroids, the doctors did, and that just made him worse. So I decided to take the bull by the horns, and I made up a concoction of medicines. I told him to throw his prescription away, which he did. He's never been bothered with his kidneys since. That was quite a few years ago. But at that time, he decided to retire because he wasn't too well. He couldn't keep up anymore with the demands of the world, so we hibernated out at our house here.

12 Dempsey Bob, born in 1948 at Telegraph Creek, is a Tahltan-Tlingit carver and artist. His first teacher was Haida artist Freda Diesing, in Prince Rupert; later, he graduated from the 'Ksan School of Art at Gitanmaax. His work has been exhibited in many cities and countries.

Whenever we leave, I can't wait to get home. I love my family and I used to love Sardis, but now when I go down there, it's like a madhouse. It's scary! Too many cars, too many people, too many houses mushrooming up everywhere. I like it here; it's so quiet. In the spring, we have the mother duck. She and her mate, they make a nest and they have little ducklings, and they make a lot of racket out there. It's just wonderful! We have hummingbirds all summer. Cliff's busy feeding them—buying pounds and pounds of sugar.

And, oh, we have lots of trouble with the bears! They come and eat our apples and the cherries and they break off the limbs. We're desperately trying to keep our trees from dying. Those bears are terrible. But since we've had this dog, Stacky, who's part wolf—we call him Steqó:ye, which of course means "Wolf" or "Wolf Clan member"—we're free of the bears. His mother was a wolf, or his father, but we got him and raised him. We've had him for about fifteen years. He makes his mark right around the place here and the bears—as long as he's here, they won't come too close, but as soon as we're gone—if we farm out old Stacky while we're away, then they all come in. That's when they wreak havoc in the garden. They wreck everything.

You say that Ken Malloway told you in the old days, around the Stó:lō fishing sites, there used to be a way of keeping the bears away from the women and the fish by leaving them fish to eat—leaving out food, around the perimeter of the camp. I've never heard anything like that.

FIGURE 33

Cliff Bolton displaying one of his moon mask carvings, fashioned from British Columbia jade (nephrite) and inlaid with abalone shell. The mask is set in a piece of polished red cedar. Photo: Richard Daly.

But it's no wonder if he said the wolves could be your allies. You see, his mother was one of my tribe. Her mother was my aunt, Antonia—and Georgina was her oldest daughter—Georgina Kelly. Antonia was married to one of the sons of James Kelly—who settled on the Kilgard Reserve with his wife, the descendant of X̱éyteleq. Antonia married Albert Kelly and there was Georgina, Myra, and Verna, Patricia, and James. Jimmy was the youngest. Georgina married Ivan Malloway, and she had all those children with him. I don't see Ken very often. He's so busy. But when his mum passed away, he phoned and asked if we'd come down, and he'd pay our way on the plane. So we did. We went down—maybe five or six years ago.

Sometimes I think about my life up here compared to where I grew up. Yes, I think about it and I often wonder, "How on earth did this ever happen to me?" I always thought all these wonderful things happened to great people—like movie stars or royalty or very rich people—but why on earth did all these things happen to me?

I had quite a hard time raising the children. It was a feat at the time, but I did it because I was young and strong. But the rest of my life, after that, was very exciting. I met a lot of people. And I've had a good life here with Cliff. He's a very kind and attentive husband. We travel well together. When he's not telling me a story, I'm telling him a story. So today we're both big-time listeners! We still have a lot to say to one another. It's as if our days aren't long enough. Well, we have our quiet times too, but usually we're tired by the end of the day. We just sit there and stretch out in front of the television. But if we're having tea, we chat, about everything under the sun. Like today, this fellow came. He unburdened himself on Cliff. And I know later on Cliff will tell me what happened to him. We'll talk about it. It's just the way things go. There are problems and they unload on certain people. We always have people from the village or from elsewhere, they come when they have something they want to talk over. They consider us to be elders, and I guess we are. I never realize the reality of it, not until I look in the mirror!

When I came up here, Cliff's children were small. Now they are grown. The youngest, the boy—he was seven at the time—his name is Lyle. The next is a girl, Karen, and the oldest one is Jill. Karen was ten or eleven. Let's say she was eleven. And Jill was fourteen. I don't want them to think I forgot about them or anything. They lived with me in my own home in Terrace for a while, and when we moved here, they lived with us. That's why Cliff had to build a big Joey shack for all our beds. Then, when we moved into this house, which wasn't completed at the time, they had their rooms upstairs, but they wanted to sleep in our bedroom! They were used to sleeping with us and were afraid to sleep in their own rooms. You see, we slept in the Joey shack for four years and we all got used to it. In the old days, it didn't really matter where you slept. But today, the way this modern society is, if children don't have their own rooms, they could take your children away from you! So you do what you are told, or else![13]

FIGURE 34
*Cliff and Rena in 2010, exchanging stories over tea at the kitchen table.
Photo: Richard Daly.*

13 With regard to fear of government intervention in their private family lives, I have, for years, noticed a high degree of psychological trauma. On one occasion, I arrived at the house of a Xwélmexw family with whom I was working and found them all very tense. A stranger had come to the door to sell them insurance. They did not understand what he was talking about, but he kept repeating "blanket coverage," and they stole glances at the grey blanket covering their old sofa. Sometime after my visit, not wanting to get into trouble with the government or to risk having their children taken away from them because they might be classified "dysfunctional," they went out to Abbotsford and used their welfare money to buy new slipcovers for their furniture.

Baskets and Textiles

When I first came up here, I started teaching the women at Kitsumkalum, trying to get them going on their local craftwork. I got a grant from the First Citizens' Fund to pay some people to come in and teach them to make button blankets and these other things. I had to get Annette out to get her to do beading. And later, when she brought the beading back into circulation, we paid her to teach others to do it. Oh, it was quite a time. But to do the research myself, on the Tsimshian styles, or the North Coast weaving, I didn't get anything or anybody to help me. I just did it on my own, because I didn't know if I was going to keep it up or if I was going to quit. There were times when I threw my hat up in the air and said, "That's it!" It drove me crazy—the techniques of the weaving. It's really difficult!

But then a year or two would go by and I'd start in again. I'm talking about the northern basketry, making hats and capes. I had to master the North Coast cedar-bark weaving first, and I *couldn't*. It was so difficult! Mrs. Sutton had taught me how to make a mat. And I saw some of the techniques there. But how to make it round, in a circle, you know, like a basket? *I couldn't figure it out!* Like making a little Easter basket?

FIGURE 35
Rena working on a northern-style basket. Photo courtesy of Rena Point Bolton.

Well, if you're going to make a little Easter basket, you can hold it together with clothes pegs or bobby pins or something as you go, but if you are going to make a huge big basket, you can't use clothes pegs. They didn't have them in the old days, anyway. So how on earth—they didn't put one round on at a time, I figured that one out—but how on earth did they get those many rounds on the basket?

One day, I was sitting in our little shack, and I was desperately trying to figure it out. I was wishing Agnes Sutton was still here—and I was going crazy trying to figure it out. I could put one strand on at a time, building it upwards, but that would be too slow, tedious—and how on earth do you keep it on once it's there? Because you don't use glue anywhere. So I was sitting there, and for some reason—I don't know what happened to me—I said, "Will someone please help me? I cannot understand how they did this kind of weaving."

It was as though all of a sudden something took hold of me. I had this strange feeling. It was like somebody said in my head, "Turn your basket the other way, upside down. You're weaving the wrong way!" Then I thought, "What do you mean?"

I had my basket upright, with the warps going upwards. And the voice inside me said, "Lay it down on its side. You are weaving the wrong way." So I lay the basket on its side and the voice said, "All right. Pick up two or three wefts and put them on like Mrs. Sutton taught you how to make the mat, only you are putting them on the basket now. And weave it the way she taught you to weave it."[14]

And just like that, click, the light bulb went on in my head. I started weaving, not with the warps standing upwards, but with the warps lying down—working with the force of gravity, not against it. And I put three wefts on the basket and started weaving them the way she had taught me. I wove three strands all the way around the basket. And that's how I learned. You can build a big basket with as many wefts as you can hold in your hand, and you can change the colours, or whatever. And so I learned how to do the bark weaving.

14 See Steltzer's *Indian Artists at Work* (1976) for fine photos of this process as practiced at Haida Gwaii: Eliza Abraham, of Masset, works on a cedar-bark hat (39), and Florence Davidson on a spruce-root hat (45).

FIGURE 36

Rena at work on a North Coast spruce-root basket, much like the one standing on her workroom table. Once the base is complete, the basket is turned so that the warp fibres hang down, and the weft is then applied to build the sides. Photo courtesy of Rena Point Bolton.

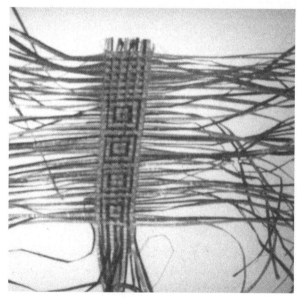

FIGURE 37
The first rows:
beginning a North
Coast basket.
Photo: Richard Daly.

But it took me another year, or two years—we were already in this house by then—before I learned to finish the basket the way the Tsimshians finished the rim. That is very difficult. But I still finish it that way. I taught myself, for the most part. I'd seen the finishing on a basket—an old lady, Cliff's auntie, Auntie Miriam, she had two baskets that belonged to her own grandmother. So I knew they were made a long, long time ago. I would look at the rim until I was going cross-eyed.

"How the devil did they do that rim???" But I wouldn't give up. I tried and tried and tried for years. Finally one day, I was in the bedroom upstairs, by myself, when all of a sudden, I got it. Since then, I've never lost it. Whenever I haven't been weaving for a while, I almost forget, but I won't give up until I get it back. I have kept it all these years. I've tried to teach it to others. I teach my stepsister Annette. She's another one who has learned to do weaving. She was in one of my courses, my classes. But she cannot retain it. She will do it while I'm watching her, but as soon as she goes home, she forgets. It is very difficult to do the edging on the Tsimshian cedar-bark basket.

FIGURE 38

Rena edging a North Coast basket. As Rena explains, the rim on Tsimshian baskets is very intricate. Very few people now know how to produce it, and Rena had to figure it out on her own. Photo courtesy of Rena Point Bolton.

FIGURE 39

Examples of Rena's
North Coast basketry
in spruce root and
cedar bark. Photo:
Richard Daly.

I didn't get into Chilkat weaving. I know how to do it, but for political reasons I didn't do it. I was told that the chiefs' nephews had to select who would make the copy board for the women to follow. It was complicated with family relations, and there were too many things involved. I didn't want to get into something that might break into open warfare, so I just said, "No, we'll just wait until some younger Tsimshian people learn to do it."

I did a cushion cover, in Chilkat tapestry weave, just to learn how. I know the techniques. I just have never made a robe. I do baskets instead. I do the coiled weaving, the Interior Salish and the Coastal Salish—Stó:lō type—I do the fine, fine Tsimshian weaving, plus the checker weave, the Tsimshian bark weaving. This keeps me busy, really busy. I do the Salish rug weaving—the Interior Salish and the Coast Salish—both types of blankets. I do the pounded cedar-bark blankets, which no one makes anymore, but I continue to make them for my family. I have more than enough to keep myself busy.

The capes and rain hats in this Tsimshian style of root weaving are ordered by some of the big-name artists too. Bill Reid's wife ordered a fine, fine cylindrical basket that she hoped her husband would paint on. Having the two of us on one article she thought would be just great.

FIGURE 40
North Coast spruce-root hat, interior view. Photo courtesy of Rena Point Bolton.

But at the time, he wasn't well anymore, so we just dropped the idea.[15] Nowadays, I get so many orders I can't remember who has asked me. There may have been other big names, but I just can't take them on and fill their orders anymore.

I've taught several people up here along the Skeena to do the northern type of basket weaving, but I've done the easier edging when I have been teaching. There are many different edgings—finishings, if you like. And there are quite a few weavers now. I'm sure as they get older, they will teach younger people. I had courses here at Kitsumkalum and over at Kitselas. And I did teach some at the school, to teachers, because I thought—I was really desperate—I didn't know what to do. I thought if somebody learned, they would pass it on. So I had a whole bunch of teachers weaving, even men! I would take them out root digging. The men were good at root digging. The women couldn't dig at all. The easiest, and some of the best roots are the ones that grow along the length of rotten logs. Those roots are excellent—those are clean and they're easy to split. The spruce roots in general are good because they run along under the moss—if you can find a good spruce tree with lots of moss. The spruce roots don't grow too deep under the ground. But cedar, they will go way down deep and you've got to dig like heck to get them out.

---

15 Bill Reid's wife, Martine Reid, writes on Northwest Coast themes and collaborated with translator Daisy Sewid-Smith to produce *Paddling to Where I Stand: Agnes Alfred, Quiqwasutinuxw, Noblewoman* (2004), the memoirs of a noted Kwakwaka'wakw storyteller. Bill Reid (1920–98), a Haida artist and jewellery maker, is especially famous for his bronze sculptures of Haida war canoes. One casting, *The Spirit of Haidi Gwaii, the Black Canoe* (1991), stands outside the Canadian embassy, in Washington DC, and another, *The Spirit of Haidi Gwaii, the Jade Canoe* (1994), can be seen at Vancouver International Airport. His magnificent cedar carving *The Raven and the First Men* (1980), housed at UBC's Museum of Anthropology, is a much larger version of *The Raven Discovering Mankind in a Clam Shell* (1970), a tiny, but exquisite, boxwood carving, also in the museum's collection. (These and other examples of his work can be viewed at http://theravenscall.ca/en/art.) Photos of Bill Reid at work are found in Steltzer (1976, 4–8) and at the Bill Reid Gallery in Vancouver.

I have taught my girls, of course, and some of them can do the northern weaving. Wendy knows how. She was married to Rennie Lockerby up here. She wanted to teach her daughter, but I don't know if they've continued on. But she does know how to weave the cedar bark, and she does the Stó:lō type. I don't know if she does the Thompson coil yet. She's so busy. She's still raising her family and it's kind of hard. But when I did move up here and bought a house in Terrace, I moved my girls, my younger girls, up here. So a lot of them finished their schooling here, grade school. Then they went back home again. While they were here, I taught Gail basket weaving and knitting. She does spinning. Most of her work is with wool. Wendy learned to knit and to spin and to do baskets.

FIGURE 41
Rena holding one of her rare Salish fish baskets, made from split cedar boughs. Photo: Richard Daly.

My younger daughter was doing the *swéqeth* Salish wool blankets.[16] She was very good at it. She could spin and weave on the loom. Reenie is kind of slow at learning these things, but once she learns, it stays with her for good. So she pretty well knows about all of these things, but she's been busy raising her family, too. Steven wants to start weaving. He built himself a loom. But it is so big, I don't know where on earth he's going to put it. Build a shed around it outside, maybe, ha ha ha. He wants to weave *so* badly.

FIGURE 42

One of Rena's Salish textiles, which was on display for a time in Vancouver International Airport and was later exhibited at the University of British Columbia's Museum of Anthropology. Photo courtesy of Rena Point Bolton.

FIGURE 43

One of the traditional Salish robes that Rena wove for her sons (also visible in figure 26). For this robe, Rena used black and white wools, to striking effect. Photo courtesy of Rena Point Bolton.

16 Traditionally, Salish woollens were made from spun yarn that combined mountain goat hair and dog hair, sometimes with the addition of beaten cedar bark (as in Chilkat weaving) or, in the case of the *swox'wath* weave that Rena describes in chapter 5, down feathers and white clay. The cedar fibre and the clay assist with the binding of the yarn and cut down on the oily lanolin of the goal wool. Following European settlement, this yarn was superseded by sheep's wool.

FIGURE 44

A "rattle" basket, made of spruce root. A space woven inside the lid contains pebbles
or deer hooves, which rattle when shaken. Photo courtesy of Rena Point Bolton.

FIGURE 45
Producing the lid for the rattle basket. Photo courtesy of Rena Point Bolton.

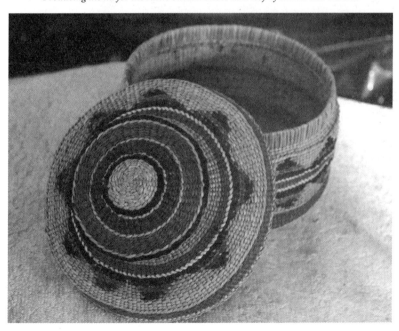

I teach in the smokehouse at Skowkale. My grandson built a big loom. So whenever I'm down there and I'm kind of at loose ends, I'll string it up and start teaching, and all the granddaughters and daughters-in-law and even the boys will come and do a few rows. I think in the old days, everybody could stop in and do a few rows when they had time, except the main weavers who were going to weave all of their lives.

FIGURE 46
Rena working on a Thompson River (Nlaka'pamux) basket, of the sort common in the upriver canyon area where Rena's father was born. Photo courtesy of Rena Point Bolton.

They were different—more professional. They were pulled aside by their elders, and they had to weave every day. Once they got into it, their mothers or their grandmothers would bring them food until they were finished with their projects. They couldn't do anything else, because if you are socializing or travelling or visiting—if you are doing something else, your mind is taken away from your work, and the elders did not like that. They wanted you to stay with your project—focused on it—until it was finished.

So, as a result, you had a very close relationship with your piece of work, especially if it was a large blanket. Your teacher would be there with you quite a bit of the time, checking up to see if you were doing it right. They would bring your food. And you would sleep alone. You would have a bed there by your work, so that it was almost as if you were married to your work. If you were a married woman already, then you would have to leave your husband's bed until you were finished. And it wouldn't be good if you had a baby because the baby would be on your mind and your mind would not be on your work. So they tried to find a girl or a woman who, at the moment, was free and then they would teach her. But usually someone like me, who was born into the caring for all these things, I would have no choice. I would have to learn. But others who wanted to learn, they had to be free to do so without interruption.

Girls started learning at different ages. It varied. Say there was a young girl who wasn't interested in the weaving to begin with but gradually, as she got older, she realized how much she wanted to learn, and she would speak to her elders and ask if they would give permission for her to learn. But it wasn't a rigid thing. It was the same with basket weaving. If you wanted to learn and you were older, there was nothing to stop you, but if you were a carrier of the culture and traditions, you had to learn, and you had to be taught at a specific time in your life cycle.

When I am working, my mind, well, it travels. I try to remember things. I hear voices. I hear my elders speaking in Halq'eméylem. A lot of times, I hear them say words I must have heard them say when I was little, because I have forgotten a lot of my language, most of it, but at times when I'm weaving, or making a basket, or spinning, I hear them talking, and I hear words that I have forgotten for many, many years. And so, I try to use the word. I feel like they have given it back to me, so I must use it. So I talk to myself and I use the word as if I am speaking with someone. I have my daughter's picture, and my sister's, in there where I work, so when I hear a new word, I'll talk to them and have a little conversation. And, oh, I hear songs, songs that I've never heard before—beautiful songs. Some of them I retain, others I just get to hear them as they are passing. They seem to visit me and then they are gone and I never hear them again. But I have heard several beautiful songs that I have kept. And where they come from, I don't know.

I remember as a child I heard a beautiful Scottish song, or a tune, whatever it was. It was being played by bagpipes. My granny, Annie Jamieson, she was half-Scottish, and she used to always tell me when I was a little girl, "Your great-grandfather was a Scotchman. You mustn't forget him." This was her dad she used to tell me about. And so, I don't remember too much, but I do remember a bagpipe song. I used to hear it in my head every now and then, especially when I was working. I would hear this tune played by bagpipes. It used to haunt me, and I'd get a picture of my grandmother taking me by the hand, and we'd be walking beside the pipers. And yet we were in a strange place that I had never seen before. I don't know if this was a dream or if it was real.

One day, I was telling Steven about it, just recently. And I told him, "You know, next time I go to Victoria, I'm going to ask your piper if he will learn this song and play it, because I often hear it when I'm working."

And so he said, "Will you sing it for me, Mother? And I'll tape it. Right now." He took out his little tape recorder, and so I hummed it along. He was really astonished and said, "My goodness. That sounds like a real Scottish song."

He brought it home [to Government House] and had his piper—his name was Tom—play it over and listen to it. He said, "You know, this sounds like an old, old funeral march or something." So he took it to the rest of the pipers he knows in Victoria and talked to them about it. Now they are busy putting it together. They say it sounds like a tune from years and years ago that no one has played for—well—maybe a hundred years. They don't know. So they are putting it together, and Steven says, "Next time you come out, Mother, they're going to play it."

So I don't know where these things come from. The mind is a mystery. Even the scientists think so. Sometimes, I get songs from the Kanakas, from the Hawaii connection. I hear beautiful songs that sound like they are Polynesian songs. But I have never learned any of them. They just seem to come and go. My brother used to write Polynesian songs. He sang a beautiful Polynesian song he called "Honolulu Moon." But I don't really remember too much about it. He used to say, "One day, Sis, we'll go to Hawaii and look for our great-grandfather's people." But we never did go.

What happens in my head when I am working is sort of—what's the word? Yes, that's right, visualizing. It's part of the way we were trained by old people, like travelling inside yourself. The old people usually knew what they had to do, or what they wanted to do. They didn't have radios or television or computers to interrupt them. So if they wanted to meditate, that's what they did. They would go away to the mountains for a week or two weeks to meditate, to travel inside their heads, and to fast. Like when X̱éyteleq's parents, before he was born, how they were planning to have this child? Well, they went to the mountains and they meditated.

* ❀ *

They Begin to Listen

Rewards

RICHARD DALY: For many years, Rena immersed herself in activities aimed at promoting First Nations society and culture. Like orator Mark Antony in Shakespeare's *Julius Caesar*, she was tireless in urging the public to "lend her their ears" when it came to appreciating and respecting Native cultures. Now, after many years, the public has begun to listen, as evidenced by the awards that Rena has begun to receive. In 2010, she was honoured with the BC Lifetime Creative Achievement Award for Aboriginal Art for her work in weaving and basketry. The awarding foundation stated:

> When Rena Point Bolton was growing up, potlatches and the
> creation of aboriginal art were banned. Against that backdrop,
> her life as a cultural leader began at an early age, when her
> mother and grandmother taught her the traditional songs,

history, arts and crafts of her people, passing on the responsibility to keep the traditions alive. Rena has since dedicated her life to learning and teaching the traditional arts of not only the Sto:lo and Thompson nations of her ancestors, but also the Tsimshian arts of her husband's territory. Her main concern today is for the preservation of the natural world, which is the wellspring of her art. The deep forest is where she respectfully harvests the cedar and spruce roots and cedar bark she uses to create her exquisite baskets.[1]

RENA POINT BOLTON: I have to admit it is satisfying when the awards start to roll in. I guess it is about that time of life for me! Our people have been trying to get recognition for the things we do, not as creators of quaint activities but to be recognized for our normal human skills. We have been trying for so long.

FIGURE 47
Rena holding the Coast Salish basket that accompanied her to the British Columbia Lifetime Achievement awards. The photograph was taken in front of her log house on the Zymacord River. Photo courtesy of Frontrunner Productions for the British Columbia Achievement Foundation, 2010.

---

1 British Columbia Achievement Foundation, "2010 BC Creative Lifetime Achievement Award for Aboriginal Art," http://www.bcachievement.com/firstnationsart/lifetime/recipients.php?year=2010, 2013.

The whites, or Europeans, foreigners—we call them Xwelítem—they washed up on our shores long ago and drastic changes followed their arrival.[2] The world changed for everybody. Our people have been linked to those foreigners for a long time now, but goodness, it still feels like nobody sees the Xwélmexw and how we really live. It's like we're still invisible in so many ways.

It hit me again yesterday, the fact that we've survived so much as a people. We have a culture of giving, a culture of taking in people who are in need.[3] We took in those newcomers and made sure they did not starve. We showed them how to get through a winter. We never ask for anything in return. That's not our way. But in your heart, you expect others to understand, to give something of themselves back to you. We expect give and take, but what do we find? Well, we give and give and give. And so this new culture was our downfall—because the people we now took in and helped and gave things to, they came from a very different way of living. They were used to buying and selling and owning everything and giving nothing back to others. We Native people living on this land cannot understand how you can dare sell water or sell land or sell food. To us, it was always given freely by the Creator who put us

2 According to Elder Dan Milo, the word *xwelítem*, "the hungry people" or "those who need to be fed," was originally used in reference to starving gold prospectors who arrived in Xwélmexw territory around 1860, during the Cariboo Gold Rush, and had to be given food by the local people (Carlson 1997, 65). The term was subsequently generalized to refer to white newcomers in general.

3 The spirit of giving that informs Aboriginal life is exemplified in chapter 4, where Rena talks of how Grandmother Sarah would feed and clothe itinerant victims of the Great Depression, who were "riding the rails" through Xwélmexw country and spied the camp at Devil's Run as they looked for work. In chapter 5, she explains how one is expected to leave something of oneself when one takes roots or fish or game or birds from out on the land. Since the land and Mother Nature give so much to humans, it is incumbent upon the people to reciprocate and maintain the balance for the health of both nature and society. Here, she also stresses the importance of sharing in Aboriginal cultures. This question of reciprocity is a long-standing trope in the Aboriginal monologue that continues to address the colonizing culture.

here. These things, these essentials are here to share. With us, it is still shameful to want to buy and sell these things.

The whites seem to be driven to make money, while, for the most part, our people believe that getting along with others and with the natural world is what's really important in life. Earning money is okay when you need basic necessities but not as a goal in itself. Maybe we are not as competitive and aggressive in daily life as the newcomers, the Money People. I know that lots of Native people living in towns and cities find it difficult to cope with the newcomers and their brutal ways of doing things. Some of our people still find it easier to run away and hide in alcohol or drugs—to just tune out. We are torn between toughing it out, getting trained and getting jobs and feeding the family, or heading into the bush and feeling that old freedom coming back into our soul. The white world talks about everybody having freedom, but some are much freer than others. If you are rich, you have more freedom than if you're poor, or coloured, or somebody who does not fit into the mainstream.

Children of Mother Earth

As the years have passed, we have come to see that we really have to stand up for what we believe in our hearts and minds. Somewhere along the way, we have to do this. We are being forced to break the old quiet, dignified traditions and to fight back to protect what was ours. We are learning to protect what is and what was ours. Hopefully, in the future, before everything is destroyed by greed, we may all learn to live together. Our people cannot go back to the old ways. We have lost too much already. We have to try to build a better future, where the people who have much will have to let go and not be so controlling. They will have to let the rest of us survive and work to heal the planet, to heal the Earth before it is totally destroyed.

I wrote a poem about this back in 1981 when, once again, Prime Minister Trudeau was trying to remove Aboriginal rights from the Canadian Constitution. They have taken the whole continent, but that is not enough for them. Now they even want to take the small reserves we live on. Government and industry have taken great wealth from the land. We have received nothing. Still, the Canadians complain that we, the children that the Creator put on this land—that we get special treatment and are not paying taxes—us who have been looking after the land for thousands of years and now are being banished from it! The children of Mother Earth are the Indigenous peoples of the world.

It is time to share and to heal. Part of what I wrote was the following.

Children of Mother Earth

We are the children of this land,
Born from the womb of the Earth
Seized from the giant cedar trees,
Scattered on land and surf
Blood from the mighty rivers
Bone from the mountain rocks,
Slime from the steamy swampland
And breath from the winds that talk

. . .

We shared the fruits of our loving Mother
But their need soon turned to greed,
With money, guns and dynamite
They raped her from the start

I wrote that if the newcomers did not stop their destruction and work with Indigenous people to heal the planet, then:

The blood from the rivers will cease to flow,
The bones from the mountains will crumble,
The seeds from the trees will cease to grow
And the buds from the winds will tumble.

Our life was rooted deep in the land and the river. Then the priests waded in, and the DIA was on their heels. Things seemed to change overnight. The old structures, the social order, relations between the families—all that got tipped on its head. The priests preached that women had to follow their husbands. Suddenly, the women, as soon as they married, were shipped off to live with their husband's family, where they had no roots and where they were cut off from their own family knowledge. Our women used to teach their children by example, in their home place. But now, suddenly, they were fish out of water, flopping around in some foreign medium, no longer able to breathe.

The old ways of learning from the river, the land, and the elders, it all got blown apart, and this was made worse by smallpox, the flu, and other diseases. The epidemics carried off lots and lots of people. Before this, women had the responsibility to teach the young, including the new young husbands of their daughters who married into the village. They would teach them where the family had rights to fish and hunt and collect things from the land—the salmon, the berries, and so on. But now the women were moved out to their in-laws' territories, where they were strangers. The knowledge system collapsed. The wisdom of the home place—where we were rooted—was lost. This was a big mark that the priests made on our society, and then the DIA with its rules and regulations just added to the loss. It got easy to define us out of existence. If a woman married a non-Indian, she too became, overnight, a non-Indian. She was no longer part of the culture that made her. She was legally denied her heritage.

In these ways, our peoples have lost their bloodlines, their languages, and their cultures. Today, the children don't know who they are. In the old days, there was more equality flowing between the families when young people intermarried. Often, the boys would move in and be trained and raised by their new mothers-in-law, at least when they were starting out their married life. But with marriages between distant peoples, like from Semá:th to the Nlaka'pamux or Port Douglas or Vancouver Island, this learning from the women was harder and it broke down. Things didn't work anymore the way they used to. This is one of the ways our culture has been silenced since the whites, the *Xwelítem*, came.

Another area where we were too long invisible has to do with what the old people called "the land question." This is still a difficult one. They knew that the land belonged to their forefathers, but there is so much ... so many restrictions and laws and ... problems in dealing with the land question and who controls it. Even today, our people feel close to the forest, the river, the mountains. To express who they really are, they go to the mountains and they spend a lot of time up there.

But the land is a very ... it's a sad situation, with forests being cut and homes mushrooming all over the place. We are too close to Vancouver. Even on Skowkale Reserve, there are many, many homes being built now [encroachment by the Town of Sardis/Chilliwack on the tiny reserves]. I think my family is seriously considering moving, or some of them are, to get away from this crowded situation. Some of the non-Xwélmexw people in Sardis have complained about the drumming [the ceremonial life], because they live right next to the smokehouse—people who have never, ever seen Indians—us, the people who live right under their noses—so they don't want to put up with drumming—and there have been complaints to the newspapers and the news media about this, about our spiritual life. Skowkale is such a small reserve![4]

Our home in the Fraser Valley is now on the outskirts of Vancouver. People are moving further and further out from the city into the valley. Soon, the whole valley will be nothing but houses—and then where will

4 On the subject of the Stó:lō winter dance, anthropologist Brian Thom writes:

During the winter months, many Stó:lō people gather in "smokehouses," in order to take part in the winter dance ceremonial. This is an extremely important part of Stó:lō culture and spirituality. Up to several hundred people gather in one smokehouse to witness the dancers do their work. Dances take place at night, and involve almost continuous singing, drumming, and dancing, until the early hours of the morning. Many of these smokehouses are located in urban areas, such as Chilliwack and Sardis. What happens when the non-Aboriginal neighbours, who were neither invited to the dance nor explained the importance of the ritual, were disturbed in their sleep every night for the entire winter? Whose cultural values should be taken as more important? How can this be decided? Is multiculturalism only acceptable as long as it doesn't step on the toes of the dominant cultural values? (Thom 1996)

the people go? Where can we go to be Xwélmexw again? Remember what I told you before? It is important to who we are. Stó:lō means "the big river." It is not the people. And *Stótelō* is "little river." The "real people" are Xwélmexw and their language is Xwélmexwtel, and they live by the Stó:lō, the big river.[5] Anyway, it's really getting terrible. It is horribly crowded, with the malls and gas stations and everything coming up around us.

So these are some of the consequences of us being too silent and too invisible in the face of *all* the development around us. Younger people have taken over the political work we were so wrapped up in. I hope someday people realize the contribution that women have made to improving life on the reserves.

As for the rest, at least some of my work will be left behind for the coming generations. My work has been shown in various exhibitions, and some of it sits in museum collections and in private hands. I have baskets in the Museum of Civilization in Ottawa. I have a collection called "Salmon in Cedar." They also have a half a dozen mats, a metre by a metre square, six of them. The Royal Ontario Museum in Toronto, I think they have a small wall hanging and two or four baskets, I'm not sure. The Bishop Museum in Honolulu has one or two. The Vancouver School District has a large collection of my baskets that they use, I guess, for "show and tell." They have more fancy names for it now, but the baskets travel all over to different schools. The Museum of Anthropology at the University of British Columbia has three.

I've also contributed to many shows and exhibitions. I had a show in Ottawa where I was the only Native Canadian. This was the Universal Year of the Woman, in 1975, and I was chosen to represent the Native women of Canada. I was two weeks there, demonstrating my weaving. I had another show at Harrison Hot Springs, at a weaving symposium

5   As a language, Xwélmexwtel is not an undifferentiated whole but encompasses a range of local dialects of Halq'eméylem—those spoken by people indigenous to the lower portion of the Stó:lō or Fraser River. In Rena's reckoning, this language community extends at least to those who reside between Matsqui and Semá:th, downriver, and to the upriver Tii:t people who live within the first five miles of the Fraser Canyon.

where many nations came to weave, and again I was the only Canadian Native woman. There have been two shows at UBC and others in Vancouver. I had another show in the summer months of 2001 at UBC. I have turned down so many shows. I would just never have had time to stay home and get any work done if I attended them all. One place I would like to go is Arizona, but I can't do that. It's just too far. Anyway, those were the bigger shows.[6]

Xwelíqweltel and the Queen

Recognition of our people comes in different ways. You wanted me to talk about how and why Steven became lieutenant-governor of British Columbia [2007–12]. Well, you have to go back some years. After he had been appointed a judge and had been in his post for ten years, I believe it was ten years as a judge, Steven was approached by the prime minister—what was his name? Harper. Yes, Stephen Harper was the one who nominated Steven, my son Steven, for the appointment as lieutenant-governor. They asked him if he would accept, and he phoned me and asked what I thought about it.

I told him—well, I knew that he was becoming depressed by his work on the bench, because the system was like a treadmill and it was depressing him. The same people were coming up before him all the time—people with little going for them, being judged according to the law. It just seemed the same old story, and it seemed as though he wasn't getting anywhere.

So I told him, "Maybe you need a change. This would be something different for you. You'd meet a lot of new people." Steven loves people. He likes being with people and he likes to travel.

So I told him, "You know, give it a try, and if it works, carry on. It'll be good for the esteem of our people. We have been invisible for too long. There will be those, a few people, who have negative things to say,

6 In 2010, Rena was also among the selected North American weavers featured in an exhibition entitled "Smash" at the Art Gallery of Greater Victoria.

but that you find everywhere and in everything. There are always people who will disagree."

I told him our people need a lift and I thought it would be good for everyone to see a Native Indian up there representing the Queen, you know. It may not look right to a lot of people, but in this day and age, it really doesn't matter what it is you do, you will still be criticized.

So I told him, "You think about it." He did and then he decided he would go through with it. He decided to accept the offer.

When it happened, the ceremony, it was a great thing. The people, the Native people from all over came to his swearing in. There were hundreds of people. Older ladies were crying. Many groups came to sing with their drums. People came from back East who said it was wonderful. "At last, our people are being recognized."

We were invited to go—Cliff and I. We went down to Victoria to attend his swearing in. Different things happened there at the Parliament Buildings. I remember getting lost. I needed to go to the washroom.

Cliff said, "Would you like me to come with you?"

"Oh, no. I'll be fine. It isn't so huge that I'll get lost."

Somebody said, "Okay, down this corridor."

I went down this long corridor. I kept going because I didn't see any washroom signs. Finally, I opened one door and went through. Then a lady approached and asked me what I was doing there. I said, looking for a washroom. So she showed me to a door and I went in. When I came out, she was still there.

I was trying to go back to where I came from. She says, "Oh, you can't go in there. They are having the swearing in of the new lieutenant-governor."

"Well," I said, "I'm the lieutenant-governor's mother, and I want to go back to where I was sitting."

She said, "Oh, no. I can't open that door for you." She didn't seem to believe me.

Just then a maid, or housekeeper or whatever, she came along. She had her arms full of cleaning stuff. She pushed the door open and before anybody could say a word, I ducked through that door and scurried back to my seat. Everybody whispered, "Where did you go? We were looking for you?" I told them, "I got lost. I almost got locked out forever!" Ha ha ha!

Anyway, after the swearing in, we came outside and the media got ahold of me. I hadn't been involved with the media for so long, I became frightened and disoriented. Someone took me by the arm and brought me to an office and hid me away there. So I was safe for a while. Then they brought us out to the front of the building, in front of the House of Parliament where they had us sit down in chairs. I watched a tall man walking in front of all these RCMP officers who were lined up—a whole troop of them in their beautiful red coats. And I saw this tall man with this big, strange-looking hat on, and this dark classy uniform with all its gold braid. I said to Cliff, "What's going on? Who is that man up there walking in front of all the RCMP officers?"

He grins and says, "That's Steven!" He had on his new work clothes, his L-G uniform and I didn't even recognize him! He was inspecting the troops. After that was over, all those guns went off, firing a salute. I almost jumped out of my skin! Sitting there every time the guns went off—I was just petrified! Everybody came over and hung onto me so I wouldn't lose my mind. I don't know how many guns went off, but they were so loud! I was just shaking.

When it was over, we were packed into limos and whisked away, down to Government House. There were so many people there. I could never remember everybody. The ceremonies started at the Parliament Buildings before moving to Government House. The whole family was there, but Cliff and I were out front—like where Steven was sitting. We were down beside him. The rest of the family, they were up in the galleries, or whatever they call them.

We came out of the Parliament and there was a crowd out there, and the press and cameras and the whole works. It was a beautiful day, from what I remember—I do remember Reenie hanging on to me and telling me, "Don't be afraid, Mother. These are all friendly people. They are just trying to be polite to you."

But after living up here along the Skeena in the peace and quiet for so many years—and I really wasn't well at the time—but my eldest daughter, Reenie, was there trying to take care of me.

Later on, Steven took us upstairs at Government House and showed us around, showed us all the rooms, the huge ballroom. He took us in, and I turned to him and said, "D'you think the Sxwóyxwey would fit in here? Could we hold a ceremony here, Steven, in the Queen's ballroom?"

He says, "I suppose they'd fit, Mother." He starts to laugh, you know. He thought that was funny, picturing the Sxwóyxwey dancing in the royal ballroom.

He took us all over. We went upstairs and saw the Queen's apartment. The hallways were unlit—a lot of the hallways—and I said to him, "This is kind of spooky, you know."

He said, "Well, you know, Mother, we have a ghost here. He's a friendly ghost. He doesn't harm anyone, but we do see him every now and again. You can feel that he's around." I wasn't too happy to get that news.

We had our own little quarters there. Whenever we weren't at meals or visiting, we'd be in our little apartment. When we were there, I just wouldn't go out the door. I'd see the long hallways. It was so spooky. I think it was all in my head, but I was a bit scared. Government House is *so* huge. I thought of all the many lieutenant-governors whose pictures were on the walls, and I wondered if they were all hanging about somewhere—lurking, you know. I was just very nervous. And who knows, it could happen that Queen Victoria herself might be walking the halls. You never know. But that was my visit to the big Government House. It rained all the time after the ceremony. Then the second time we were there, it rained all the time and we didn't get to go anyplace. I wanted to see the gardens outside, but I didn't get to. One day perhaps, I'll go when the weather's nice and I'll see the gardens.

Just as a little "PS" here: We were invited back to stay at Government House during the Winter Olympics in 2010. This time, we felt more at ease. The ghosts seemed to have settled down and accepted us. We had no bad experiences in those long hallways. The cook couldn't do enough for us. He even agreed to feed us salmon twice a day! Of course, we had to do without the heads and backbones, but it was very nice to have fresh salmon in the winter. It did not rain every day and we got to see the gardens and make our own way around. I even set up my roots and my bark and got some basket work done every day in our royal apartment.

There is something else that happened recently. Steven, as lieuten-ant-governor, has these meet-the-public sessions from time to time in Victoria. I think they are called "levees." At one of those sessions, he met a lawyer by the name of Jamieson. Steven told him that he too had a Jamieson in his ancestry, a William Jamieson, who came out to Canada over a century ago. They found out that they were both descended from the same William Jamieson, and this man gave Steven some suggestions about finding out more. Later, when Steven and his wife, Gwen, were in Brussels or Belgium on some official visit, they went on from there to visit Edinburgh in Scotland. They talked to the curator of the highland clans museum up in the north of Scotland and learned that William Jamieson was from Clan Gunn and that they had some of their roots in the Vikings who came down from Scandinavia. They found out where the Jamiesons came from, and they brought me the Gunn plaid and the clan pin when they came home. I guess our next venture will be to find out more about Pete Silva's father's side, about Chile, or wherever Rafaelito da Silva came from. Then, of course, there's the Polynesian connection, Paluya, to follow up, too.

FIGURE 48
A marriage of two worlds: Rena beginning work on a basket at Government House, in Victoria, where she and Cliff stayed during a visit to her son Steven, after his appointment as lieutenant-governor. Photo courtesy of Rena Point Bolton.

Still a Long Way to Go

Your wife suggested that one theme for this book was "breaking the silence," and I think that makes sense. Our people had to remain without a voice for years and years. Our lands were taken, and our children, too. Between the Department of Indian Affairs and the churches, we faced a lot of insecurity. For years, we survived by keeping our heads down. Our elders wanted to let sleeping dogs lie. Our traditional laws and the social order of the families were replaced by the laws and the pecking orders of the government and the churches.

When the whites arrived, we had a hereditary system of government and we had land. But they called us nomads with no government and no fixed address. From day one here on the West Coast, government and the churches worked hand-in-glove to remove the power of the hereditary chiefs, our *sí:yá:m*. They also removed power and authority from women in the families, who were the carriers of the culture. We women had the responsibility to guard and protect the old ways and pass them on. Women knew the lineages and they held the knowledge. Under the directives of the missionaries, they were forced to follow their husbands to the man's home village. Often, they were stuck far away from home. Home was where the family knowledge was held, quietly and without fuss. The old people were left at home with the knowledge, and the young ones to whom they would normally have passed it on were away at residential schools, or logging camps, or married into distant villages. So they said to themselves, "We'll let it die out, just to avoid trouble with the new authorities."[7]

7 In the 1950s, when Wilson Duff wanted to make a written record of Stó:lō customs and traditions, he made his way to members of the community who had a reputation for knowing the old ways. Duff reported that these elders (such as Mrs. August Jim) told him that they knew nothing of the old ways. It now seems that this response was an attempt to avoid further cultural indignities from Canadian society. Silence, at that time when Aboriginal cultures had been so traumatized by Canadian rules and regulations, was deemed the most dignified and safest response to those asking to bring out into the light of day, and to record, these peoples' cultures, customs, and practices. See Duff (1952b, Appendix) for more on the frustration he felt when people would not talk to him.

In my case, we were Steqó:ye, the People of the Wolf. X̱éyteleq was like our governor, but by the end of his life, our ways were being destroyed by the new order. The same thing happened to other Xwélmexw families. Everything from the old people's world was dismantled, and they were left sitting in silence, frustrated, robbed and dispossessed. Our ways used to flow down through the generations, but then the flow trickled to a stop. We had no more identity. Everything that defined us—spirit dancing, ancient songs, our ceremonies, potlatch feasts—all the activities that used to take place in the *híkw' lalém* (big house)—everything was banned and made illegal. The *híkw' lalém* was our government house, our parliament. We were left without drums, healing ceremonies, feasts.

I happened to be the last link with the old ways in our family. For years, I felt frustrated at not being able to speak out. I taught my children who they were, who they had descended from. I taught them to respect their elders and the land. Thank goodness, they have tried to follow the old instructions as they have lived their lives. I don't know what is going to happen to our ways in the future.

The churches condemned the old ways. They called them heathen practices, the work of the devil—the wages of sin. They terrorized our old people, who were very tuned in to the world, and sensitive, and the intimidation from schools and churches helped the government control Indian people everywhere.

I have spent much of my life going around trying to let people know that it is not wrong to take what's good from the past and use it to move on toward the future. I've spent lots of time working with the youth. Many of them feel they don't belong *anywhere*. They don't feel welcome in their homes or in the main society. They don't have a sense of identity or a sense of home. They feel lost. When I worked with the young, they wanted to bring back some of the old ways, the language and the crafts, and they wondered why the elders were hesitant to help them. The elders were afraid, and so many of the young had no guidance. They fell into alcohol, drugs, trouble with the law. They began to feel hatred and destruction, especially self-hatred and self-destruction.

Many people, both Native and non-Native, remain brainwashed by the old prejudices that seem to be spread by religion, school, and government. This brainwashing has to be overcome. The need to pass on what is best from the old ways is something that challenges every new generation.

In our family, we stress education. We think it's important to educate as many Native people as possible, to increase the education levels of families. Our people have to find ways to get off welfare and stand on their own feet again. This was part of the reason for our involvement in promoting a renewal of arts and crafts. We offered a program that would subsidize elders who were willing to teach the old ways to the younger people. This was so that members of the community would have something of their own to work at, something they could excel at.

You know, we made a little dent with the work we did, when we went around the province from village to village, but it was only a dent, because as fast as one generation learned and started doing things with their culture, a new generation was growing up with nobody to pass things on to them and guide them. It's a difficult problem, and all we could think of as a solution was more education in order to attack that terrible feeling of being stuck on a reserve with nothing—no education, no resources, no self-worth—feeling that you are not allowed to develop. Maybe we did start something. I don't know.

At least there are a lot more of our young people getting higher education. They at least have a sense of pride in who they are. For example, there is the APTN TV station for the performing arts now. This is a good outlet that allowed our peoples to learn the business of entertainment, especially humour. Indian humour is effective—criticizing injustices by poking fun. I like to think that things like this are the result of our work on getting arts and crafts passed down and allowing these things to come out into the open, especially through the performing arts and through sharp wit and laughter. All these things give us a place to belong, but still there are lots of villages without this, and they continue to feel like they are stuck in a rut.

We still have a long way to go to understand our years of silence. It is very good to know who we are and who we have been for thousands of years. It's good to know that we did live in harmony with the environment, that we exercised good stewardship over the lands and the rivers.

Our old people took care of everything. They had to be active to make a living, but they did it without destroying the living world around them. You don't have to kill the environment to live well. We have to find a happy medium. We are acutely aware of all the destruction around us, but we no longer make the rules. It's not our laws that are being followed.

9

* ✤ *

Life Cycles

When We Come Back

One of the things I have tried to impress on my children is that when new life is coming to our family, when the girls or women have babies, they have to recognize that these new babies are bringing forth old life. We are true believers in reincarnation. They must always receive the newborn with dignity and humility and respect.

If young girls make a mistake, as young girls do sometimes, and they bring forth a life out of wedlock, they must not be ashamed. They must receive the child because an old spirit has come back to the living. They must honour that child and take care of it. We must never, ever be ashamed of new life. There is no shame tied to new life, despite what the churches have tried to teach us. They tried to make us ashamed. There were strict rules for young girls in our Xwélmexw world too, rules that are no longer in use. But today it is very difficult when young girls are allowed to do as they wish, going to the public schools and mixing with other people where they can do and say whatever they wish, and then it gets difficult. They have to come home to strict parents. So, many mistakes are made. I have had this talk with my family. I explain that they must *never, ever look down on new life.*

When babies return, at the moment they are born, they are elders coming back. They are people who have gone through life before, at some earlier time. First, we welcome them into the family; then, we try to find out who they are. Or who they were. We look for behaviour traits. Are they like Grandmother or Grandfather? If somebody died young, they might be coming back soon afterward to try life again. Or a baby might have markings at birth, a birthmark or something. My mother herself was born with pierced ears.[1] Important signs like that can help a person realize herself. As a basket maker, Mother was a perfectionist like certain of her recent ancestors. It was the same for Grandmother Sarah. She was a good weaver and also knew herbal medicines like her predecessors. Grandfather Pete took pride in his work. He was also a herbalist, and a spiritual healer, too. He understood these things and was trained earlier by Louie Sqw'átets. Pete Silva did the lower Stó:lō burnings, and Louie Sqw'átets did the upriver ones. They were both ancestors coming back, using family talents, returning these arts and practices to the family again.

It's funny, but my mother told me that every so many generations we have a child born with a sixth toe. And the toe is like a claw. And she said that this is so that we will remember that we were, at one time, wolves. This is the way the Creator does not let us forget where we came from. My brother carries that. My youngest brother, Alfred, carries the claw. I remember telling my mother, "You should have it surgically removed"—because she used to have quite a time getting shoes to fit him.

1 In Northwest Coast cultures, pierced ears denoted status and prosperity—possession of the wealth needed for earrings or labrets, usually of copper, bone, and abalone shell. Hence, being born with pierced ears is taken as a sign of genetic connection to high-born ancestors. Cultural continuity through beliefs concerning, and practices associated with, reincarnation are found in many cultures in the Americas (see Mills 1998; Mills and Slobodin 1994).

But she said, "No, he was chosen for us to remember who we are, and so we must not remove it." There are other features of the wolves we feel strongly about in our family, like having strong mothers. Very strong mothers. Our mothers have to take care of and control their families, being careful about not letting outsiders come in so they could exert the wrong influence—they have to guard against the influences of other people on our wolf children. We must always be careful that the teachings we give our children are followed. Also, whatever the stronger members of the family receive—food or anything else—they must share. They will share it with the rest. This is like bringing home food and sharing with the rest of the people. This is what the two head wolves always did—to bring food back to the rest of the family. Just watch the wolves. That's what they do. We try to carry this out. We have helpers who help to bring food in. One of the main teachings has been always to share food.

Today, the young people don't believe in rebirth. They are just too civilized! But I notice that they talk about it a lot. When I was young, a deceased soul might go and live inside an animal or a bird—like the owl, for instance—to learn things and then come back to Earth as a human. We still go through life knowing there is a lively life out there "on the other side." The other side of life, that is. There are passageways; at death, the doors open to the other side, and the living can be drawn in if they are not careful. This lasts for four days. It takes a soul four days to free itself from the bodily remains. During this time, others can be drawn across to join them on the other side. It is a dangerous time. If the deceased cannot bear to leave a husband, a wife, or a child, this person may be pulled toward the door to the other side. Then, on the fourth day, the soul leaves and the door closes.

As I explained earlier, we hold our burnings on the fourth day after someone dies, to send off the soul with as much consolation as possible. Food and personal effects are burned as offerings that the soul can take along to the other side. When we burn, it is to honour not only the deceased but also those who owned and looked after the land where we now live, long, long ago. We keep on the good side of those who went through life before us.

Sitting here by the river at Kitsumkalum, I often feel the old Tsimshian people around me. Like me, they too were from the Wolf Clan.[2] I talk with them when I am working, and I feel very much at home with them.

You can keep coming back from the other side, until you finally act according to the standards of an adult and are able to live a good life without harming anybody else, doing good to make up for past mistakes. You have many, many chances to come back and improve your performance in this life. You can also undergo a healing process on the other side, too.

For a long time after I lost my youngest daughter, I felt I had not lived up to my duty and the responsibilities that I had been taught. I was sure I had failed her. She began to come to me when I was dreaming. The first time she came to me was in the form of a little girl. She was walking toward me through a field of wildflowers. I was standing at the edge of the field. She came near and said, "Don't feel bad, Mum. What I did to myself, I had to do. I had to be an example to teach the family what not to do. I have been a warning to them. I will be staying here for a while until I have healed. Don't worry, I'll come back and talk to you. You have done nothing wrong. Things were beyond your control."

We both stood there. It was a warm scene, very nice. She said, "I have to go."

Down through the years, she has returned and talked to me in dreams. The last dream was here, in my chair upstairs. She came to me as a full-grown woman. "I am free now," she said. "I'm cured. My spirit has healed and I am going to wait for you. I will wait for you and help you across."

What this tells me is that even if you have lived badly and made mistakes, you can heal your spirit on the other side. The spirit recovers and returns healed. It can come back to earth again when that happens. The scientist in me says it would be nice to know more about this! I guess some day we will find out.

---

2 Rena is referring to Lax Gibuu, the Wolf Clan of the Kitsumkalum Tsimshian people.

Water and the Cycle of Life

The river is home, as far as I'm concerned. Water is the cycle of life. My grandparents raised me and we moved to Devil's Run. Our smokehouse was right there above the river. I lived there off and on as a child. We even spent a couple of winters at the old smokehouse. The river was our highway. Canoes moved everything and everybody. We had freight canoes and smaller ones for travelling. Medium-sized ones were used for fishing.

We dressed the fish by the river and returned the innards and bones to the water. After the flesh of the first salmon had been honoured and shared every spring by everybody, the bones were given back to the river as an offering. This is how we give back life and appreciation to the salmon for the next generation and the next fishing season. The salmon is our brother. First-berry and first-root ceremonies are the same. They are signs of respect for our relatives among the other creatures. We hold them to make sure that people remember there is continuity to life.

When we come out of the sweat lodge, we bathe in the river or in a creek. The cold, clear snow water of the river is the source of power and cleansing. It brings peace and destruction, life and death. Fishermen fall into the water and drown. The river, which gave them life, takes them back again. Louie Sqw'átets and Pete Silva were *shxwlá:m*. They used a stone basin with water in it for healing. The power of the water was their medicine. They used it to cleanse a house of bad luck, and this made it safe for people who had to live there. The soul leaves your body at night when you sleep and dream. That's why a medicine man or lady has a bowl of water by the bed at night, to draw the soul home to the body by daybreak.

Water brings life and food to us humans. A bowl of water is very important. Louie Sqw'átets was very powerful with water. He used it to cure different sicknesses in different ways. If a doctor is a good healer, he puts a current through the water he uses. It is very important for the Sxwóyxwey people. Water is their power. You need water for life and for the spirit.

There is a cycle to life. Our ancestors have lived here for thousands of years. And by that I mean the ancestors of all of us, not only the ancestors of the humans; our other ancestors are the animals—the fish, the birds and insects. All who have gone on before us, our elders. Our elders have left their bodily remains—their dust, their footprints, and their breath—spread across the surface of the land. The land is covered with the remains of our ancestors. The living generation feeds itself from what the ancestors have produced and left behind—all the generations who have passed on.

The storms come in from the ocean, over the Pacific, and their clouds hit the mountains and burst into rain. The rains run down the mountainsides and wash the dust of the ancestors into the river valleys. The plants eat these remains. The birds eat the berries and their droppings fall on the hills and mountains. The cycle continues.

We worship all our ancestors—the old people and all the Old Ones from among the birds and fish and animals and insects. Water holds the decay and the dust of the bodies of our ancestors. It mixes with the rain and forms the lakes and the rivers. The rivers and creeks carry the essence of our elders. We run across the surface of the Earth in the early mornings until our bodies are heated; then we bathe in the river whenever we want to be strong. The river is the blood and the body fluids of our elders.

The river is sacred to us. All we produce—all we eat and drink—eventually goes back, out the river, down to the sea. In the ocean, it gets purified. It comes back as the rain and the mist. It comes back along the valleys as *slhákw'em,* the breath of our ancestors. *Slhákw'em* is both your breath and your spirit.

I have not talked much about this in life. It is something very sacred to us. These things demand respect.

We must care for our ancestors, all our deceased, including our brothers and sisters in the animal world. We are no better or worse than the plants and animals. We have to purify our bodies before hunting or fishing, so that we do not insult any of these ancestors. Back when we lived directly off animals, birds, and fish, we wasted nothing. We found a use for everything. With the animals, even the bones, hooves, and innards were used in the old times. Bones that are not used are to be burned. Fish bones are to be returned to the river.

We humans can talk and make tools. "We have an advantage over the animals," my Grandfather Pete used to say. "So we have a duty to take care of them." Those of us who do not show such respect and responsibility, we run the risk of coming back to Earth, being born again, but as an animal that is badly treated by humans. It is not easy to outwit and kill an animal. You have to respect it first. We are taught not to be cruel to the animals, especially the game animals and the fish. Their fortunes are our fortunes, and our futures are linked with each other.

We must be able to respect ourselves if we are going to live a good and decent life. If we do not respect all our ancestors among the people and the other creatures, then we do not respect ourselves and we cannot feel the heartbeat of all the life around us. When we feel the life around us, we respect the past and the present and we can live in a humble way, as equals among all the creatures. This is how we understand the wonderful but fragile cycle of life and death on this Earth. It is our duty to pass on this understanding and to hope that our grandchildren will pass it on to theirs.

For the Young

The Fraser Valley is filling up with people, and I don't know what the answer is for the future. Right now, members of my family are carrying on with the teachings that their parents have taught them. It all ties in with the Sxwóyxwey and the longhouse, the mí'lha—all the rules and regulations tie in with the land and the water. The younger people who become initiated or who dance in the Sxwóyxwey, they all learn these things, respectfully. But otherwise, I guess we'd have to start teaching them by taking a course! But our family is not like that. Everything we talk about, we go out and we live it. So the children are there. When they are two or three years old, they are put in a canoe. They grow up in a canoe. So they don't have to study it or take a course. It's just something they grow up with. They go up into the mountains. It's just part of their upbringing.

Last night [at Skowkale], I did talk to the young ones who were coming out for their puberty rites. I told them that as young adults now, they have to start taking responsibility for themselves, as well as for all the things around them. One of the things I really stressed was that they listen to their elders, and to hear what the elders tell them whenever the elders talk to them, instead of just shrugging their shoulders and acting bored. They should pay attention when elders speak to them because elders have a lot of things to say about the past. I can't even remember all the things I said, but I did warn them about the bad things outside the village that could happen to them if they strayed too far from home. Then there were many things I would like to have told them, but we didn't have time because there were other speakers waiting to speak to them.

But I guess, perhaps, some of the things we could do is to teach them how to take care of what's left and to respect things the way our elders and our ancestors respected everything around them—because we are related to everything in the environment. Our relatives are everywhere. They are in everything. We could not survive alone. We have always had to get along with nature—with the animals, the birds, and the trees as our fellow creatures, our brothers and sisters. We had to respect everything and live in harmony with everything around us. So we took care of them. If we are to continue living on this planet, we're going to have to take care of what's left and not be so careless and act as if everything is going to be there forever, because it isn't.

Oh, one of the things I did tell the children last night was that there is nothing wrong with being poor. When I say poor, I don't mean destitute. I mean, poor without all the material things that everyone seems to think they have to have. As long as you have enough food to eat, as long as you're warm and you have shelter, and you are healthy, and your families are cared for, then you don't need to have all kinds of money to throw around. Everything that we had before—it has all been destroyed—and all because of money.

People seem to think that they have to have more than they need, and that's wrong. We should be happy just to have enough to live comfortably, and therefore try to save the forests and the fish and the animals and the birds—take care of all those relatives, what the newcomers call "the environment." We should not be so quick to destroy things just because we need more money.

These are things that children should hear. Maybe in the future, they will remember some of these words. I told them to respect their elders and take care of them. This is what we did in the old days. Always be patient and ready to help elders and not throw them away, put them away where people don't care about them. In the old days, we took care of them because they were wise people. They had lots of stories to tell us, about the mistakes they made and the things they did. We could learn from their mistakes as well as from the good things they knew how to do.

I guess we could also tell them that they have to pass on the knowledge they gather in life to the next generation coming up after them. This is their duty. Every generation should pass on the culture so that the people coming up will always know how to behave and treat one another properly, instead of destroying everything. It can't end with just one generation—"my" generation—getting some knowledge. This has to go on always to the next generation. There must be continuity. *Always remember, the land—as our elders said to us—does not belong to us. It belongs to our grandchildren and, in turn, to their grandchildren.* We must always think of it that way. We must teach the children as they grow up that we are preserving things, looking after things around us, so that when they grow up they can teach those who come up behind them.

We must look after everything and save what's left. Maybe we ought to be planting trees or looking after the few things we have left instead of destroying them. And the water, we have to be so careful with it and make sure it is in good health. I think that pretty well covers it.

Epilogue

* ❀ *

RICHARD DALY: Rena found peace and creative inspiration living in her log home by the Skeena River. In the course of our interviews, she sometimes talked about living in one culture and watershed (that of her husband) while being tied in a thousand ways to another in southern British Columbia, where she was born and raised and where her descendants live.

RENA: I think living up here is a good thing in a way. Because I'm not involved in the many little problems all families have on a daily basis. These, they take care of, down there at home. They have family meetings and they take care of their own problems, unless a big event is coming up and they want my input—which usually isn't too much. It's just protocol. They can then say, "We spoke to Mother on this and that." But usually they take care of everything. So, in a way it's good that I'm up here. I don't have to tolerate all of the problems of a large family, day to day. Usually, a lot of the problems are kept from me anyway. I'm safe here with Cliff. He kind of has a connection with them, letting them know how I am and what we are doing. This keeps them satisfied. If any of them wish to come up and spend time with us for any reason, they do so. Here, it's quiet. I only hear about illnesses that may end in death, or of a relative who has passed away. Then I have the choice of coming down, or not. I don't feel pressured while I'm here.

When I'm working here, it feels like a good wedding between the north and the south. I'm referring to the work I do reviving the ancient weaving among the local people around here. That was a great feat and an honour for me to take it up and bring it back to the local people. I feel like I've done something for my husband's people. And it has kept me busy all these years—kept my mind awake. I do my own weaving, and, well, I had a course going on down there, at the smokehouse at Skowkale, but it is difficult to catch people and have them come in every day because they are all so busy, all working or going to school. But I always think one day I will have another course.

Another thing that hampers the weaving is that there are no more large trees. They have all been cut down. The second-growth roots aren't very good. They are not old enough to have grown long and straight. They taper too quickly and they're not very good for weaving—so it's very difficult to get smooth joins and tight, even rows with such roots. It's not very easy to pick up and start teaching, unless we go into a place where they still have some old-growth trees. That's kind of hard to find these days. You go on private property and you get shot!

It just seems like since the arrival of the new people, there has been a steady decline of everything. More and more people are coming into the country. There are more people to feed and they want more money. There is just no end to it. I don't know what will happen—the decline of the salmon, the trees, the destruction of the land itself. They're digging up oil and gold and diamonds and whatever it is they are looking for. There is just no end to it.

We always looked on everything in nature as our relatives, but now they're looked upon as resources—even people are now called "human resources," and all the species are looked on as a way of earning more money. Things are out of balance. Right now there is a great danger of us losing everything. And that's going to affect everybody.

RICHARD DALY: As our manuscript was being prepared for publication, there was an unexpected deterioration in Cliff Bolton's health. He was taken to hospital, stabilized, and submitted to extensive testing around Easter time. Then, quite suddenly, he passed away on April 12, 2012. Rena was understandably devastated. His funeral was held in his home community at Kitsumkalum, and then Rena's children helped to move their mother back from the Skeena River to the home area in the Fraser Valley, at Skowkale in Xwélmexw territory.

Rena is now back at work daily, usually from daybreak, making her baskets and textiles. She has set up her workshop once more in the kitchen of the family's *híkw' lalém*, their winter dance house, and she lives nearby surrounded by her family. Her descendants drop in and try their hand at weaving and plaiting. They listen to her stories. She thinks over her life and the lives of her parents and her elders; she meditates as she works. She involves herself in the activities of her grandchildren. A granddaughter is working with her, making a cedar-bark dance robe, and others are learning some of the things she herself learned as a child on the riverbank at Devil's Run. Rena is giving lessons again in both northern and southern styles of basketry and textile weaving. The apprentices are local Xwélmexw youth, as well as visitors from the north and from as far away as Saskatchewan. Recently, Simon Fraser University asked her to allow some of their students to join her and to learn "by watching and doing."

RENA: Now, when we are finishing this book, I want to say that Cliff was a warm and gentle man, and I never thought there might be a day when he was not around, coming in and out, digging in the garden, cutting wood, carving in our workroom or fleshing out a new canoe in the shed outside. I never thought there would be a day when he was not always looking out for my welfare. We had a good life together. We were the best of friends, and we talked about new things every day. We never ran out of things to say to each other. I miss him very much, but I think it was fitting that in the end, he was recognized for what he achieved, especially as a master carver. In his last year, he was commissioned to design and make one of his distinctive jade carvings for the lieutenant-governor's Black Rod. This ceremonial rod is like a talking stick. It is used in the Parliament Buildings in Victoria. He finished this piece, and when it was done, it was inaugurated down there in Victoria, with the government officials. This happened not so long before Cliff left us. They took him to Victoria for the investiture of the Black Rod. He was there to receive the recognition, and that is how I hope people will remember him.

I miss our everyday life together, and I miss our log house down in the trees by the river, and the peaceful life we had, but it was right for me to come back home, to move south again to my own family and relatives, to the flow of the Stó:lō, the river where I grew up. Our people—no matter where we get to, eventually we come home. That is our way.

Family Trees

* ❋ *

Rena's family through her mother's second marriage

Alec raised by the Phillips
after his mother died

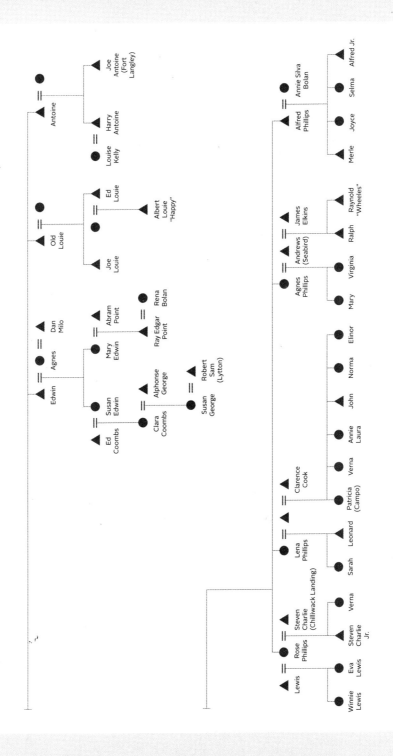

Rena's maternal grandmother's family (showing Rena's line of descent from the warrior Xéyteleq and the Steqó:ye Wolf People)

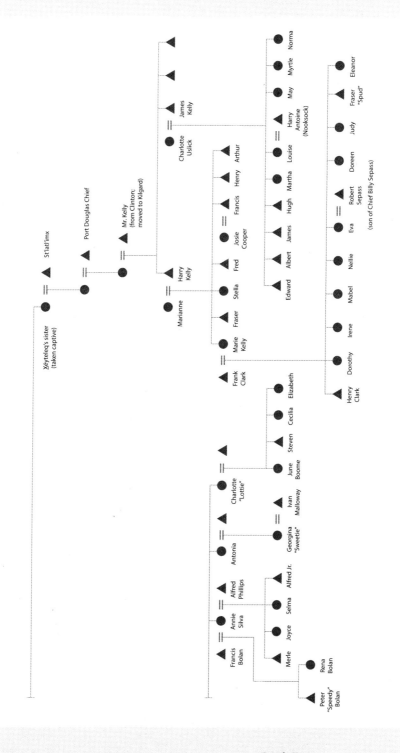

Rena's maternal grandfather's family (through which Rena became the custodian of the ceremonial Sxwóyxwey masks)

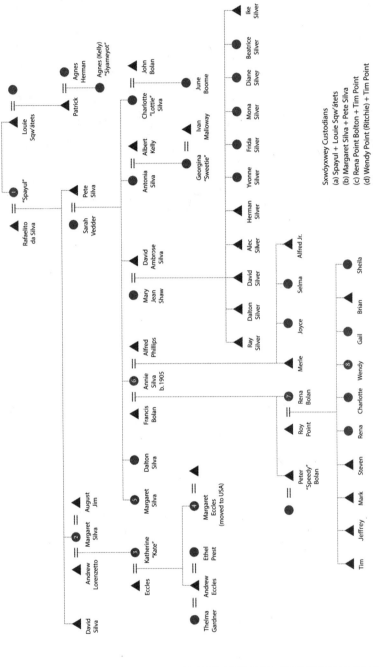

Sxwóyxwey Custodians
(a) Spayul + Louie Sqw'átets
(b) Margaret Silva + Pete Silva
(c) Rena Point Bolton + Tim Point
(d) Wendy Point (Ritchie) + Tim Point

Rena's father's family

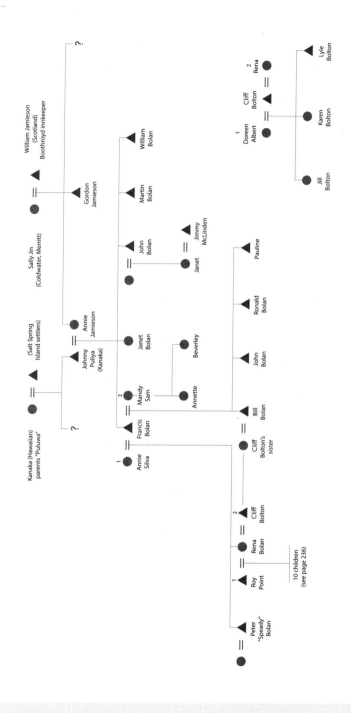

Pronunciation Guide

* ❋ *

The following is based on the key to pronunciation in Keith Carlson's *You Are Asked to Witness* (1997, v–vi). Carlson drew on linguist Brent Galloway's guide to Halq'eméylem pronunciation and orthography, "The Significance of the Halkomelem Language Material," in *The Chilliwacks and Their Neighbours* (Wells 1987, 23–27), with modifications intended to reflect local Xwélmexw pronunciation.

* ❋ *

The vowels in Halq'eméylem are written and pronounced as follows:

a   as in *fat, bat* when under an acute or a grave accent (which indicates stress) or before *w* or *y*; elsewhere, as in *when* or *bet*

e   as in *sill, bill* when between any of the sounds *l, lh, w, s, ts, ts', k, k'*; as in *pull* or *bull* when between sounds involving the lips: *m, w, kw, kw', qw, qw', xw, xw*; elsewhere, as in *mutt* or *what*

i   as in *mean, beet, eel*

o   as in *pot, mop, father*

ō   as in *no, go, crow*

u   as in *Sue, soon, moon, flu*

:   A colon after a vowel indicates that the vowel is prolonged (that is, drawn out).

239

Most vowels can be followed by *y* or *w* (in the same syllable):

aw	as in *cow*
ay	rare in English; for some dialects, as in *sang*
ew	as in Canadian English *about*
ey	as in *bait*
iw	as in *peewee*, without the final *ee*
iy	as in *see you*, without the final *ou*
ōw	as in *oh well*, without the final *ell*
oy	as in *bride*
ow	as in *bowl*

Most Halq'eméylem words have at least one stressed vowel (like *á, à,* or *í*). Vowel stress, marked with ` or ´, alters the pitch of the vowel but does not change its essential quality. A stressed vowel is pronounced more loudly and at a higher pitch than an unstressed vowel. An acute accent (´) over the vowel indicates high pitch (high stress); a grave accent (`) over the vowel indicates middle pitch (middle stress); an unstressed vowel (low pitch) is unmarked.

The consonants are written and pronounced as follows:

p	as in *pill* and *spin*
t	as in *tick* and *stand*
ch	as in *church*
ts	as in *rats*
k	as in *king* and *skill*
kw	as in *inkwell* and *queen*
th	as in *thin*, but not voiced as in *this* or *the*
sh	as in *shine*
s	as in *sill*
h	as in *hat*
m	as in *man* and *bottom*
l	as in *land* and *camel*
y	as in *yes* and *say*
w	as in *wood* and *how*

This leaves eighteen consonants that have no precise equivalent in English:

q	made by touching the back of the tongue to the very back of the soft palate (like English *k*, but the contact is further back on the palate)
qw	made like the *q* but with rounded lips

ch', k', kw', p', q', qw', t', th', ts', tl'   These ten consonants are glottalized, or "popped," by adding a glottal stop to the consonant.

'	a glottal stop, made by pulling the vocal cords together and then releasing them, as in North American English *mutton* or *button* (between the vowel sounds) or the Cockney pronunciation of *bottle* (between the *o* and the *l*), or at the beginning of *earns* in *Mary earns,* as compared to the beginning of *yearns* in *Mary yearns*
lh	pronounced like *l* but without vibration of the vocal cords; the air flows freely along the sides of the tongue, like the *l* sound in English *clean* or *climb*

In addition to these consonants, there are four blown *x* sounds. These are made by raising the main body of the tongue to narrow the passage of air until the friction of air can be heard:

x	made with the middle of the tongue raised toward the roof of the mouth, as though to make the *y* in *yawn* but without vibration at the vocal cords, as at the beginning of *hew* or *Hugh* (in some dialects of English)
xw	made with the tongue raised a little further back and with rounded lips, somewhat like *wh* in some dialects of English but with much more air friction
<u>*x*</u>	made with the back of the tongue raised near (but not touching) the soft palate where English k is made, or as in German Bach and Scottish loch
<u>*xw*</u>	made like *x* but with rounded lips

Glossary

* ❅ *

chelángen	esoteric family knowledge, as well as the inherited right and duty to protect that knowledge and bestow it on coming generations (plural: *chu'chelángen*)
gwa'ay (Gitxsanimx)	poor, of little value
híkw'lalém	the longhouse (lit. "great house")
híkw' sí:yá:m	a great chief
Kw'ekw'íqw	Kilgard (the village and the creek)
kwóxwmal	a ceremonial staff with rattling deer hooves attached
lehál. See *slehá:l*	
lhá:ts'tel	a fish-cutting knife, similar to the Inuit *ulu*
Lhi'hletálets	site at Iwówes where the Sxwóyxwey regalia and knowledge came out of the water for use in healing ceremonies
Lhókw'ōlá:leqw	"The-man-who-flew-like-an-eagle-as-he-danced," the name of the Tii:t *sí:yá:m* who lived along the Fraser River at Pópkw'em, above Chilliwack and below Hope
Líyómxetel	Devil's Run (see chapter 3, note 1)
mí'lha	winter dance ceremony during which initiates are possessed by spiritual forces (*syúwel*) and acquire power by learning to control these forces
mí'lha híkw'lalém	name given to the longhouse, or smokehouse, when it is used for the winter *mí'lha* ceremonies
móqwem	swamp tea, Hudson's Bay tea, Labrador tea

Nlaka'pamux	a First Nation (formerly known as the Thompson Indians) who occupy the upper Fraser Canyon, the Thompson Canyon, and part of the Nicola Valley
Nuu-chah-nulth	a First Nation (formerly known as the Nootkas) who occupy most of the west coast of Vancouver Island
Penelakut	the Coast Salish people of Kuper Island, in the Gulf Islands
pí:lt	to plant or bury something (the related verb *pí:lten* means to bury someone)
Pópkw'em	an upriver Tii:t village, downstream from Hope
q'ewétem	a board that used to be placed between the two teams in the *slehá:l* game
s'éliyá	dream prophecy
sélseltel	spindle whorl
Semá:th	Sumas (Sumas Lake, Sumas Prairie, Sumas Mountain)
shxwlá:m	healer, medicine man
Si:l'hiy	a giant worm or snake with a head at either end
simoogit (Tsimshian)	the very most person (that is, a chief)
sí:yá:m (also *si:em*)	honourable, esteemed, chiefly person
Skw'átets	Peters Reserve, in the Tii:t area, above Chilliwack, below Hope; the settlement of Ohamil is in the same general area
slehá:l (also *lehál*)	a game, played in teams, usually to the accompaniment of drumming and songs, that involves a group of sticks and two sets of bones, one marked and the other unmarked; one team hides bones, and the other team must guess which bones are hidden; a correct guess earns the team a stick, the object being to win all the sticks
slewil	sleeping mats woven from rushes
slhákw'em	breath, spirit; used metaphorically to denote the morning or evening mist along the river, which is said to be the breath of the ancestors
Sq'ewq'éyl	Skowkale
stlaqwem	those who have undergone spiritual initiation
Stó:lō	"the big river," used today to identify the people of the lower Fraser River region, who call themselves Xwélmexw

Stótelō	"the little river"
swéqeth	woven blankets worn as robes by high-status people
swo'hwa	dance apron
swox̱'wath	a kind of twill weave, traditional among the Steqó:ye people of Semá:th
sx̱ax̱á	taboo, banned
Sxwóyxwey	healing cult in which humans cooperate with underwater powers
syúwel	spiritual powers, mainly from the natural world, said to be capable of possessing the souls of certain receptive human individuals; also used to describe the community of *stlaqwem* (initiates)
telset	a blessing, bestowed with hands raised, palms forward
tets'eets	the welcome blessing given to guests in ceremonies and feasts
Tii:t (also Te:it)	upriver Xwélmexw people, who live in the area that extends roughly from above Cheam to Yale
ts'a:s	poor, pitiful, stingy
Ts'elxwéyeqw	Chilliwack, "the place of coming together," and, by extension, the people who live there
Xwelíqweltel	"The hungry flesh-eating speaker of the house," the name of Xételeq's uncle (the original Xwelíqwiya's brother), which Rena's son Steven now carries
Xwelíqwiya	"The flesh-eating hungry female," the name of Xételeq's mother (and Xwelíqweltel's sister), which Rena now carries
Xwelítem	white people, foreigners (see chapter 8, note 2)
Xwélmexw	"the people," that is, the people who live along the lower Fraser River, who are more popularly known as the Stó:lō
X̱éyteleq	warrior leader of the Sema:th wolf people
Yakweakwioose	a village adjacent to Sq'ewq'éyl (Skowkale) in Sardis; the name Yeqwyeqwi:ws means "place of burning"
yeqwá:ls	a shamanic journey into an altered state of consciousness, undertaken by the healer to discover the source of someone's afflictions

Works Cited

* ❊ *

Archibald, Jo-ann (Q'um Q'um Xiiem). 2008. *Indigenous Storywork: Educating the Heart, Mind, Body and Spirit.* Vancouver: University of British Columbia Press.

Baker, Simon. 1994. *Khot-La-Cha: The Autobiography of Chief Simon Baker.* Compiled and edited by Verna Kirkness. Vancouver: Douglas and McIntyre.

Bakhtin, Mikhail. 1986. *Speech Genres and Other Late Essays.* Translated by Vern W. McGee and edited by Caryl Emerson and Michael Holquist. Austin: University of Texas Press.

Barkaskas, P. M. 2009. "The Indian Voice: Centering Women in the Gendered Politics of Indigenous Nationalism in B.C., 1969–1984." MA thesis, University of British Columbia, Vancouver.

Barman, Jean. 2004. *The Remarkable Adventures of Portuguese Joe Silvey.* Madeira Park, BC: Harbour.

Bellos, David. 2011. *Is That a Fish in Your Ear? Translation and the Meaning of Everything.* New York: Faber and Faber.

Blaser, Mario, Harvey A. Feit, and Glenn McRae, eds. 2004. *In the Way of Development: Indigenous Peoples, Life Projects and Globalization.* London: Zed Books.

Boas, Franz. 1889. "Notes on the Snanaimuq." *American Anthropologist* 2: 321–28.

Boyd, Robert. 1994. "Smallpox in the Pacific Northwest: The First Epidemics." *BC Studies* 101: 5–40.

Carlson, Keith T., ed. 1997. *You Are Asked to Witness: The Stó:lō in Canada's Pacific Coast History.* Chilliwack, BC: Stó:lō Heritage Trust.

———. 2001. *A Stó:lō Coast Salish Historical Atlas.* Vancouver: Douglas and McIntyre.

———. 2003. "The Power of Place, the Problem of Time: A Study of History and Aboriginal Collective Identity." PhD diss., University of British Columbia, Vancouver.

Carlson, Keith T., and A. McHalsie. 1998. *I am Stó:lō: Katherine Explores Her Heritage.* Chilliwack, BC: Stó:lō Heritage Trust.

Collins, June M. 1952. "The Mythological Basis for Attitudes Toward Animals Among Salish-Speaking Indians." *Journal of American Folklore* 65, no. 258: 353–59.

Converse, Cathy. 1998. *Mainstays: Women Who Shaped B.C.* Victoria: Horsdal and Schubart.

Cruikshank, Julie. 2005. *Do Glaciers Listen? Local Knowledge, Colonial Encounters and Social Imagination.* Vancouver: University of British Columbia Press.

Cruikshank, Julie, with Angela Sidney, Kitty Smith, and Annie Ned. 1990. *Life Lived Like a Story: Life Stories of Three Yukon Elders.* Vancouver: University of British Columbia Press.

Daly, Richard H. 2005. *Our Box Was Full: An Ethnography for the Delgamuukw Plaintiffs.* Vancouver: University of British Columbia Press.

Dawn, Leslie. 1981. "'Ksan Museum: Cultural and Artistic Activity Among the Gitksan Indians of the Upper Skeena, 1920–1973." MA thesis, University of Victoria, Victoria.

———. 2006. *National Visions, National Blindness: Canadian Art and Identities in the 1920s.* Vancouver: University of British Columbia Press.

Duff, Wilson. 1952a. "Gitksan Totem Poles, 1952." *Anthropology in British Columbia* 3: 21–30.

———. 1952b. *The Upper Stalo Indians of the Fraser Valley, British Columbia.* Anthropology in British Columbia: Memoir, no. 1. Victoria: BC Provincial Museum.

———. 1956. "Prehistoric Stone Sculpture of the Fraser River and Gulf Islands." *Anthropology in British Columbia* 5: 15–51.

———. 1959. *History, Territories and Laws of the Kitwancool.* Anthropology in British Columbia: Memoir, no. 4. Victoria: BC Provincial Museum.

———. 1964. *Impact of the White Man.* Vol. 1 of *The Indian History of BC.* Anthropology in British Columbia: Memoir, no. 5. Victoria: BC Provincial Museum.

———. 1975. *Images Stone BC: Thirty Centuries of Northwest Coast Indian Sculpture.* Seattle: University of Washington Press.

———. 2003. "Koyah." In *Dictionary of Canadian Biography*, vol. 4. Toronto and Montréal: University of Toronto and Université Laval. http://www.biographi.ca/en/bio/koyah_4E.html.

Dufresne, Lucie Marie-Mai. 1996. "The Salish Sxwaixwe in Historic Salish Society." Masters thesis, University of Ottawa.

Galloway, Brent, with the Coqualeetza Elders Group. 1980. *Tó:lméls Ye Siyelyólexwa / Wisdom of the Elders: The Structure of Upriver Halq'eméylem, A Grammatical Sketch and Classified Word List for Upriver Halq'eméylem.* Sardis: Coqualeetza Education Training Centre.

George, Earl Maquinna. 2003. *Living on the Edge: Nuu-chah-nulth History from an Ahousaht Chief's Perspective.* Winlaw, BC: Sono Nis Press.

Gustafson, Paula. 1980. *Salish Weaving.* Vancouver: Douglas and McIntyre.

Haeberlin, Herman K. 1918. "SbEtEtda'q: A Shamanic Performance of the Coast Salish." *American Anthropologist,* n.s., 20, no. 3: 249–57.

Harding, Sandra, ed. 2004. *The Feminist Standpoint Theory Reader: Intellectual and Political Controversies.* London: Routledge.

Harris, Ken. 1972. *Visitors Who Never Left: The Origin of the People of Damelahamid.* Vancouver: University of British Columbia Press.

Hawthorn, H.B. 1966–67. *A Survey of the Contemporary Indians of Canada: A Report on Economic, Political, Educational Needs and Policies.* 2 vols. Ottawa: Department of Indian Affairs.

Hawthorn, H.B., C.S. Belshaw, and S.M. Jamieson, eds. 1958. *The Indians of British Columbia: A Study of Contemporary Social Adjustment.* Berkeley: University of California Press.

Jenness, Diamond. 1955. *The Faith of a Coast Salish Indian.* Anthropology in British Columbia: Memoirs, No. 3. Victoria: BC Provincial Museum.

Jilek, Wolfgang G. 1974a. "Indian Healing Power: Indigenous Therapeutic Practices in the Pacific Northwest." *Psychiatric Annals* 4, no. 11: 13–21.

———. 1974b. *Salish Indian Mental Health and Culture Change: Psychohygienic and Therapeutic Aspects of the Guardian Spirit Ceremonial.* Toronto: Holt, Rinehart and Winston.

———. (1982) 2004. *Indian Healing: Shamanic Ceremonialism in the Pacific Northwest Today.* Victoria: Hancock House.

Johnston, Basil. 1995. *The Manitous: The Spiritual World of the Ojibway.* New York: HarperCollins.

Kew, J.E. Michael. 1990. "Central and Southern Coast Salish Ceremonies Since 1900." In *Northwest Coast,* vol. 7 of *Handbook of North American Indians,* edited by Wayne Suttles, 476–80. Washington, DC: Smithsonian Institution.

K'HHalserten, William. (1963) 2009. *Sepass Poems: Ancient Songs of Y-Ail-Mihth.* Mission, BC: Longhouse.

Laforet, Andrea, and Annie York. 1998. *Spuzzum: Fraser Canyon Histories, 1808–1939.* Vancouver: University of British Columbia Press.

Lamb, W. Kaye, ed. 1960. *The Letters and Journals of Simon Fraser, 1806–1808.* Toronto: Macmillan.

MacDonald, George F. 1983. *Ninstints: Haida World Heritage Site.* Vancouver: University of British Columbia Press.

Maclachlan, Morag, ed. 1998. *The Fort Langley Journals, 1827–30.* Introductions by Morag Maclachan and Wayne Suttles. Vancouver: University of British Columbia Press.

Magosci, Paul Robert. 1999. *Encyclopedia of Canada's Peoples.* Toronto: University of Toronto Press.

McCall, Sophie. 2011. *First Person Plural: Aboriginal Storytelling and the Ethics of Collaborative Authorship.* Vancouver: University of British Columbia Press.

Mead, George Herbert. 1932. *The Philosophy of the Present.* Chicago: Open Court.

———. (1934) 1967. *Mind, Self and Society: From the Standpoint of a Social Behaviorist.* Edited and introduction by Charles W. Morris. Reprint, Chicago: University of Chicago Press.

M'Gonicle, Michael, and Wendy Wickwire. 1988. *Stein: The Way of the River.* Vancouver: Talonbooks.

Mills, Antonia C. 1988. "A Comparison of Wet'suwet'en Cases of the Reincarnation Type with Gitksan and Beaver." *Journal of Anthropological Research* 44, no. 4: 385–415.

Mills, Antonia, and Richard Slobodin, eds. 1994. *Amerindian Rebirth: Reincarnation Belief Among North American Indians and Inuit.* Toronto: University of Toronto Press.

Mjelde, Liv. Forthcoming. "The Personal Is Political: The Woman Question." In *The Personal and the Political in Cross-Cultural Perspective,* edited by Anja Heikkinen, Lorenz Lassnigg, and Manfred Wahle. Tampere: University of Tampere Press.

Mohs, Gordon. 1987. "Spiritual Sites, Ethnic Significance and Native Spirituality: The Heritage and Heritage Sites of the Sto:lo Indians of British Columbia." MA thesis, Simon Fraser University, Vancouver.

———. 2000. *Devil's Run.* Mission, BC: Longhouse Press.

Moran, Bridget. 1988. *Stoney Creek Woman, Sai'k'uz Ts'eke: The Story of Mary John.* Vancouver: Tillacum Library.

Narby, Jeremy. 1999. *The Cosmic Serpent: DNA and the Origins of Knowledge.* New York: Penguin.

Opheim, Justin. 2009. "A Biographical Examination of Chief Emmitt Liquitum." Final paper, Ethnohistory Field School, University of Victoria. http://web.uvic.ca/vv/stolo/pdf/Justin%20Final%20Paper%20-%20Liquitum.pdf.

Pennier, Hank. 2006. *"Call Me Hank": A Stó:lō Man's Reflections on Logging, Living and Growing Old.* Edited by Keith Thor Carlson and Kristina Fagan. Toronto: University of Toronto Press. First published as *Chiefly Indian: The Warm and Witty Story of a British Columbia Half Breed Logger* (West Vancouver: Graydonald Graphics, 1972).

Plant, Byron King. 2009. "'A Relationship and Interchange of Experience': H. B. Hawthorn, Indian Affairs, and the 1955 BC Indian Research Project." *BC Studies,* no. 163 (Autumn): 5–31.

Reid, Martine J., ed. 2004. *Paddling to Where I Stand: Agnes Alfred, Quiqwa-sutinuxw, Noblewoman.* Translated by Daisy Sewid-Smith. Vancouver: University of British Columbia Press.

Rios, Theodore, and Kathleen Mullen Sands. 2000. *Telling a Good One: The Process of a Native American Collaborative Biography.* Lincoln: University of Nebraska Press.

Samuel, Cheryl. 1987. *The Raven's Tail.* Vancouver: University of British Columbia Press.

——. 1990. *The Chilkat Dancing Blanket.* Norman: University of Oklahoma Press.

Sarris, Greg. 1993. *Keeping Slug Woman Alive: A Holistic Approach to American Indian Texts.* Berkeley: University of California Press.

Schutz, Alfred. 1967. *The Phenomenology of the Social World.* Evanston, IL: Northwestern University Press.

Shiell, Les. 1990. "Native Renaissance: Renewing Pride and Dignity with the Once-Outlawed Spirit Dance." *Canadian Geographic* 110, no. 4: 60–67.

Sider, Gerald, and Gavin Smith, eds. 1997. *Between History and Histories: The Making of Silences and Commemorations.* Toronto: University of Toronto Press.

Simon Fraser University Museum of Archaeology and Ethnology. 2008–9. "A Journey into Time Immemorial." http://www.sfu.museum/time/en/panoramas/long-back/hatzic-rock/.

Sleigh, Daphne. 1983. *Discovering Deroche: From Nicomen to Lake Errock.* Abbotsford, BC: Abbotsford Printing.

——. 1999. *One Foot on the Border: A History of Sumas Prairie and Area.* Deroche, BC: Sumas Prairie and Area Historical Society.

Smith, Dorothy E. 1999. *Writing the Social: Critique, Theory and Investigation.* Toronto: University of Toronto Press.

——. 2005. *Institutional Ethnography: A Sociology of People.* Lanham, MD, and Oxford: AltaMira Press.

——. 2012. "Telling the Truth After Postmodernism." *Sosiologisk Årbok* 1: 57–99. Originally published in *Studies in Symbolic Interaction* 19, no. 3 (1996): 171–202.

Steltzer, Ulli. 1976. *Indian Artists at Work.* Vancouver: J. J. Douglas.

Stern, Bernhard Joseph. (1934) 1969. *The Lummi Indians of Northwest Washington.* Reprint, New York: AMS Press.

Suttles, Wayne. 1974. *The Economic Life of the Coast Salish of Haro and Rosario Straits.* New York: Garland.

——. 1982. "The Halkomelem Sxwayxwey." *American Indian Art* 1: 56–65.

——. 1990. "Central Coast Salish." In *Northwest Coast,* vol. 7 of *Handbook of North American Indians,* edited by Wayne Suttles, 453–75. Washington, DC: Smithsonian Institution.

Suttles, Wayne P., Diamond Jenness, and Wilson Duff, eds. 1956. *Katzie Ethnographic Notes.* Victoria: British Columbia Provincial Museum.

Tataryn, Anastasia. 2009. "What *Is* in a Name? Identity, Politics and Stó:lō Ancestral Names." *University of the Fraser Valley Research Review* 2, no. 2: 54–72.

Thom, Brian. 1994. "Telling Stories: The Life of Chief Richard Malloway." Unpublished manuscript prepared for the Sto:lō Tribal Council. http://www.web.uvic.ca/~bthom1/Media/pdfs/ethnography/tell-stories.htm.

———. 1996. "Canadian Multiculturalism and *Sto:lô* Cultural Identity." *Sto:lô* Curriculum Consortium. Kwikwetlem, BC. http://www.web.uvic.ca/~bthom1/Media/pdfs/ethnography/MULTICUL.htm.

———. 2003. "The Anthropology of Northwest Coast Oral Traditions." *Arctic Anthropology* 40, no. 1: 1–28.

Tolmie, William Fraser. 1963. *The Journals of William Fraser Tolmie, Physician and Fur Trader.* Vancouver: Mitchell Press.

Treben, Maria. 1980. *Health Through God's Pharmacy: Advice and Experiences with Medicinal Herbs.* Steyr, Austria: Ennsthaler Verlag.

Venne, Sharon. 1997. "Understanding Treaty 6: An Indigenous Perspective." In *Aboriginal and Treaty Rights in Canada: Essays on Law, Equality and Respect for Difference,* edited by Michael Asch, 173–207. Vancouver: University of British Columbia Press.

Vološinov, Valentin N. (1929) 1986. *Marxism and the Philosophy of Language.* Translated by Ladislav Matejka and I. R. Titunik. Cambridge, MA: Harvard University Press.

Wade, Edwin L. 1976. "The Art of the Salish Power Dances." *American Indian Art* 1, no. 4: 64–67.

Wells, Oliver N. 1966. "The Return of the Salish Loom." *The Beaver,* Outfit 296 (Spring): 40–45.

———. 1969. *Salish Weaving, Primitive and Modern, as Practiced by the Indians of South Western British Columbia.* Sardis, BC: Author.

———. 1987. *The Chilliwacks and Their Neighbours.* Edited by Ralph Maud, Brent Galloway, and Marie Weedon. Vancouver: Talonbooks.

Wickwire, Wendy. 1994. "To See Ourselves as the Other's Other: Nlaka'pamux Contact Narratives." *Canadian Historical Review* 75, no. 1: 1–20.

Wike, Joyce Annabel. 1941. "Modern Spirit Dancing of Northern Puget Sound." MA thesis, University of Washington, Seattle.

Wolf, Eric R. 1982. *Europe and the People Without History.* Berkeley: University of California Press.

York, Annie, Richard Daly, and Chris Arnett. 1994. *They Write Their Dreams on the Rock Forever: Rock Writings of the Stein River Valley of British Columbia.* Vancouver: Talonbooks.

Index

* ❀ *

child rearing: and transmission of culture, 88–91
Chilkat weaving, 174–75, 189
Chilliwack: origin of name, 50
Chrétien, Jean, 150–51
Clark, Marie and Frank, and children of, 38
Coombs, Clara, 49
Cooper, Josie (wife of Francis Kelly), 39
Cooper, Mrs. Albert (of Soowahlie), 136–37
Coqualeetza Elders' Group, xxxv, 153*n*
Coqualeetza Residential School, 16, 27, 69–75, 103, 168
Coutts, Emily (wife of Charlie Point), and children of, 43, 85
Cruikshank, Julie, xxxviii, xlii–xliii
Cultus Lake, BC, 39, 99, 137–38, 155

Da Silva, Rafaelito, 47–48
Davidson, Claude, 74, 168
Davidson, Robert, 168
Deming, WA, 21, 82–83
Deroche, BC, 48, 49
Devil's Run (Liyómxetel), 17, 19, 51–59
Dewdney, BC, 55, 57
dialogue: reading as, xliv; silence as form of, xxi; and social construction of meaning, xli–xlv; storytelling as, xxxvi–xxxix, xl, xlvi. *See also* told-to narratives
Diesing, Freda, 180*n*
"double-tracking case," xviii*n*
Douglas, Albert, 105, 155
Douglas, Charlie, 105
Duff, Wilson, 147–49, 167*n*
Duncan, BC, 170

Eccles, Andrew, 48
Eccles, Margaret ("Chickee"), 48
Edwin, Agnes, 29, 49, 85
Edwin, Mary (née Point, wife of Dan Milo), 49, 85
Edwin, Susan, 49
elders: and cultural continuity, xxiii, 82–83, 86–88, 104–6, 110–11, 127–28, 150, 155–56, 162–63, 166, 170–72, 199, 204, 213–14, 223–25

Fernandez, Mrs. Raymond, 84
First Citizens' Fund, 147–49, 165–66, 184
first salmon ceremonies, 221
forest, respect for, 78, 88, 91, 200
Fort Langley, BC, 40

Galloway, Brent, 153*n*, 239
Gardner, Charles, 66, 67*n*
Gardner, Eddie, xxiv
George, Alphonse, 49, 105
George, Antoine, 105
George, Dan, 159
George, Earl Maquinna, xxx–xxxi
George, Jimmy, 105
Gitsegukla village, 168–69
Gosnell, James, 74
Green, Essie, 16
Greene, Rena (Mrs. Stan Greene, née Point), 92, 95, 129*n*, 192, 209
Greene, Stan, 129

Hagwilget village, 169
Hall, Johnny, 18
Halq'eméylem, xviii, 51*n*, 52*n*, 56–57, 63, 71, 95, 117*n*, 153–54, 195, 206*n*, 239–41
Hanson, Erin, 138, 140
Harper, Stephen, 207
Harris, James (Jimmie), 153
Harris, Kenneth, 168
Harris, Walter, (Simoogit Ge'el), 166–67
Hawthorn, Harry, 147–49
healer (*shxwlá:m*), 33
hierarchy, social. *See* social hierarchy
Hilaire, Amelia, 39, 43, 84
Hilaire, Ben, 43
Hilaire, Frank, 39, 41, *42*, 43, 84
Hilaire, Joe, 43
Hilaire, Veronica, and children of, 43
Holm, Bill, 167*n*
Hope, Lena, 11, 151*n*

Indian Act, xxvi–xxvii
Indian Arts and Crafts Society, 143–44, 150, 170
Indian Homemakers' Association, 138–41, 142*n*, 143–46. *See also* Wigwam Homemakers
Insley, Ida, 105

menstruation. *See* puberty, ceremonies
  surrounding
mi'lha (winter dance ceremonies),
  31–32, 44, 88, 105–9, 111, 121, 165,
  205*n*, 223
mi'lha híkw' lalém (longhouse for
  ceremonial use), 90, 108–10, 147, 213
Milo, Dan, 10, *29*, 30–31, 49–50, 84–85,
  111–12, 151*n*, 153, 154*n*, 160, 201*n*;
  mother of, 111
Milo, Mrs. Dan. *See* Edwin, Mary
Milo, Jacob, 30, 60, 98, 153
Moricetown village, 169
Mount Baker, 83
Mount Currie, 37–38
Muldon, Earl (Simoogit Delgamuukw),
  167*n*
Museum of Anthropology, University
  of British Columbia, 147*n*, 148,
  167*n*, 190*n*, 192, 206
Museum of Civilization (Ottawa), 12*n*,
  206
Musqueam (village and people), xix,
  27, 32, 35, 40, 41, 43–45, 84–85, 104,
  105*n*, 135, 137, 151
Mussel, Billy, 150
Mussel, Burns, 97, 155
Mussel, Jones, and family: and canoe
  racing, 97–99

Ned, Annie, xlii
Ned, Edna, 48
Nicomen Island, BC, 17
Ninstints, House of, 16–17
Nlaka'pamux, xxii, 12–13, 17*n*, 30, 176
non-status Indians, xxviii*n*; rights
  denied to, 5, 63, 73
Nooksack village, WA, 21, 48–49, 83,
  105, 153*n*

Ohamil village, 45, 49, 116, 121, 244
Old Pierre (Katzie spiritual leader), 110

Pasco, Duane, 167*n*
Paul, Annie, 105
Paul, Evelyn, 147–49
Paul, Randall, 110
Pennier, Hank, 3

Pennier, Maggie (wife of Hank Pennier),
  105
Peter, Karl, 151
Peters, Mary, 151
Phillips, Agnes, and children of, 49
Phillips, Alfred, Sr., 17–18, 49, 59; chil-
  dren of (Merle, Joyce, Selma, and
  Alfred Jr.), with Annie Silva, 17, 49
Phillips, Alfred, Jr., 49, 218
Phillips, George (second husband of
  Annie Jamieson), 12, 65
Phillips, Joseph (Joe Punch), 17–18, 48, 111;
  wife (Josephine) and children of, 49
Phillips, Lena, and children of, 49
Phillips, Louie (of Deroche), 18, 48
Phillips, Louie (of Lytton), 12*n*
Phillips, Nancy (née Joe) 18, 48
Phillips, Rose, and children of, 49
Pierre, Victor, 169
Point, Abram, 43, 49, 85
Point, Brian, 86, *92*, 95, 112
Point, Cecilia, 44
Point, Charlie, 41, 43, 84. *See also* Coutts,
  Emily
Point, Charlotte, 87, *92*, 95–96
Point, Gail, *92*, 95, 191
Point, Gwen, 211
Point, James, 40, 43, 104, 137
Point, Jeffrey, 86, *92*, 93–94, 104, 110, 114,
  121, 147, 156
Point, Johnny, 43–44; children of, 43
Point, Mark, xviii, 65, 86, *92*–93, 94,
  97–98, 100, 110, *129*, 156
Point, Rena. *See* Greene, Rena
Point, Roy, xxxi, 45, 49, *84*, 85, 112, 177
Point, Sheila, *92*, 95, 220
Point, Steven, xviii, 32, 38, 64, 86, 87, *92*,
  94, 95, 110, 130, 145, 156–57, 192, 196, 207
Point, Tim, 64, *84*, 86, 90, *92*, 93, 110,
  128–29
Point, Wendy, 87, *92*, 95, 191
Pópkw'em village, 30
Port Douglas, BC, 38
Port Essington, BC, 14, 80
potlatch ban, xxvi, 105, 133, 213; text of
  "potlatch law," xxvii*n*
Prince George, BC, 169
Prince Rupert, BC, 168, 175

puberty, ceremonies surrounding, 35–36, 82–83*n*, 121, 223; first menstruation, 54, 83; and Sxwóyxwey masks, 120, 125

Punch, Joe. *See* Phillips, Joseph

Punch, Josephine (wife of Joseph Punch): brothers of, 49; children of, 49

Punch, Louie. *See* Phillips, Louie (of Deroche)

Qwi'qwítlam (chief of Coquitlam), 45, 85

raids and raiding parties, xxv, xxviii, li, 21, 25, 32, 40–41, 61; Xéyteleq and, 17, 36–37, 40

Raley, the Reverend George H., 69–70

Reid, Bill, 189, 190*n*

Reid, Martine, 189, 190*n*

reincarnation, 217–20, 218*n*

residential schools, xxi, xxii*n*, 12, 73*n*, 176, 212. *See also* Coqualeetza Residential School

respect, 213, 217, 222–25; loss of, 87; for natural world, 88, 90–91, 172, 200, 221

Roberts, Johnny, 48

Roberts, Bill, 48. *See also* Joe, Rose

Robinson, Gordon, 74

Rogers, Mrs. William, 135–36

Royal Ontario Museum (Toronto), 206

runners, boys trained as, 34, 41

St. George's Residential School (Lytton, BC), 12, 176

Salis'tsian people, 168

Salt Spring Island, BC, 12

Sam, Robert (of Lytton), 12, 49

Sands, Kathleen, xxxviii–xxxix

Sargent, Polly, 167–68

Sarris, Greg, xxxix–xl

Scott, the Reverend Robert C., 71–72

Sela:miya (mother of Charles Gardner), 67*n*

Semá:th (Sumas), xxx, 3, 5, 10, 14, 25, 26, 30, 33–45 *passim*, 51, 58, 66, 67*n*, 69; and Steqó:ye Wolf People, 21, 31, 128, 130

Semá:th Lake (Sumas Lake), xix, xx*n*, xlix, 19–22, 35, 46, 52, 59–60

Sepass, Billy (Chief William K'HHalserten Sepass), 38

Sepass, Robert, 38

sharing, 91–92, 172, 201–2, 219; with nature, 77, 201*n*

Shaw, Mary Jean (wife of David Ambrose Silva), and children of, 79

sí:yá:m (hereditary chief): assault on power of, 212; duties of, 55, 56*n*, 93

silence, cultural, xxi–xxiv, xxvi, xxix–xxxiv, 22, 27–29, 149, 204, 212–14

Si:l'hiy (two-headed snake): crest, 112–113; slaying of, 111–12

Silva, Annie (Bolan Phillips), 5, 7, 11, 14–15, 17–18, 44, 45–46, 61, 65, 75–76, 119, 128–29, 218

Silva, Antonia, 44, 45–46, 70–71, 75, 182

Silva, Charlotte ("Lottie"), 45, 80

Silva, David (Pete's brother), 48

Silva, David Ambrose, 15, 40, 42, 44, 64, 79–80

Silva, Margaret (wife of August Jim), 44, 45, 48, 64, 119, 129, 137, 151

Silva, Pete, 6–7, 13–14, 22, 43, 44, 45, 47–48, 52, 55, 57–58, 62, 64, 72, 84, 98, 128, 160, 211, 218, 223

Silver, Ambrose. *See* Silva, David Ambrose

Silver, Ray, 43, 80

Skeena River, xviii, xix, 4, 66, 67*n*, 168, 173, 178, 190, 209, 227, 229

Skowkale (Sq'ewq'éyl) village, xx, 18*n*, 29, 31, 38, 84–85, 93–95, 98, 108, 110, 112

Skwah (Sqwehá) village, 98

Skw'átets (Peters) village, 45

slavery, 22–23, 37, 39

slehá:l, 99–100, 244

smallpox, 31, 41, 204

Smith, Dorothy, xl*n*, xliv–xlv

smokehouse, activities in, at Devil's Run, 53–55. *See also* mí'lha híkw' lalém

social hierarchy: and stewardship of culture, 27–28

Soowahlie village, 39, 110–11, 136, 154

spirit guides, 10, 111–13

Spuzzum, BC, 10

Squamish, BC, 37–38